V. E. SCHWAB

SHADES OF MAGIC

THE STEEL PRINCE

THE REBEL ARMY

Titan
COMICS

SHADES OF MAGIC
THE STEEL PRINCE
THE REBEL ARMY

ALSO AVAILABLE FROM V.E. SCHWAB AND TITAN BOOKS

The Near Witch

Vicious | Vengeful

This Savage Song | Our Dark Duet

A Darker Shade of Magic | A Gathering of Shadows | A Conjuring of Light

The Dark Vault

ALSO AVAILABLE FROM V.E. SCHWAB AND TITAN COMICS

Shades of Magic: The Steel Prince

Shades of Magic: The Steel Prince: Night of Knives

Shades of Magic: The Steel Prince: The Rebel Army

SHADES OF MAGIC: THE STEEL PRINCE
THE REBEL ARMY

Senior Creative Editor
David Leach

Managing Editor
Martin Eden

Senior Designer
Andrew Leung

Editorial Assistant / Phoebe Hedges
Production Controller / Caterina Falqui
Senior Production Controller / Jackie Flook
Art Director / Oz Browne
Sales & Circulation Manager / Steve Tothill
Publicist / Imogen Harris

Direct Marketing Officer / George Wickenden
Head of Rights / Jenny Boyce
Editorial Director / Duncan Baizley
Operations Director / Leigh Baulch
Executive Director / Vivian Cheung
Publisher / Nick Landau

STANDARD EDITION ISBN 9781787731158
B&N EDITION ISBN 9781787735644
FORBIDDEN PLANET EDITION ISBN 9781787735637

A CIP catalogue for this title is available from the British Library.

First Edition May 2020
10 9 8 7 6 5 4 3 2 1
Printed in Spain

www.titan-comics.com
Follow us on twitter@ComicsTitan | Visit us at facebook.com/comicstitan
For rights information contact: jenny.boyce@titanemail.com

Published by Titan Comics, a division of Titan Publishing Group, Ltd. Titan Comics is a registered trademark of Titan Publishing Group, Ltd. 144 Southwark Street, London SE1 0UP

V. E. SCHWAB
SHADES OF MAGIC
THE STEEL PRINCE
THE REBEL ARMY

ARTIST
ANDREA OLIMPIERI

COLORIST
ENRICA EREN ANGIOLINI

ART ASSISTS ISSUES #3 & #4
ALESSANDRO CAPPUCCIO

COLOR ASSISTS
ALICE KINOKI

LETTERING
ROB STEEN

Titan
COMICS

V. E. SCHWAB
SHADES OF MAGIC
THE STEEL PRINCE
THE REBEL ARMY

Introduction

"The Steel Prince," said Sol-in-Ar, and then, reading Maxim's expression:
"It surprises you, that the tales of your exploits reach beyond your own borders?"
The Faroan's fingers grazed the edge of the map. "The Steel Prince, who tore the heart
from the rebel army. The Steel Prince, who survived the night of knives.
The Steel Prince, who slayed the pirate queen."

Maxim finished his drink and set the glass aside.

"I suppose we never know the scale of our life's stories.
Which parts will survive, and which will die with us."

–A Conjuring of Light

Previously...

The Pirate Queen, defeated. The Night of Knives, survived.

Each victory adds to the growing myth of the Steel Prince. Each victory is part truth, and part lie.

Maxim Maresh has earned his place at the helm of the Verose regiment. He has earned the scars on his
skin, and the respect of at least some of his soldiers. But none will prepare him for what's coming.

Up and down the Blood Coast, a mysterious band of pirates called the Rebel Army is growing. Led by three
extraordinarily powerful magicians, the Army claims port after port, adding the strongest to its ranks,
and leaving only death and fire in its wake.

And it is coming for Verose.

For Maxim.

With Isra at his side, and the might of the soldiers he's trained—and the citizens
he hasn't—will Verose be able to stand against the Rebel Army?

Or will it fall, as all things have, beneath the rising tide?

CAST OF CHARACTERS

MAXIM MARESH

Crown Prince of Arnes. Magically gifted with the ability to bend steel to his will. He is known to be a talented fighter and soldier who has led troops at the forefront of the Arnesian army, but he desires to do more.

NOKIL MARESH

King of Arnes. Frustrated with his son's preoccupation with the other realms, he banishes Maxim to Verose. He hopes to redirect his son's attention toward matters in their own world and kingdom.

TIEREN SERENSE

Head Priest of the London Sanctuary and the adviser to the king. Wise and powerful in his own right, he has watched over and trained Maxim in magical combat and matters of leadership and statecraft.

ISRA

A royal guard serving in the Arnesian army base in Verose. Toughened by the harsh streets of the Blood Coast, she leads a matchless team with her loyal companions, Osili and Toro.

ROWAN

An Antari magician and architect of the Night of Knives. The deadliest magician that Maxim has ever encountered, he is determined to destroy the prince and the Maresh Empire.

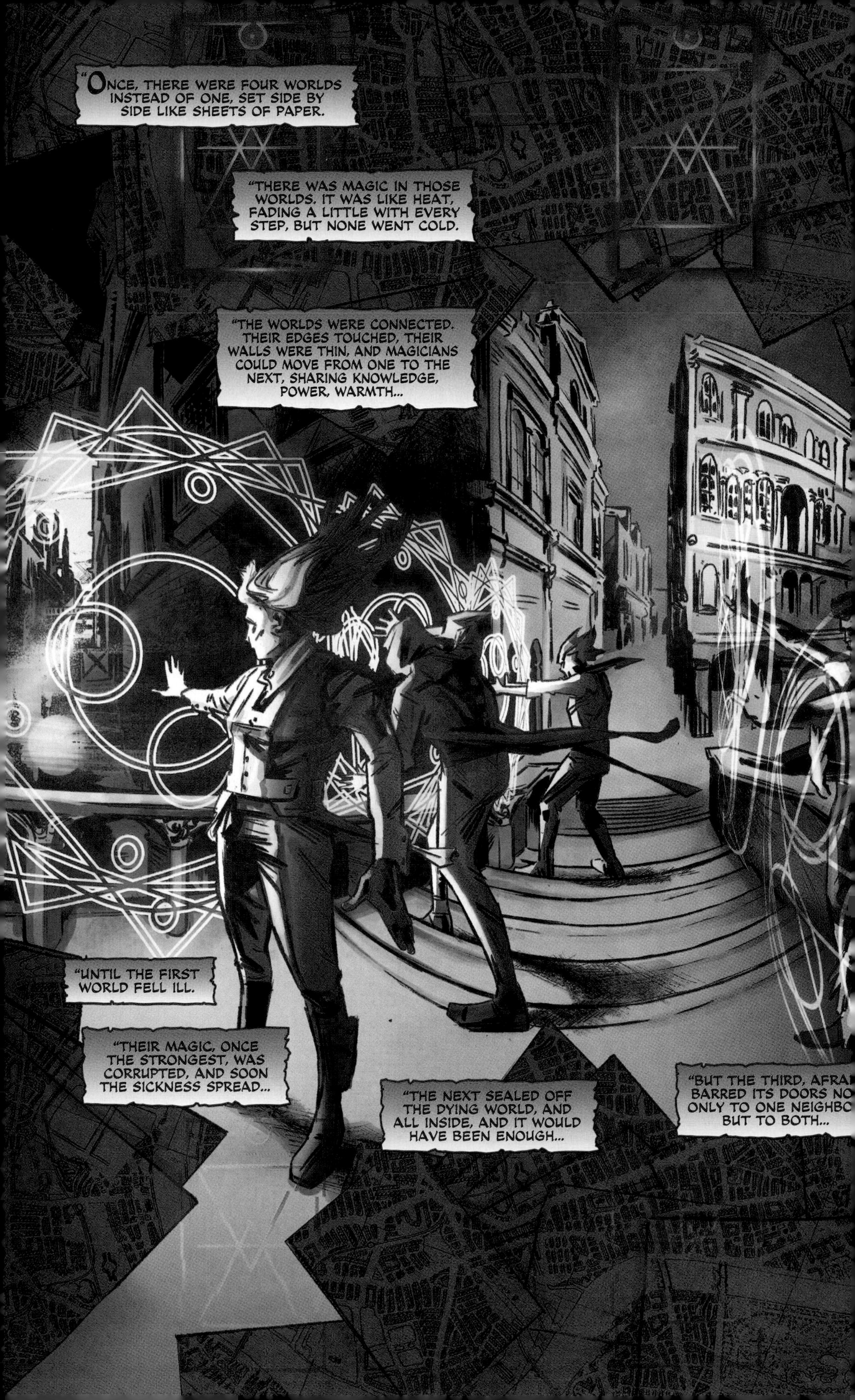
"ONCE, THERE WERE FOUR WORLDS INSTEAD OF ONE, SET SIDE BY SIDE LIKE SHEETS OF PAPER.
"THERE WAS MAGIC IN THOSE WORLDS. IT WAS LIKE HEAT, FADING A LITTLE WITH EVERY STEP, BUT NONE WENT COLD.
"THE WORLDS WERE CONNECTED. THEIR EDGES TOUCHED, THEIR WALLS WERE THIN, AND MAGICIANS COULD MOVE FROM ONE TO THE NEXT, SHARING KNOWLEDGE, POWER, WARMTH...
"UNTIL THE FIRST WORLD FELL ILL.
"THEIR MAGIC, ONCE THE STRONGEST, WAS CORRUPTED, AND SOON THE SICKNESS SPREAD...
"THE NEXT SEALED OFF THE DYING WORLD, AND ALL INSIDE, AND IT WOULD HAVE BEEN ENOUGH...
"BUT THE THIRD, AFRAI BARRED ITS DOORS NO ONLY TO ONE NEIGHBO BUT TO BOTH...

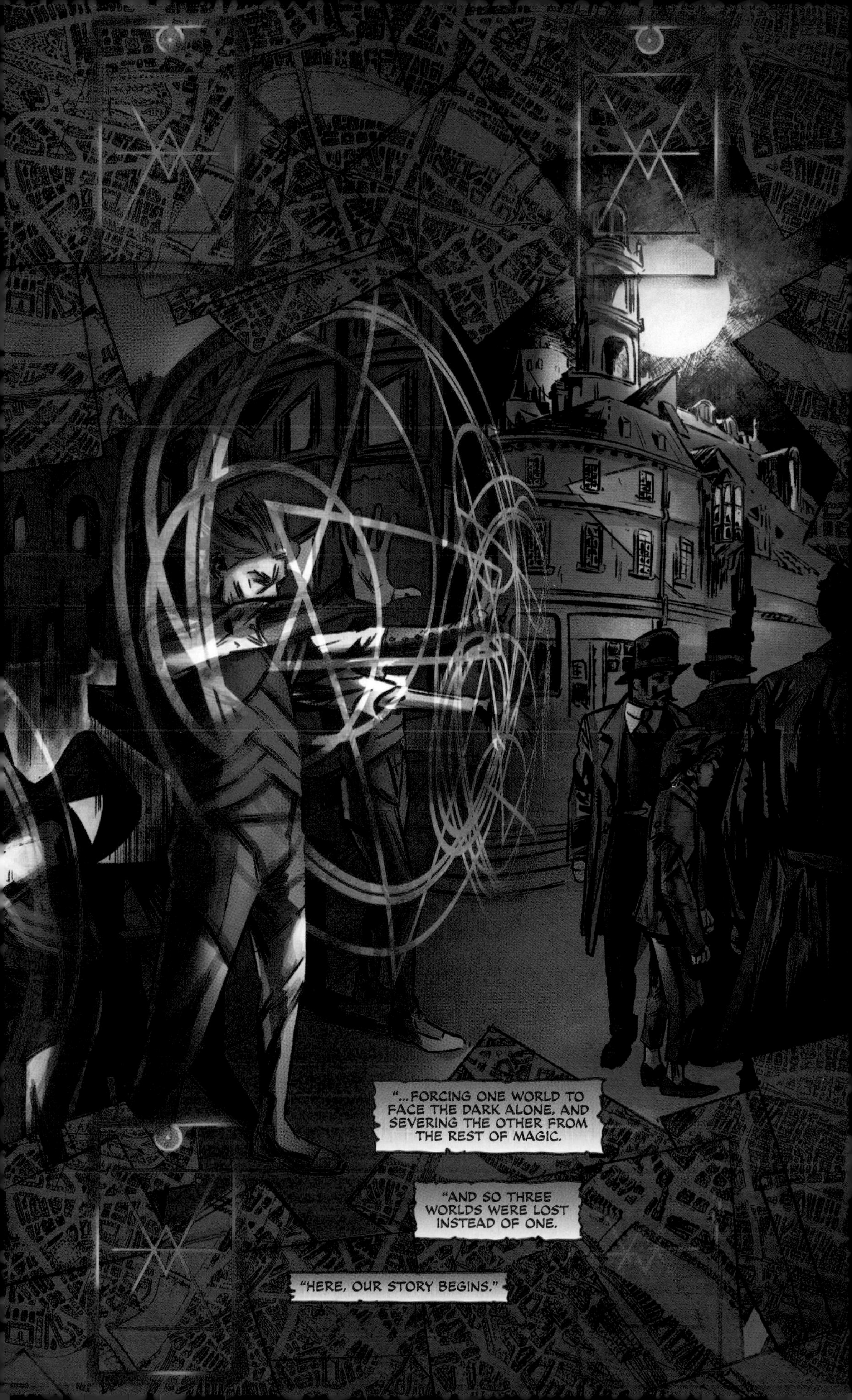
"...FORCING ONE WORLD TO FACE THE DARK ALONE, AND SEVERING THE OTHER FROM THE REST OF MAGIC.
"AND SO THREE WORLDS WERE LOST INSTEAD OF ONE.
"HERE, OUR STORY BEGINS."

#1

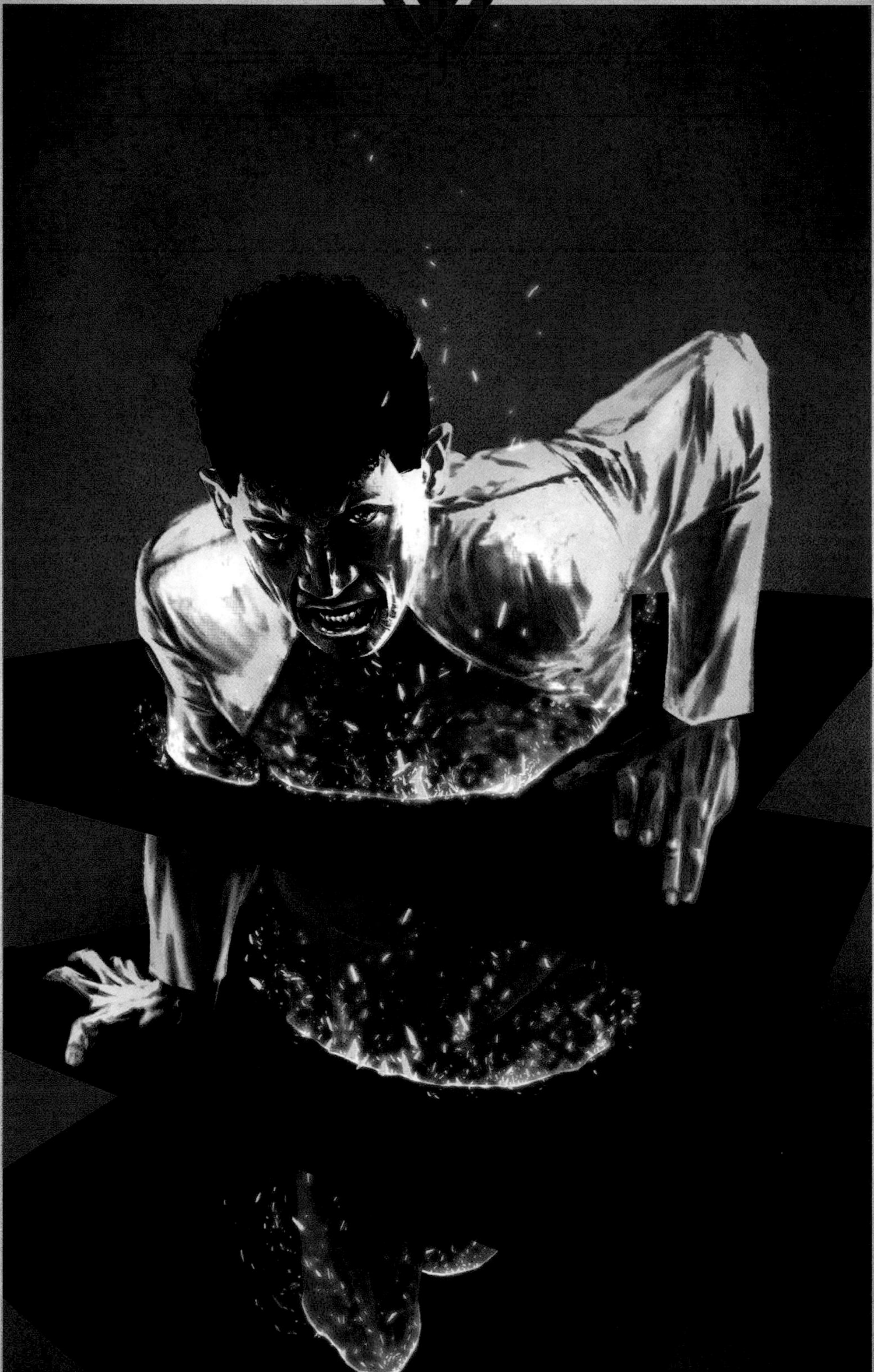

ILLUSTRATION BY ANDREA OLIMPIERI

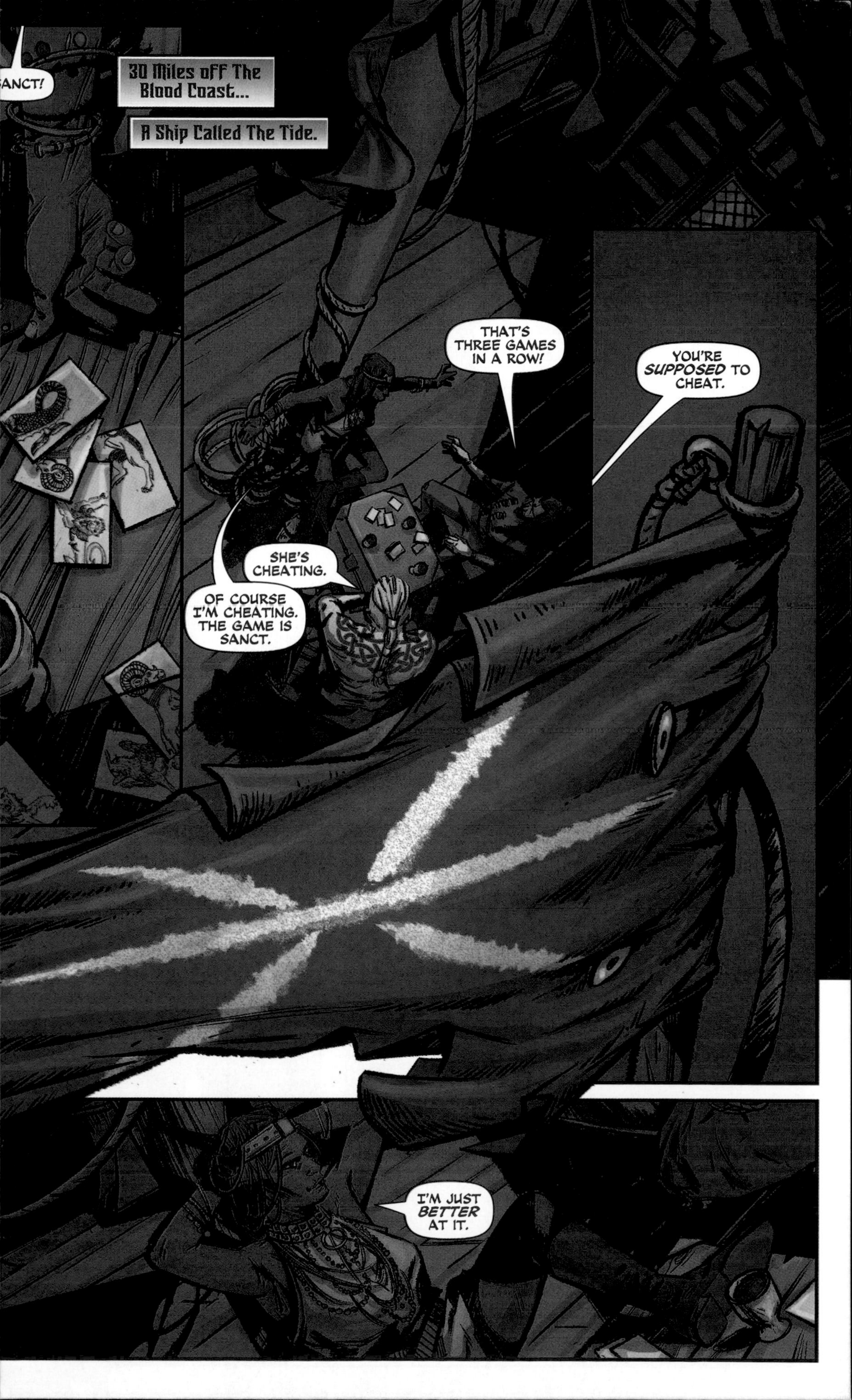
SANCT!
30 Miles off The Blood Coast...
A Ship Called The Tide.
THAT'S THREE GAMES IN A ROW!
YOU'RE SUPPOSED TO CHEAT.
SHE'S CHEATING.
OF COURSE I'M CHEATING. THE GAME IS SANCT.
I'M JUST BETTER AT IT.

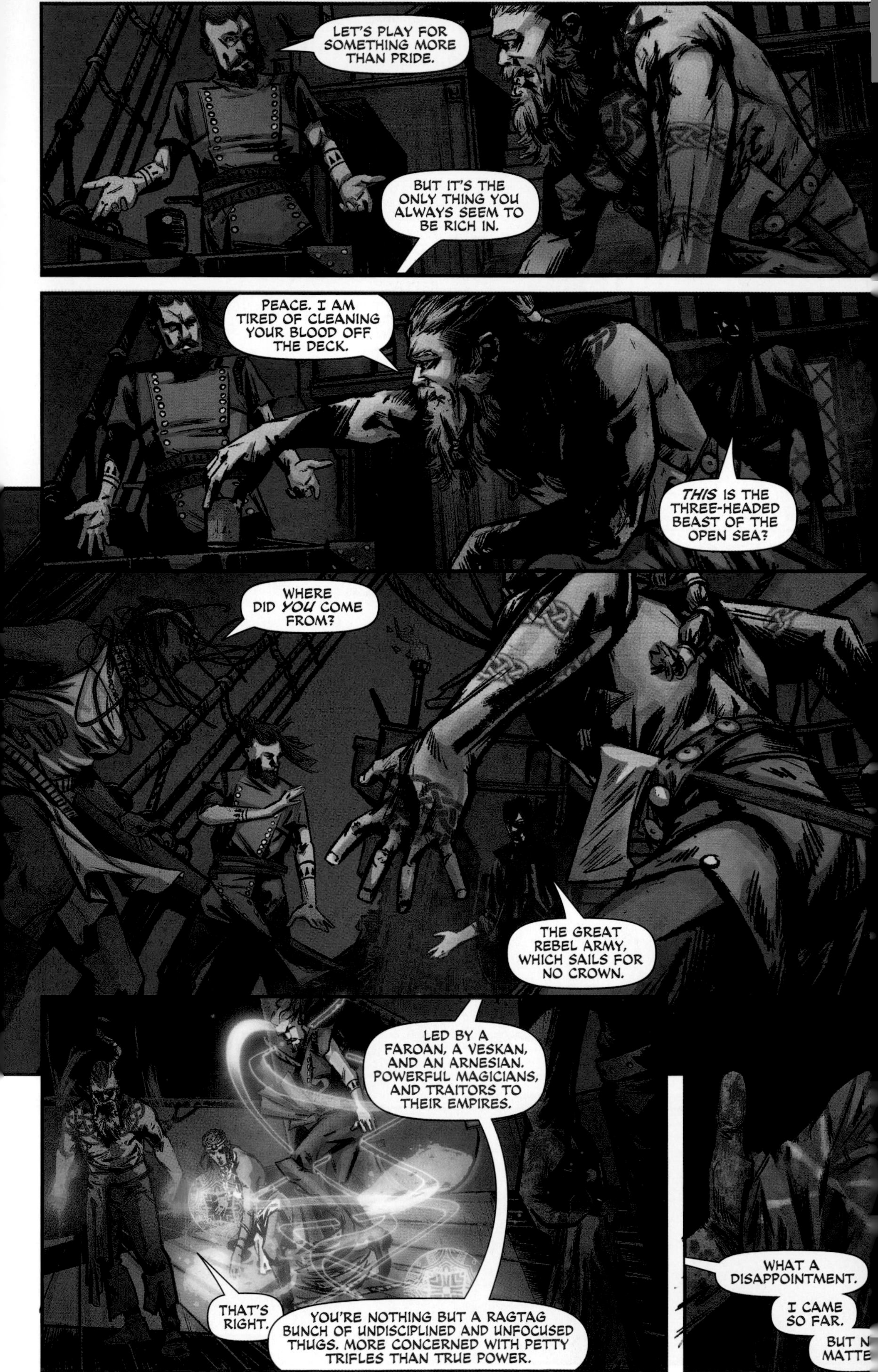
LET'S PLAY FOR SOMETHING MORE THAN PRIDE.
BUT IT'S THE ONLY THING YOU ALWAYS SEEM TO BE RICH IN.
PEACE. I AM TIRED OF CLEANING YOUR BLOOD OFF THE DECK.
THIS IS THE THREE-HEADED BEAST OF THE OPEN SEA?
WHERE DID YOU COME FROM?
THE GREAT REBEL ARMY, WHICH SAILS FOR NO CROWN.
LED BY A FAROAN, A VESKAN, AND AN ARNESIAN. POWERFUL MAGICIANS, AND TRAITORS TO THEIR EMPIRES.
THAT'S RIGHT.
YOU'RE NOTHING BUT A RAGTAG BUNCH OF UNDISCIPLINED AND UNFOCUSED THUGS. MORE CONCERNED WITH PETTY TRIFLES THAN TRUE POWER.
WHAT A DISAPPOINTMENT.
I CAME SO FAR.

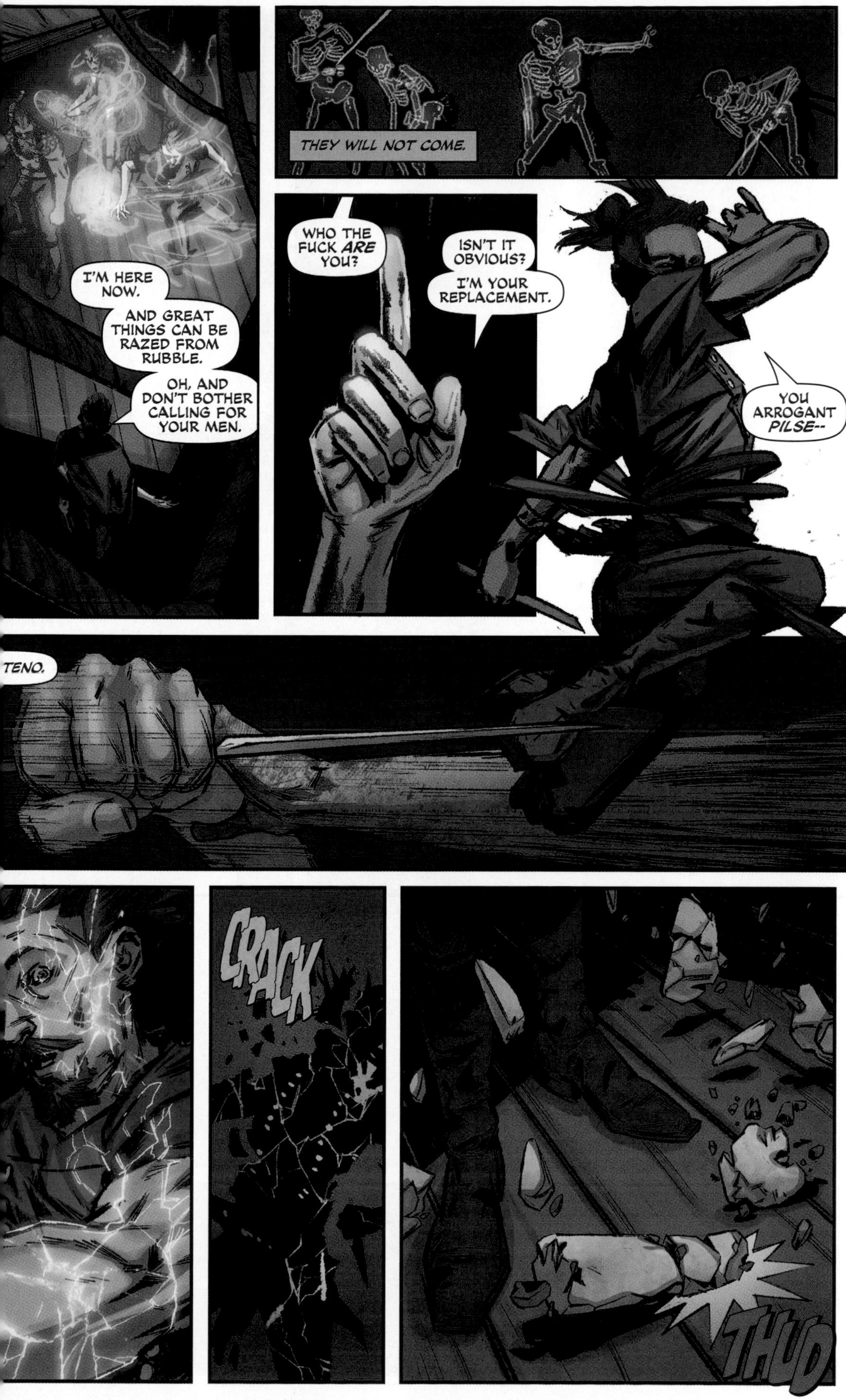
THEY WILL NOT COME.
I'M HERE NOW.
AND GREAT THINGS CAN BE RAZED FROM RUBBLE.
OH, AND DON'T BOTHER CALLING FOR YOUR MEN.
WHO THE FUCK ARE YOU?
ISN'T IT OBVIOUS?
I'M YOUR REPLACEMENT.
YOU ARROGANT PILSE--
TENO.
CRACK
THUD

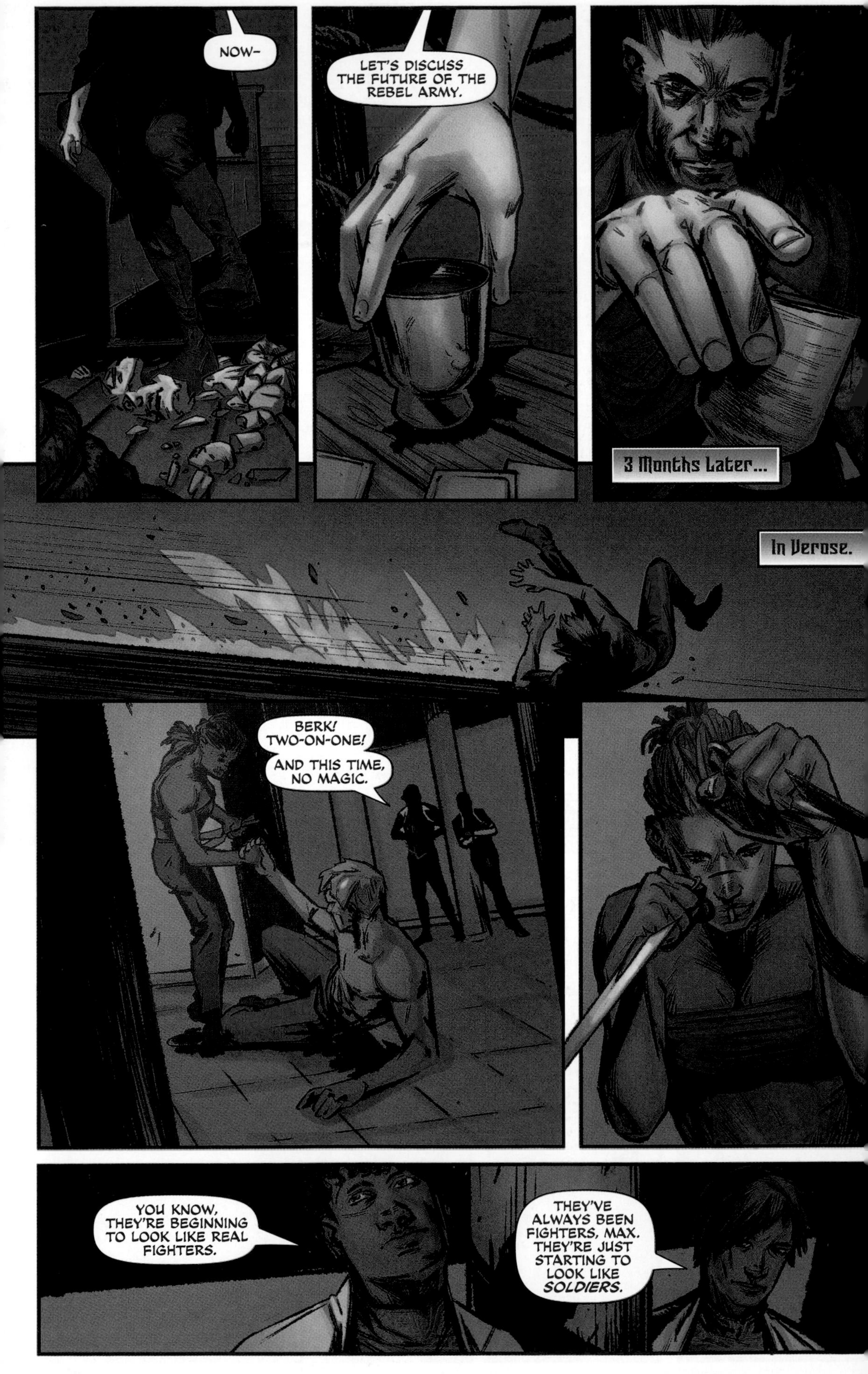
NOW-
LET'S DISCUSS THE FUTURE OF THE REBEL ARMY.
3 Months Later...
In Verose.
BERK! TWO-ON-ONE!
AND THIS TIME, NO MAGIC.
YOU KNOW, THEY'RE BEGINNING TO LOOK LIKE REAL FIGHTERS.
THEY'VE ALWAYS BEEN FIGHTERS, MAX. THEY'RE JUST STARTING TO LOOK LIKE *SOLDIERS*.

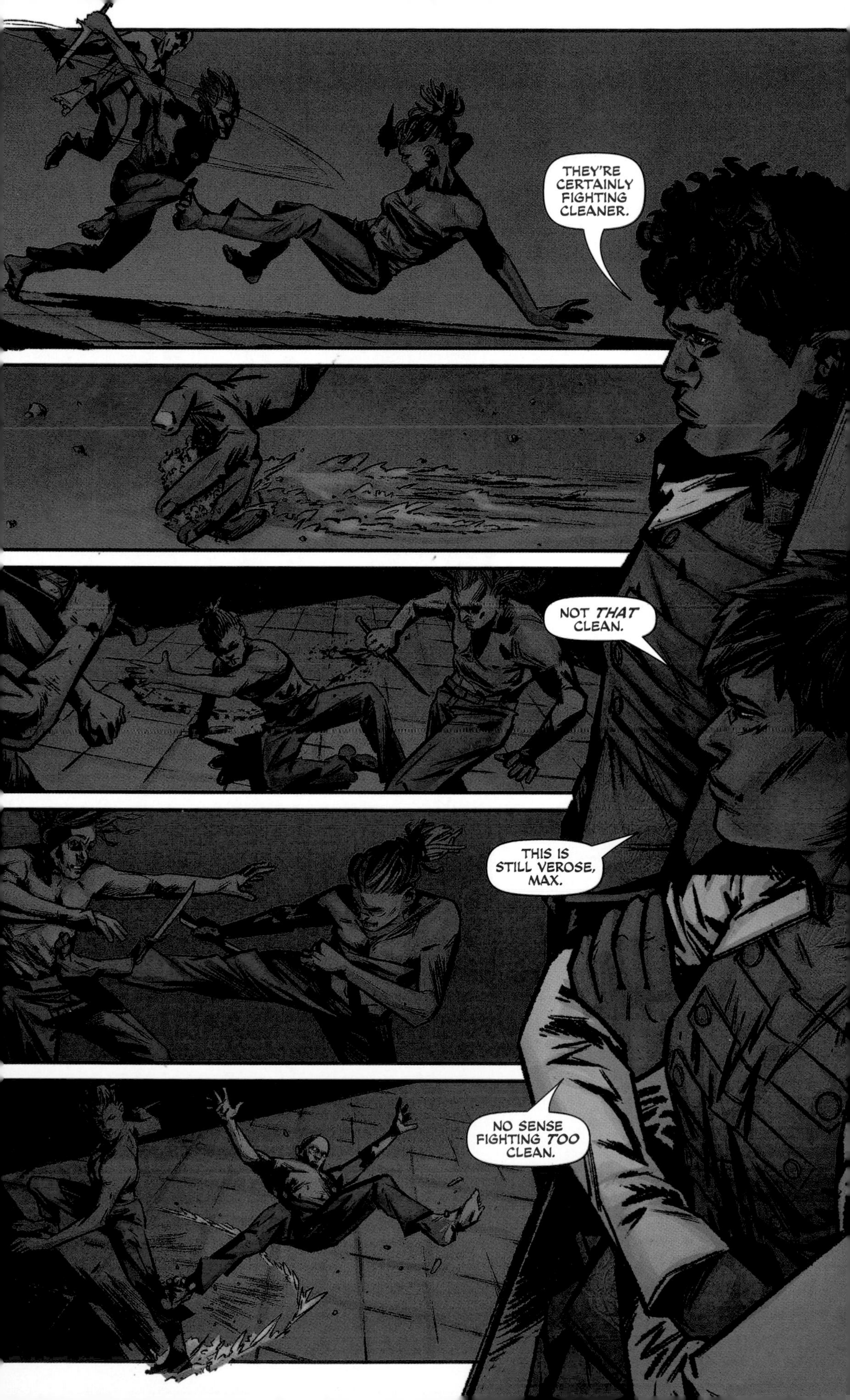
THEY'RE CERTAINLY FIGHTING CLEANER.
NOT *THAT* CLEAN.
THIS IS STILL VEROSE, MAX.
NO SENSE FIGHTING *TOO* CLEAN.

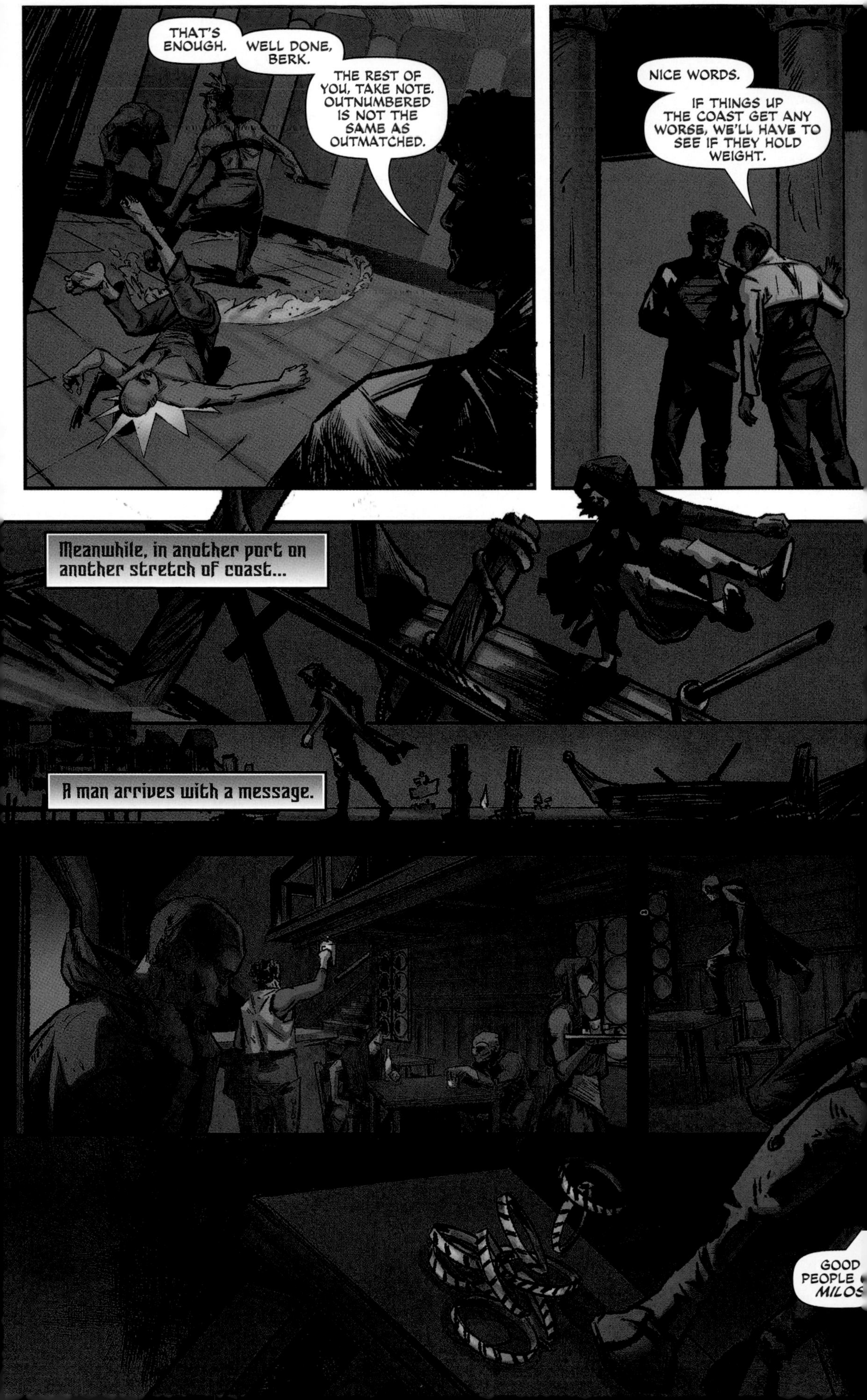
THAT'S ENOUGH.
WELL DONE, BERK.
THE REST OF YOU, TAKE NOTE. OUTNUMBERED IS NOT THE SAME AS OUTMATCHED.
NICE WORDS.
IF THINGS UP THE COAST GET ANY WORSE, WE'LL HAVE TO SEE IF THEY HOLD WEIGHT.
Meanwhile, in another port on another stretch of coast...
A man arrives with a message.
GOOD PEOPLE
MILOS

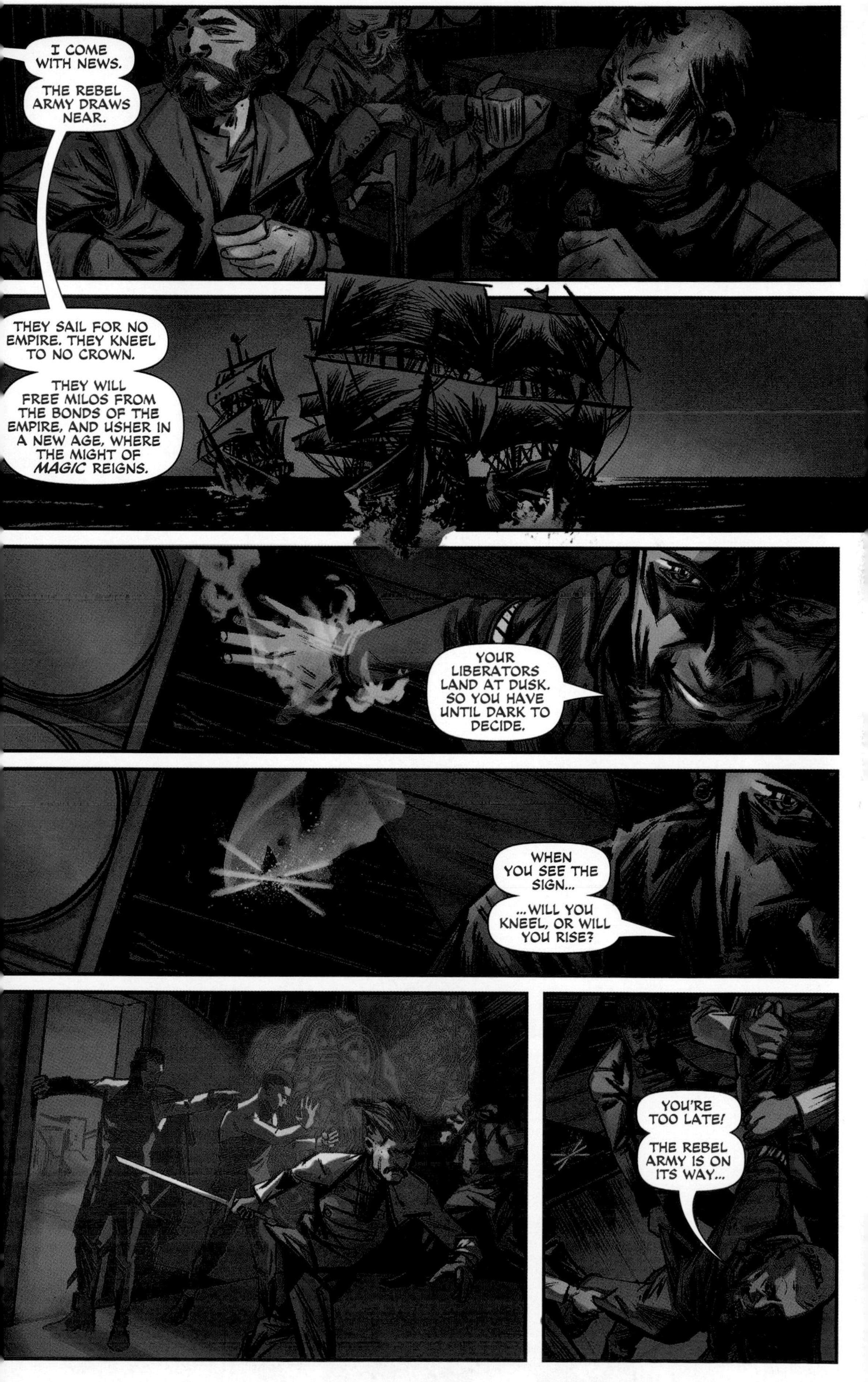
I COME WITH NEWS.
THE REBEL ARMY DRAWS NEAR.
THEY SAIL FOR NO EMPIRE. THEY KNEEL TO NO CROWN.
THEY WILL FREE MILOS FROM THE BONDS OF THE EMPIRE, AND USHER IN A NEW AGE, WHERE THE MIGHT OF *MAGIC* REIGNS.
YOUR LIBERATORS LAND AT DUSK. SO YOU HAVE UNTIL DARK TO DECIDE.
WHEN YOU SEE THE SIGN...
...WILL YOU KNEEL, OR WILL YOU RISE?
YOU'RE TOO LATE!
THE REBEL ARMY IS ON ITS WAY...

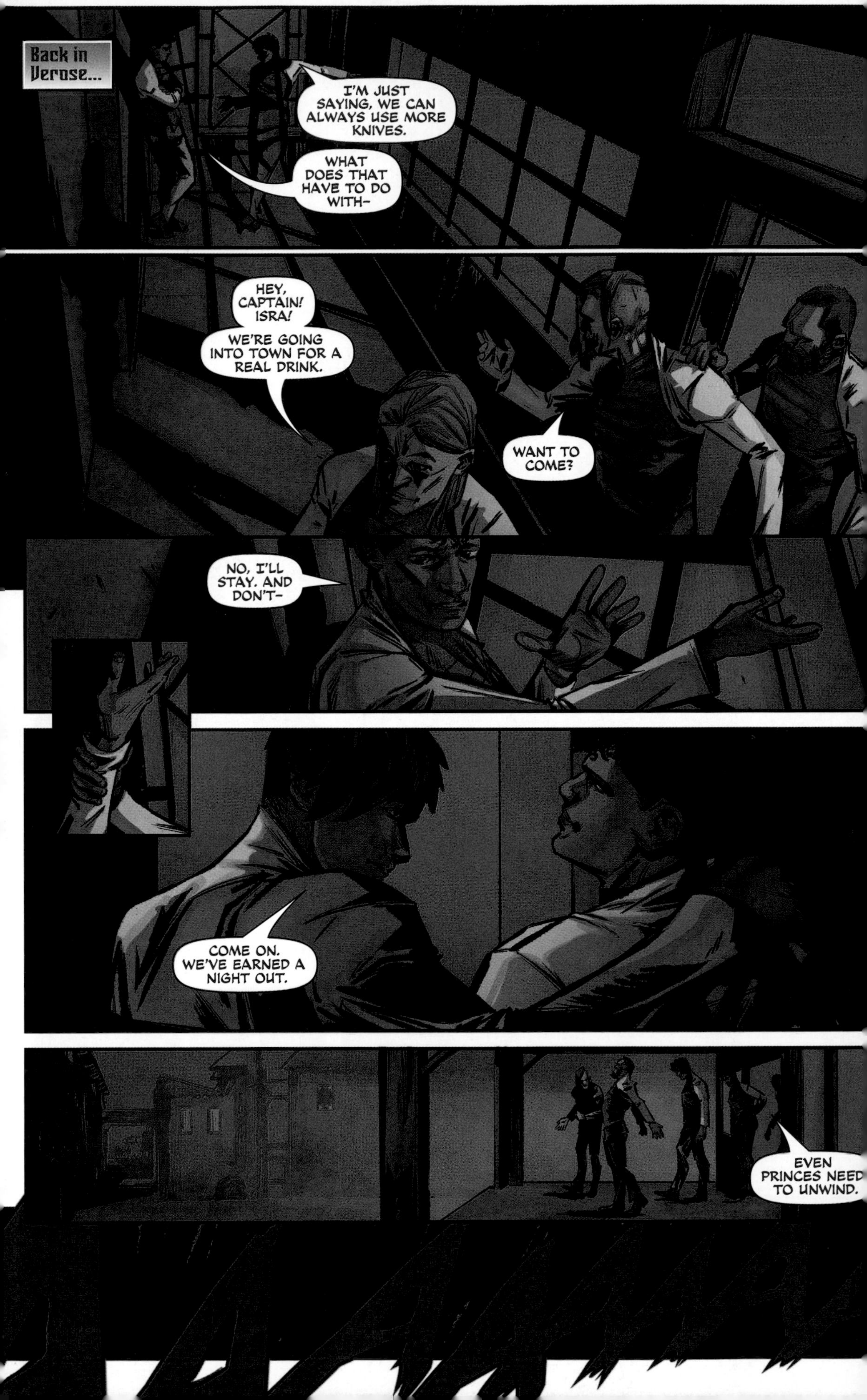
Back in Verose...
I'M JUST SAYING, WE CAN ALWAYS USE MORE KNIVES.
WHAT DOES THAT HAVE TO DO WITH-
HEY, CAPTAIN! ISRA!
WE'RE GOING INTO TOWN FOR A REAL DRINK.
WANT TO COME?
NO, I'LL STAY. AND DON'T-
COME ON. WE'VE EARNED A NIGHT OUT.
EVEN PRINCES NEED TO UNWIND.

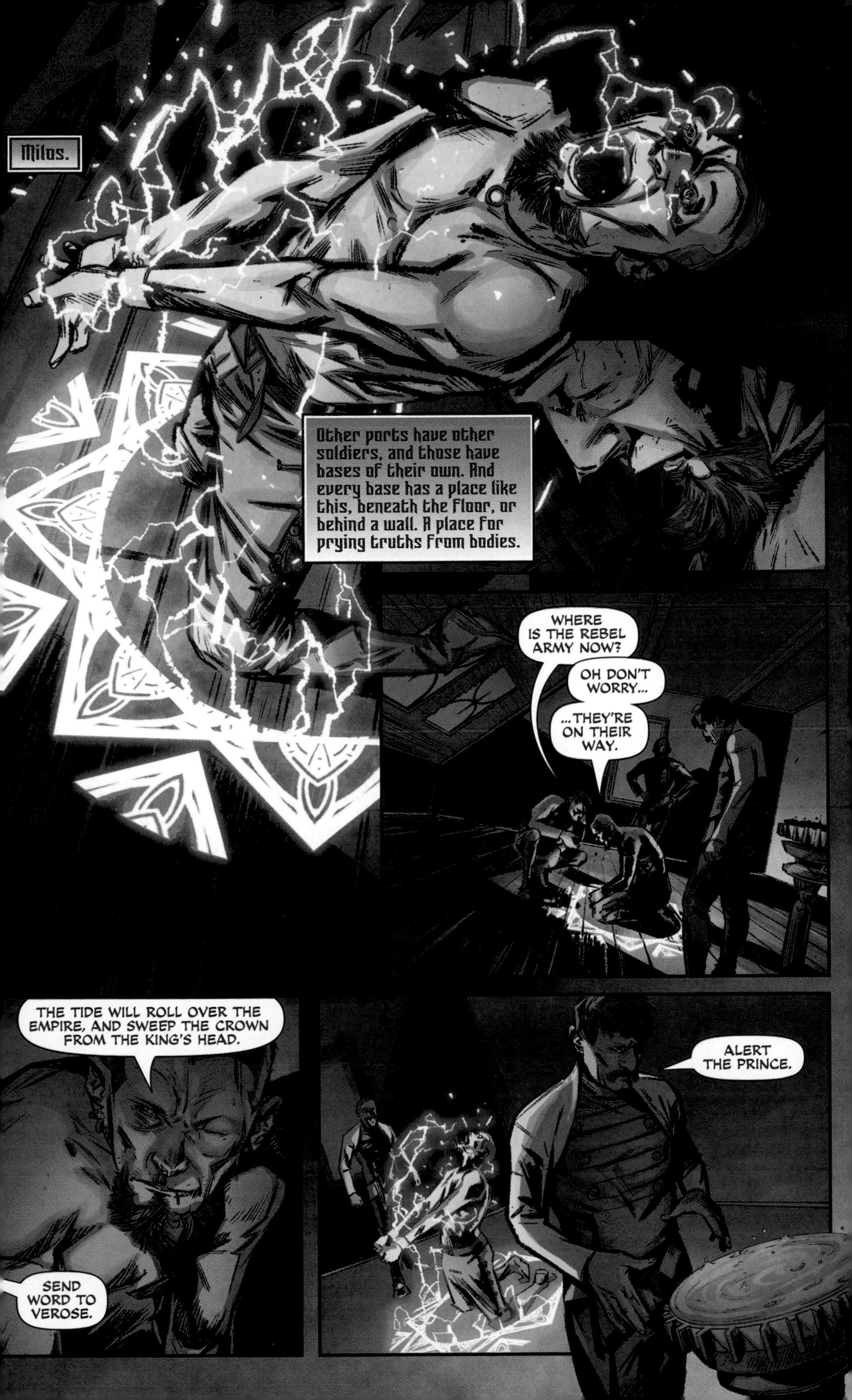
Milos.
Other ports have other soldiers, and those have bases of their own. And every base has a place like this, beneath the floor, or behind a wall. A place for prying truths from bodies.
WHERE IS THE REBEL ARMY NOW?
OH DON'T WORRY...
...THEY'RE ON THEIR WAY.
THE TIDE WILL ROLL OVER THE EMPIRE, AND SWEEP THE CROWN FROM THE KING'S HEAD.
SEND WORD TO VEROSE.
ALERT THE PRINCE.

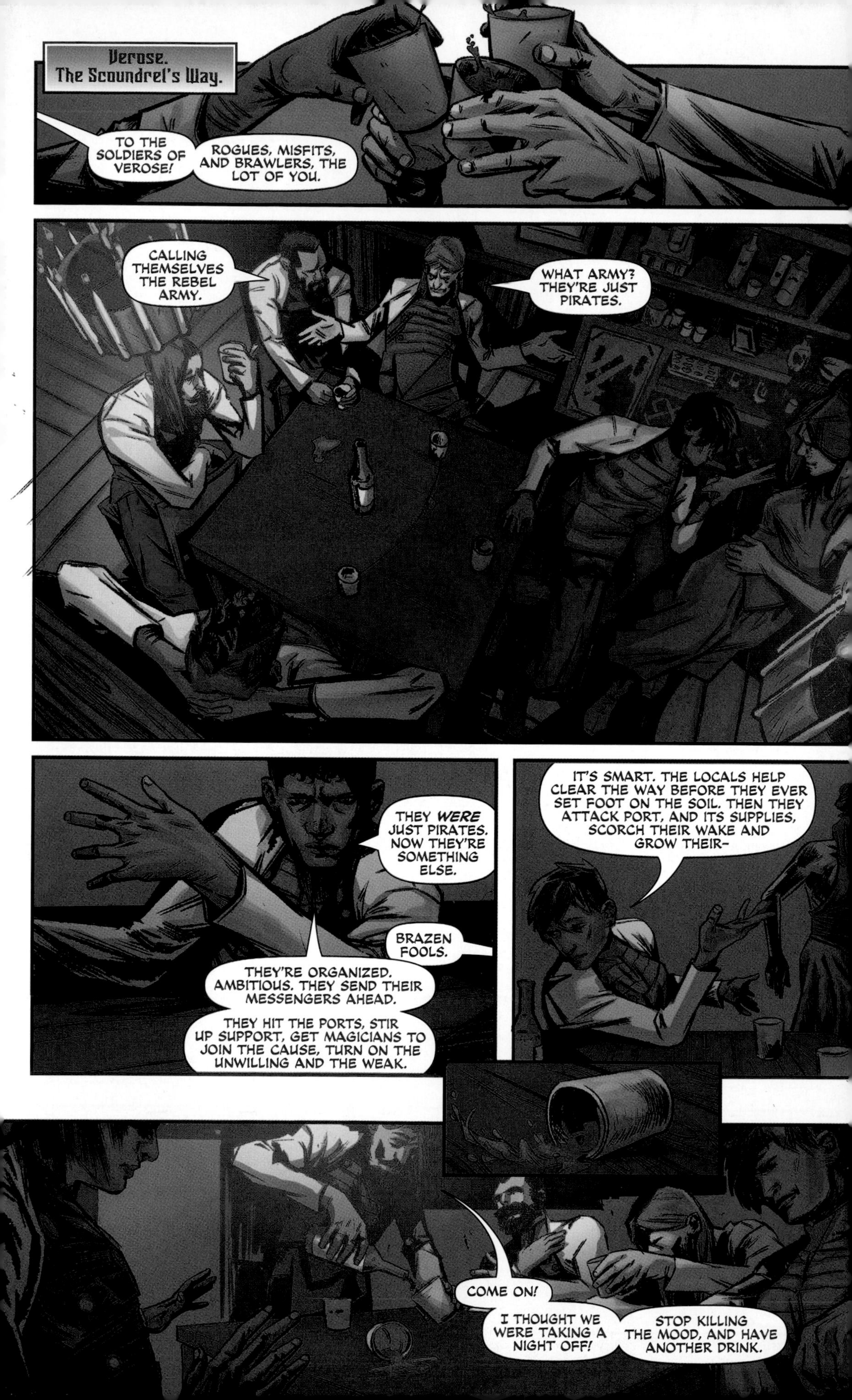
Verose.
The Scoundrel's Way.
TO THE SOLDIERS OF VEROSE!
ROGUES, MISFITS, AND BRAWLERS, THE LOT OF YOU.
CALLING THEMSELVES THE REBEL ARMY.
WHAT ARMY? THEY'RE JUST PIRATES.
THEY *WERE* JUST PIRATES. NOW THEY'RE SOMETHING ELSE.
BRAZEN FOOLS.
THEY'RE ORGANIZED. AMBITIOUS. THEY SEND THEIR MESSENGERS AHEAD.
THEY HIT THE PORTS, STIR UP SUPPORT, GET MAGICIANS TO JOIN THE CAUSE, TURN ON THE UNWILLING AND THE WEAK.
IT'S SMART. THE LOCALS HELP CLEAR THE WAY BEFORE THEY EVER SET FOOT ON THE SOIL. THEN THEY ATTACK PORT, AND ITS SUPPLIES, SCORCH THEIR WAKE AND GROW THEIR–
COME ON!
I THOUGHT WE WERE TAKING A NIGHT OFF!
STOP KILLING THE MOOD, AND HAVE ANOTHER DRINK.

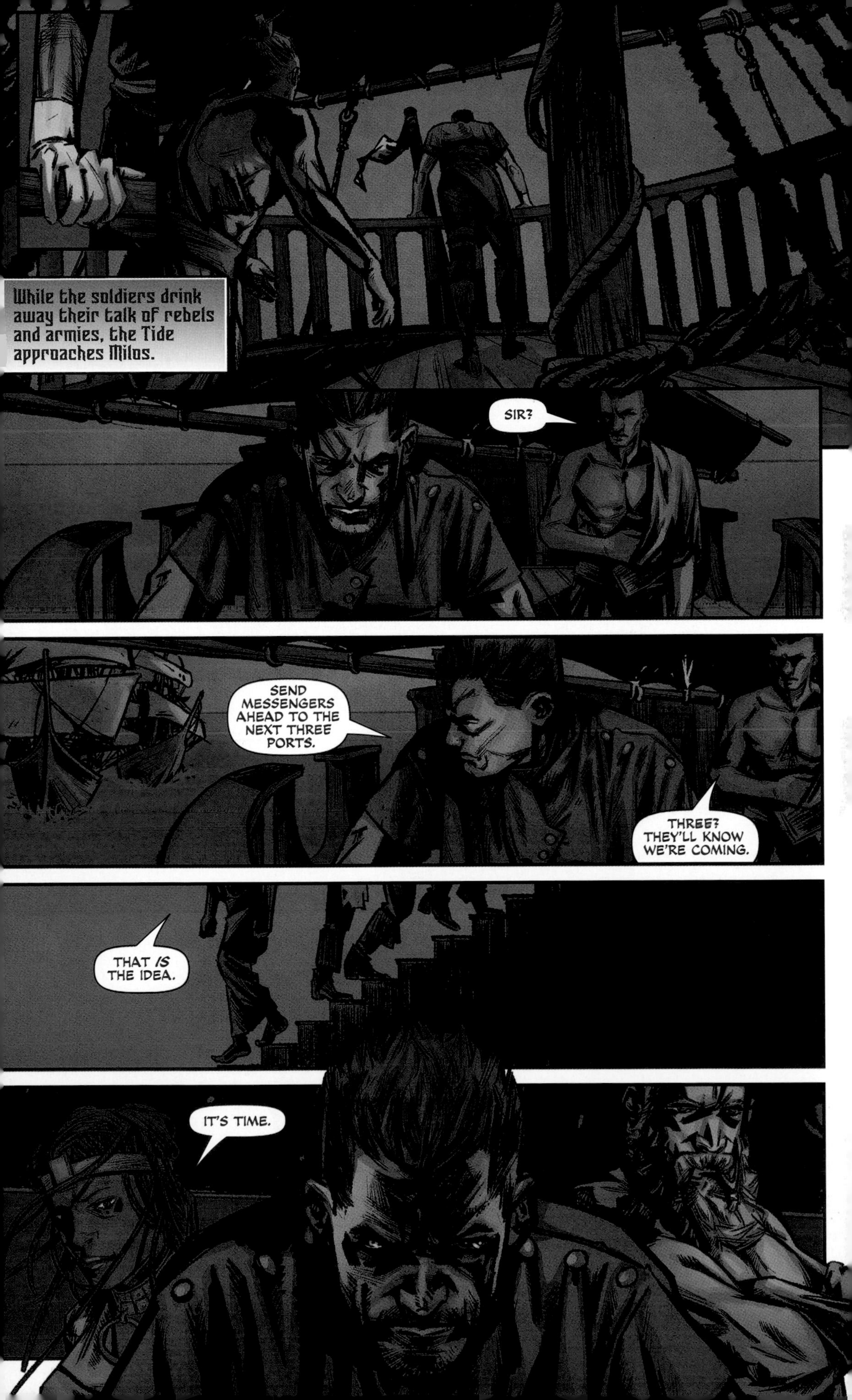
While the soldiers drink away their talk of rebels and armies, the Tide approaches Milos.
SIR?
SEND MESSENGERS AHEAD TO THE NEXT THREE PORTS.
THREE? THEY'LL KNOW WE'RE COMING.
THAT IS THE IDEA.
IT'S TIME.

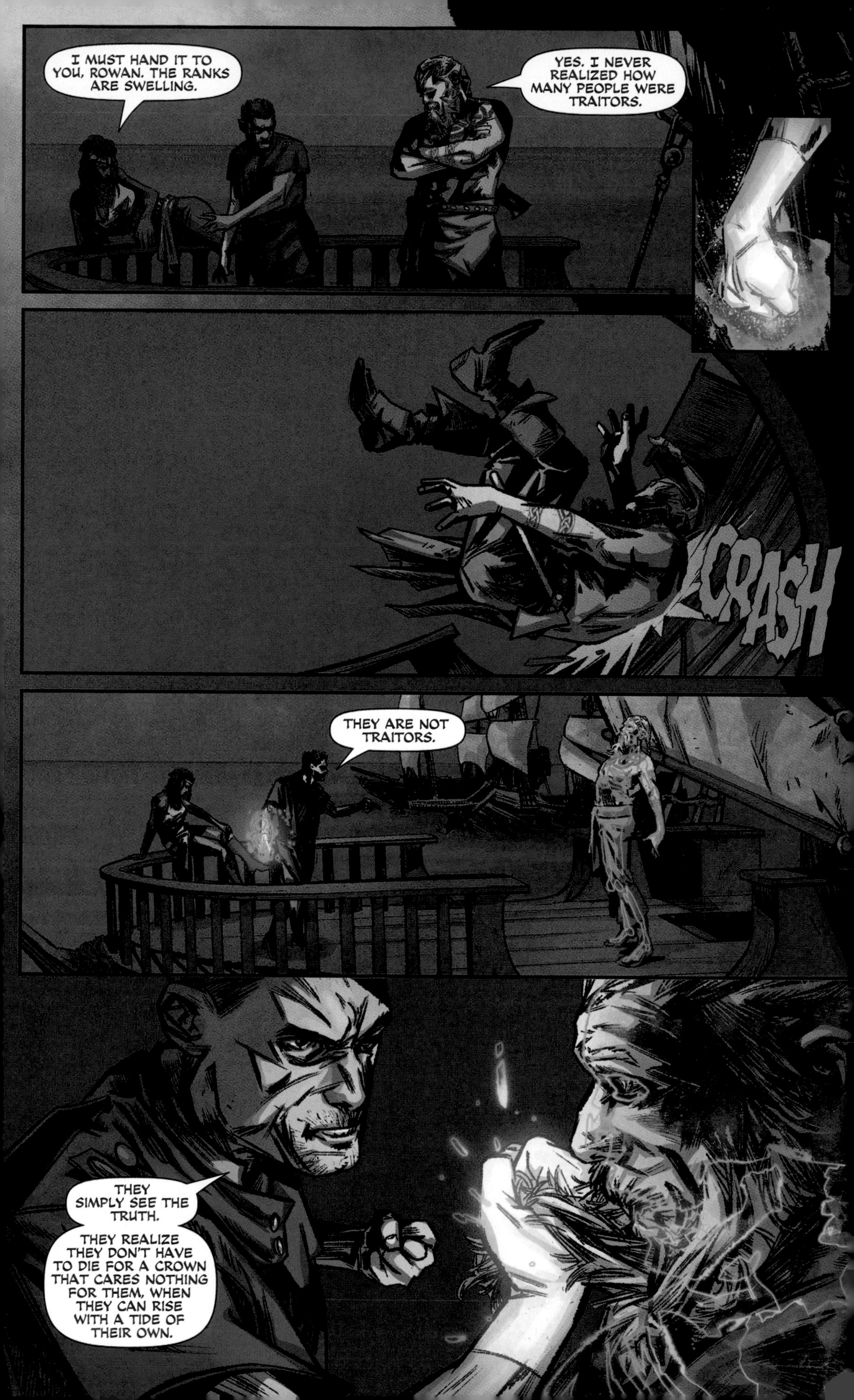
I MUST HAND IT TO YOU, ROWAN. THE RANKS ARE SWELLING.
YES. I NEVER REALIZED HOW MANY PEOPLE WERE TRAITORS.
CRASH
THEY ARE NOT TRAITORS.
THEY SIMPLY SEE THE TRUTH.
THEY REALIZE THEY DON'T HAVE TO DIE FOR A CROWN THAT CARES NOTHING FOR THEM, WHEN THEY CAN RISE WITH A TIDE OF THEIR OWN.

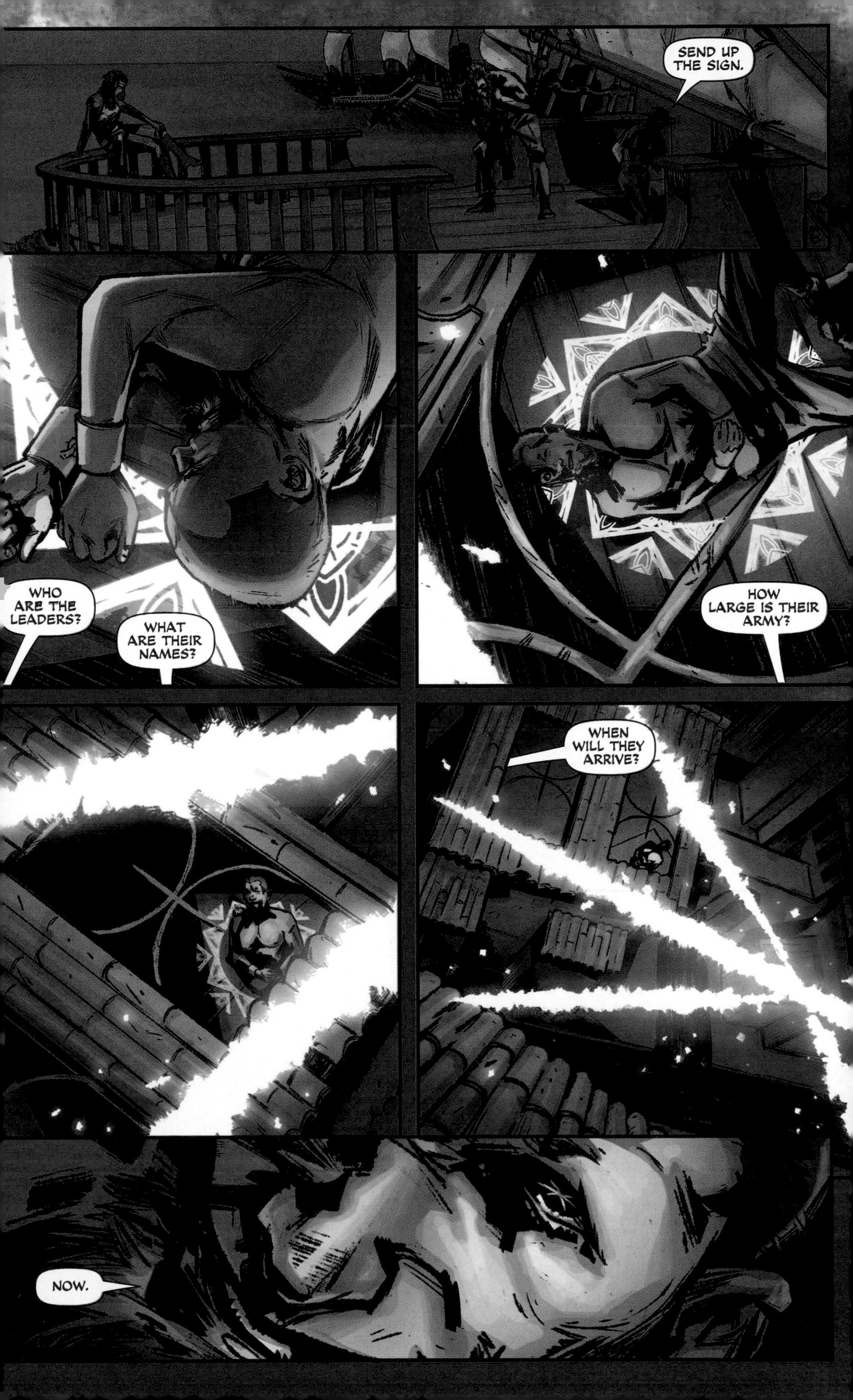
SEND UP THE SIGN.
WHO ARE THE LEADERS?
WHAT ARE THEIR NAMES?
HOW LARGE IS THEIR ARMY?
WHEN WILL THEY ARRIVE?
NOW.

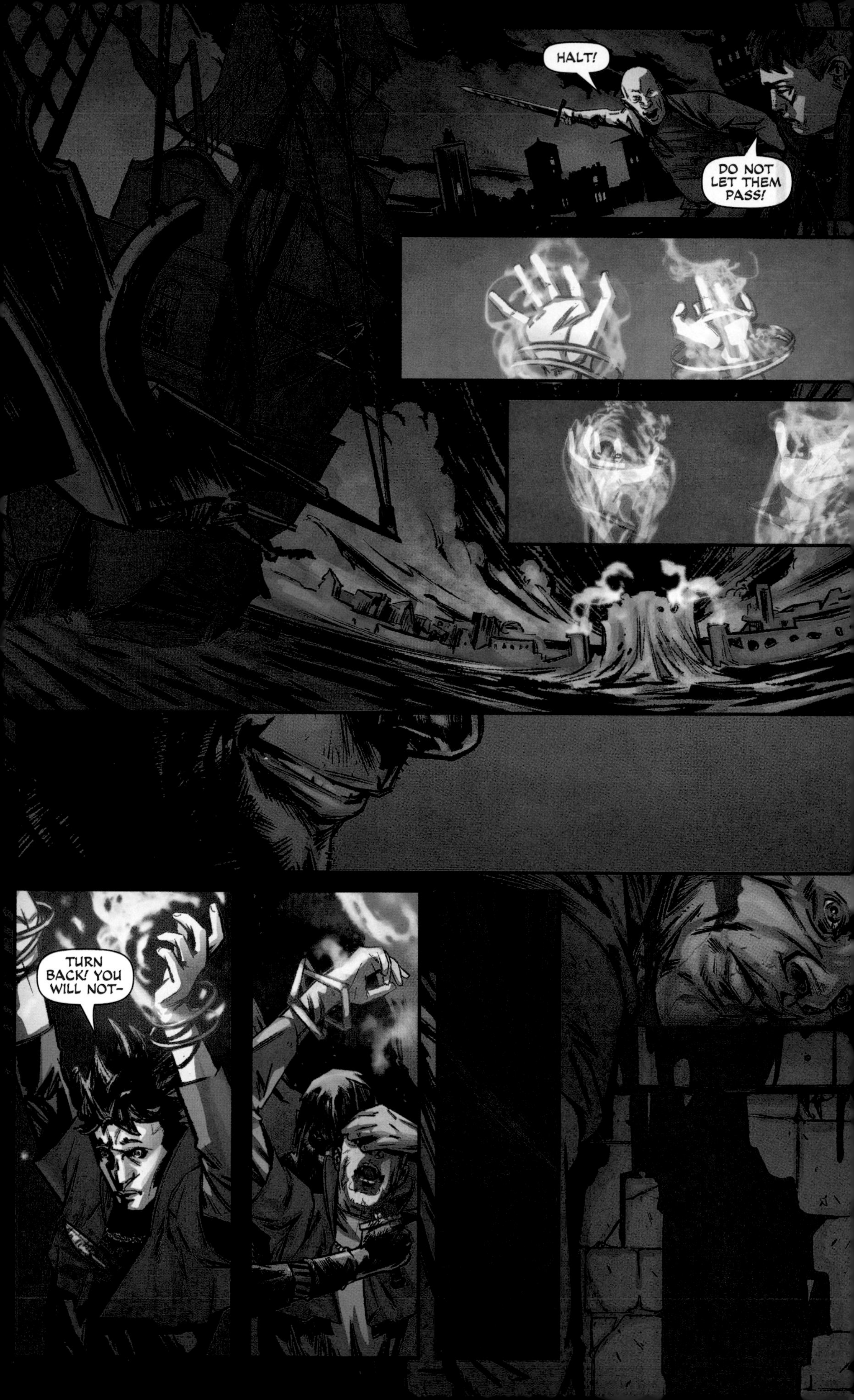
HALT!
DO NOT LET THEM PASS!
TURN BACK! YOU WILL NOT-

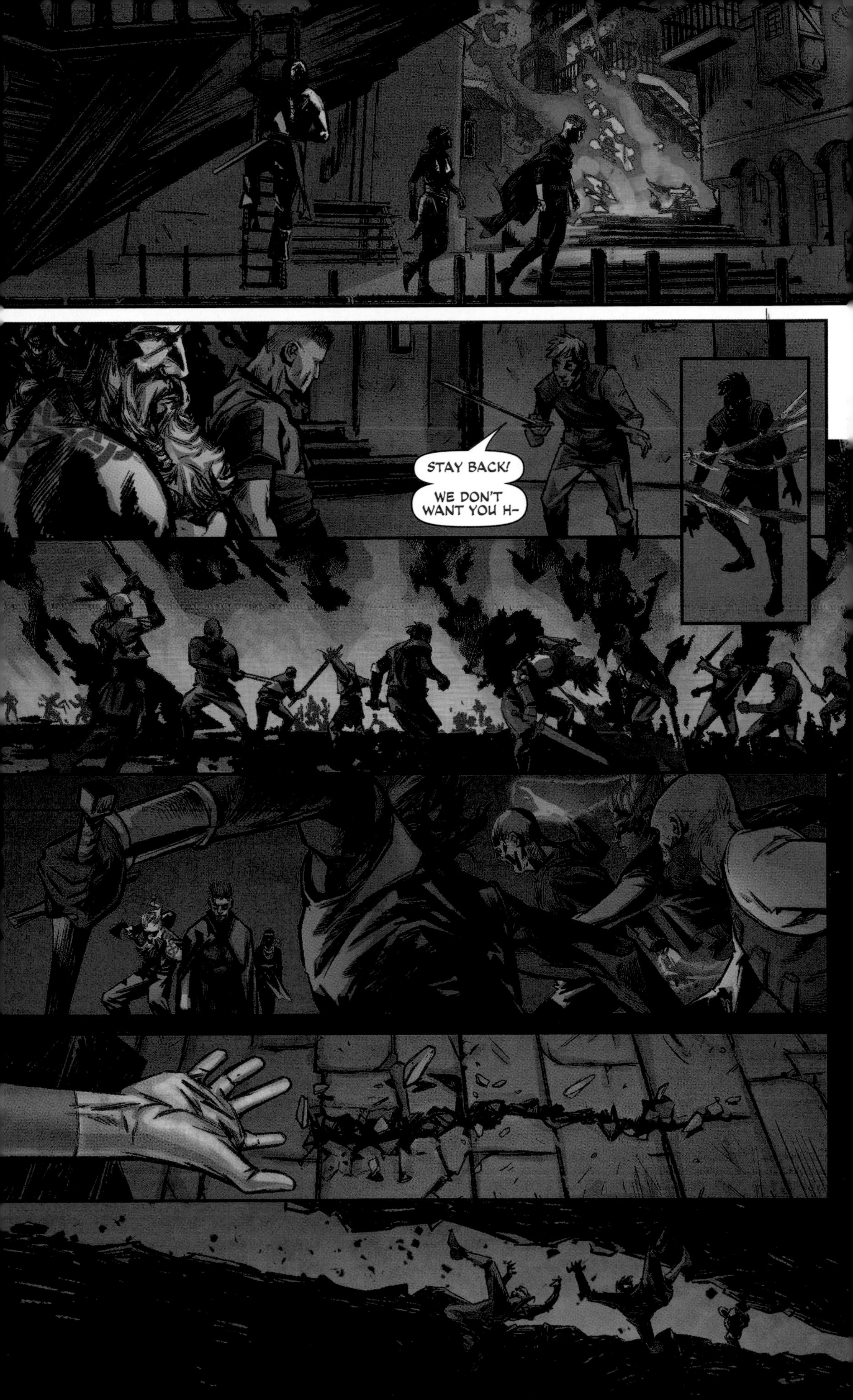
STAY BACK!
WE DON'T WANT YOU H-

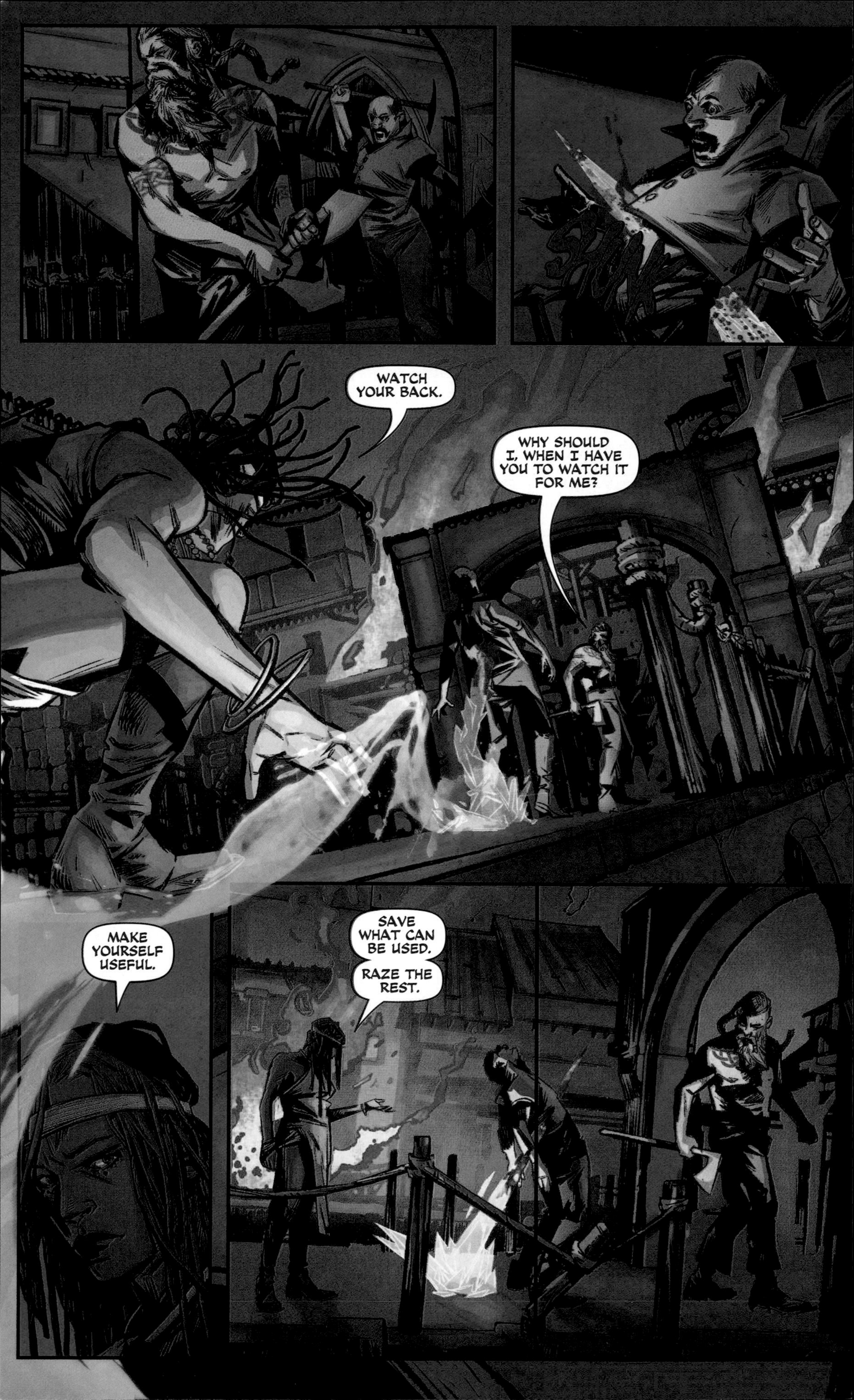
WATCH YOUR BACK.
WHY SHOULD I, WHEN I HAVE YOU TO WATCH IT FOR ME?
MAKE YOURSELF USEFUL.
SAVE WHAT CAN BE USED.
RAZE THE REST.

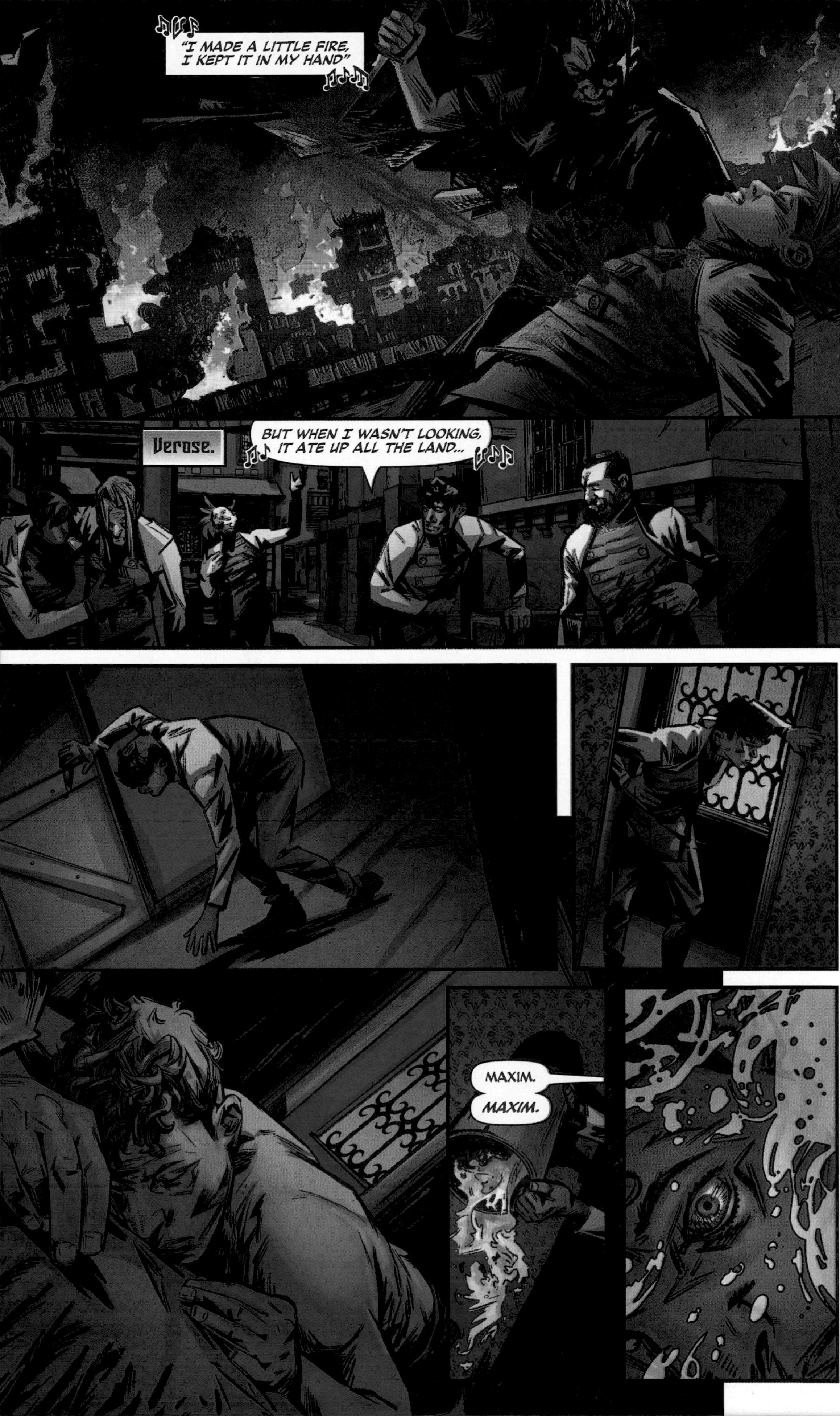
"I MADE A LITTLE FIRE, I KEPT IT IN MY HAND"
Verose.
BUT WHEN I WASN'T LOOKING, IT ATE UP ALL THE LAND...
MAXIM.
MAXIM.

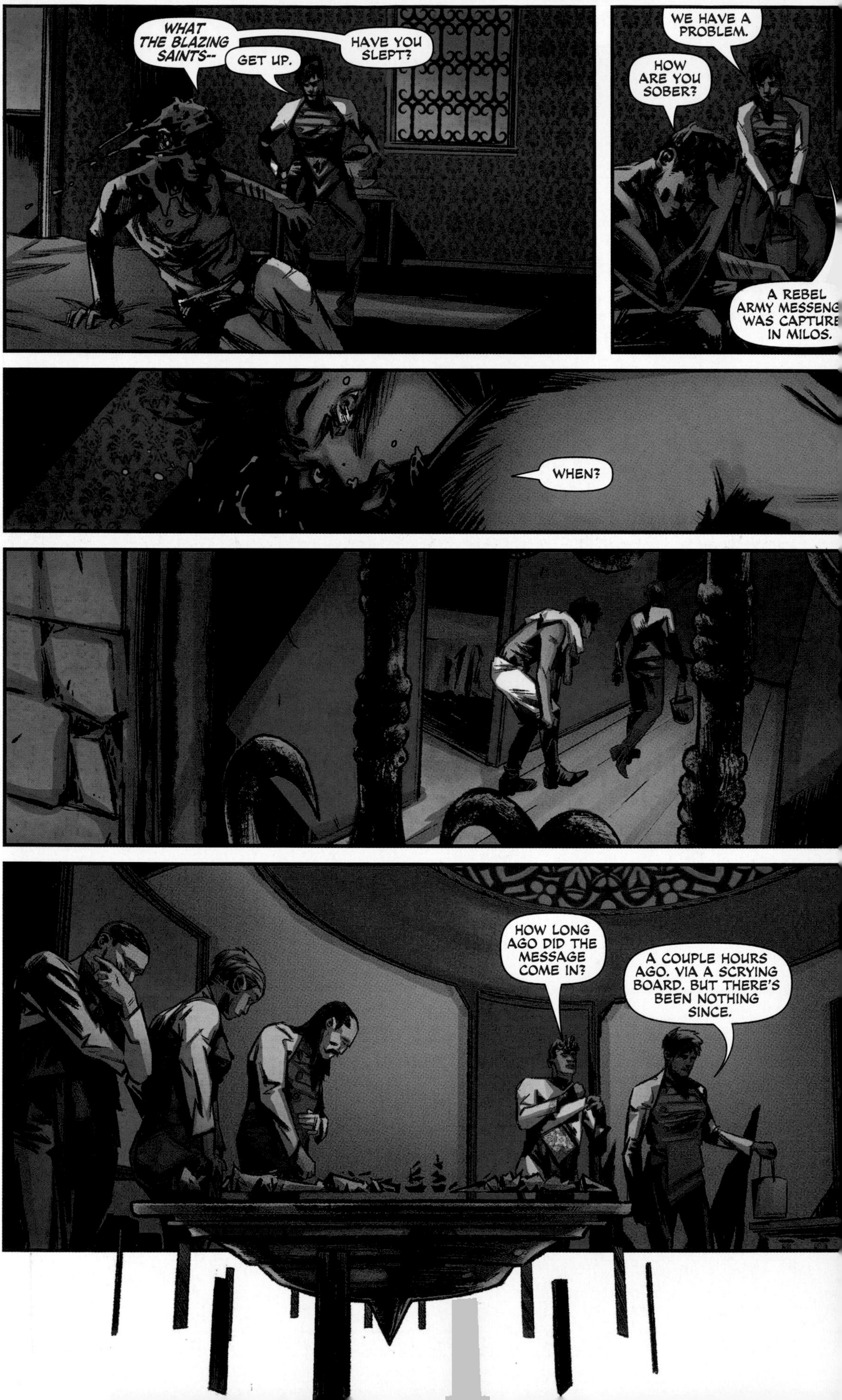
WHAT THE BLAZING SAINTS--
HAVE YOU SLEPT?
GET UP.
WE HAVE A PROBLEM.
HOW ARE YOU SOBER?
A REBEL ARMY MESSENG
WAS CAPTURE
IN MILOS.
WHEN?
HOW LONG AGO DID THE MESSAGE COME IN?
A COUPLE HOURS AGO. VIA A SCRYING BOARD. BUT THERE'S BEEN NOTHING SINCE.

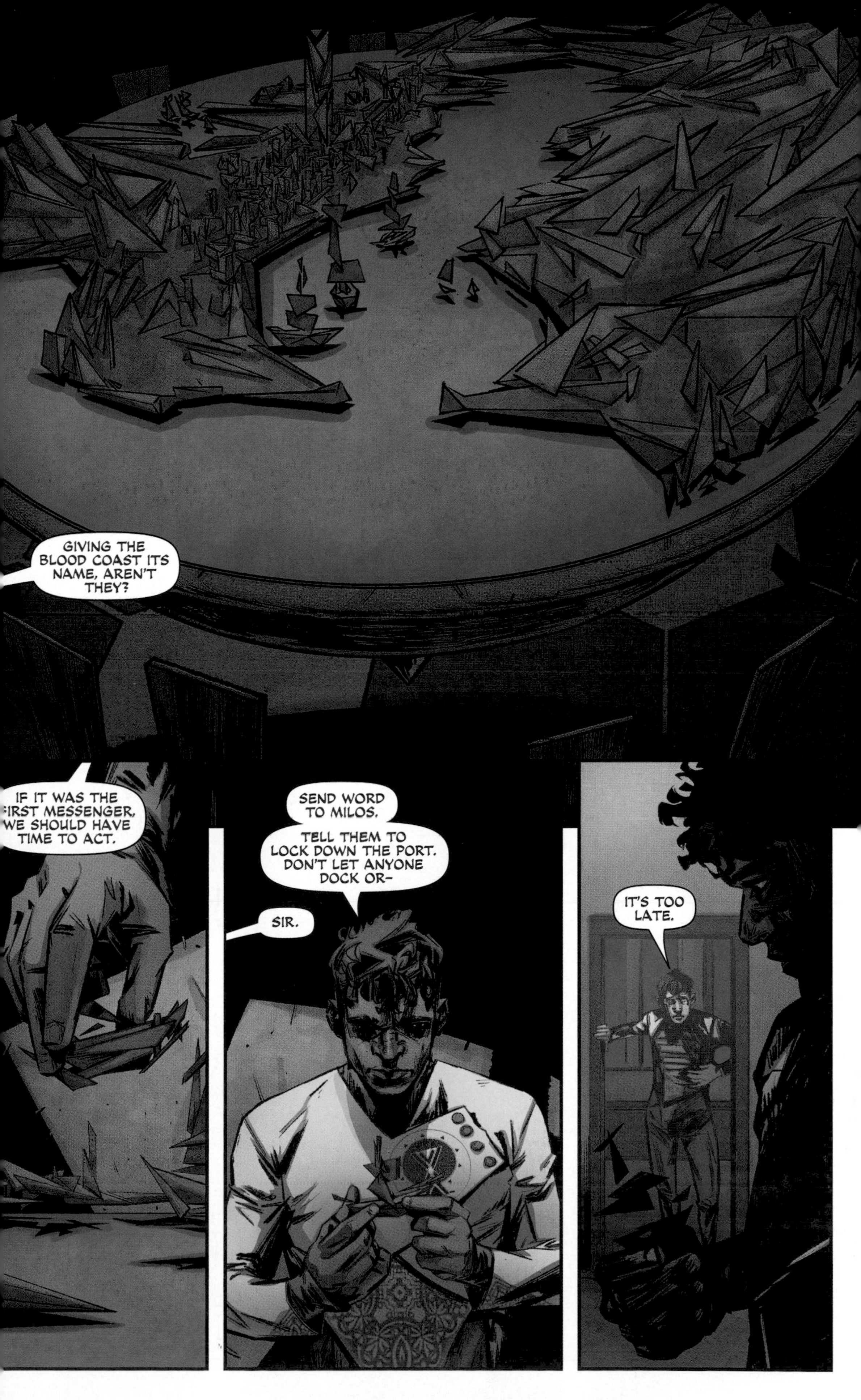
GIVING THE BLOOD COAST ITS NAME, AREN'T THEY?
IF IT WAS THE FIRST MESSENGER, WE SHOULD HAVE TIME TO ACT.
SEND WORD TO MILOS.
TELL THEM TO LOCK DOWN THE PORT. DON'T LET ANYONE DOCK OR-
SIR.
IT'S TOO LATE.

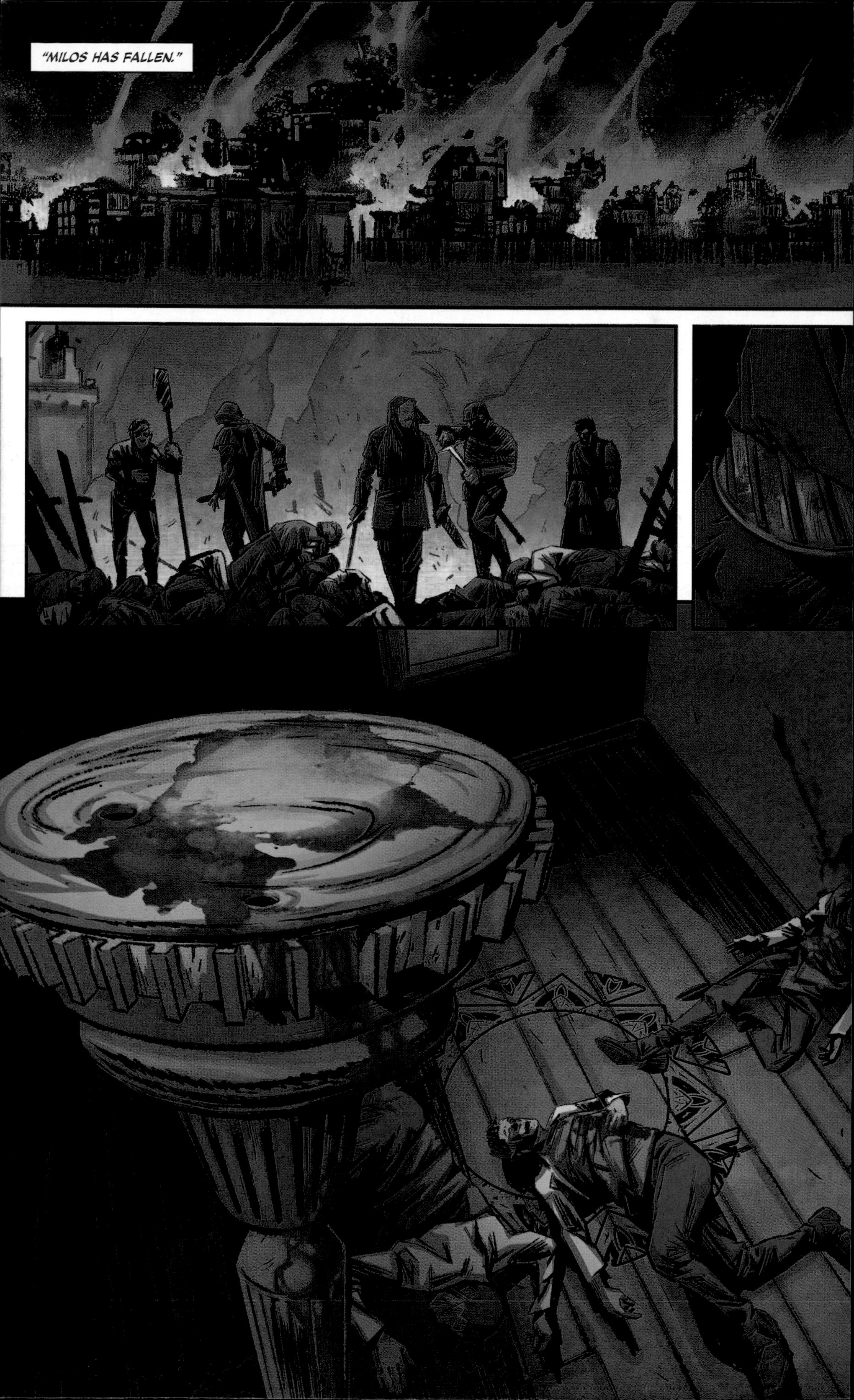
"MILOS HAS FALLEN."

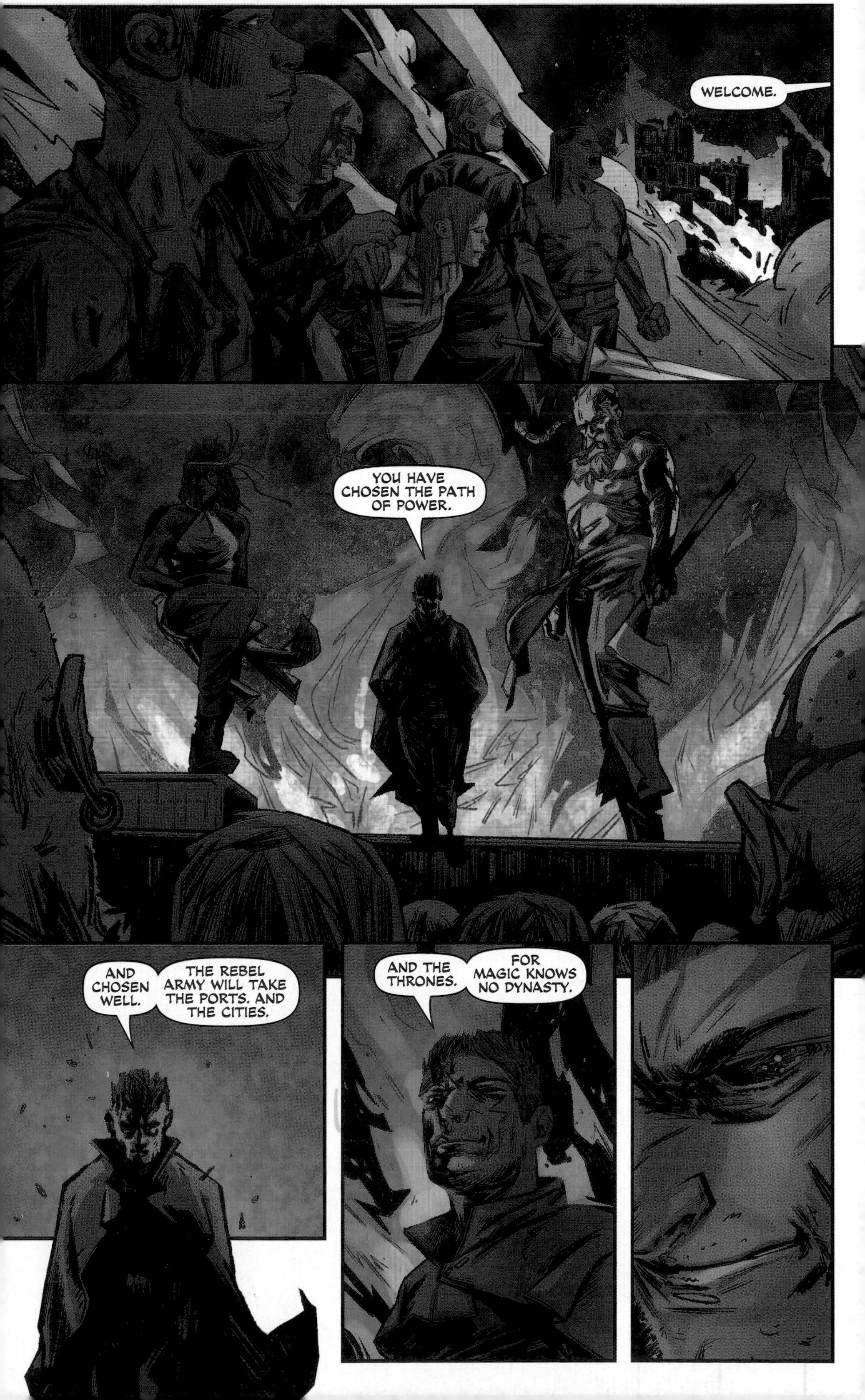
WELCOME.
YOU HAVE CHOSEN THE PATH OF POWER.
AND CHOSEN WELL.
THE REBEL ARMY WILL TAKE THE PORTS. AND THE CITIES.
AND THE THRONES.
FOR MAGIC KNOWS NO DYNASTY.

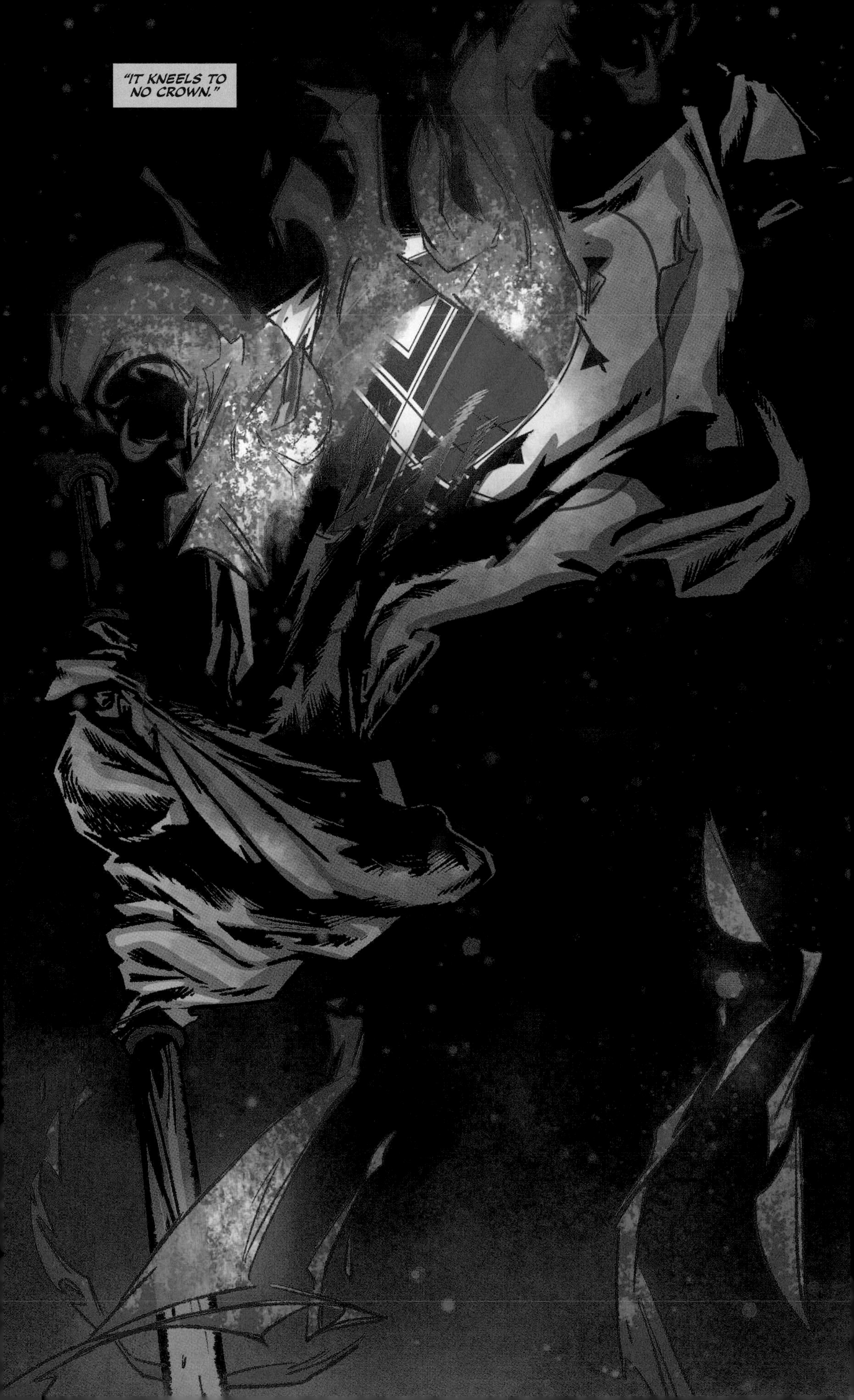
"IT KNEELS TO NO CROWN."

#2

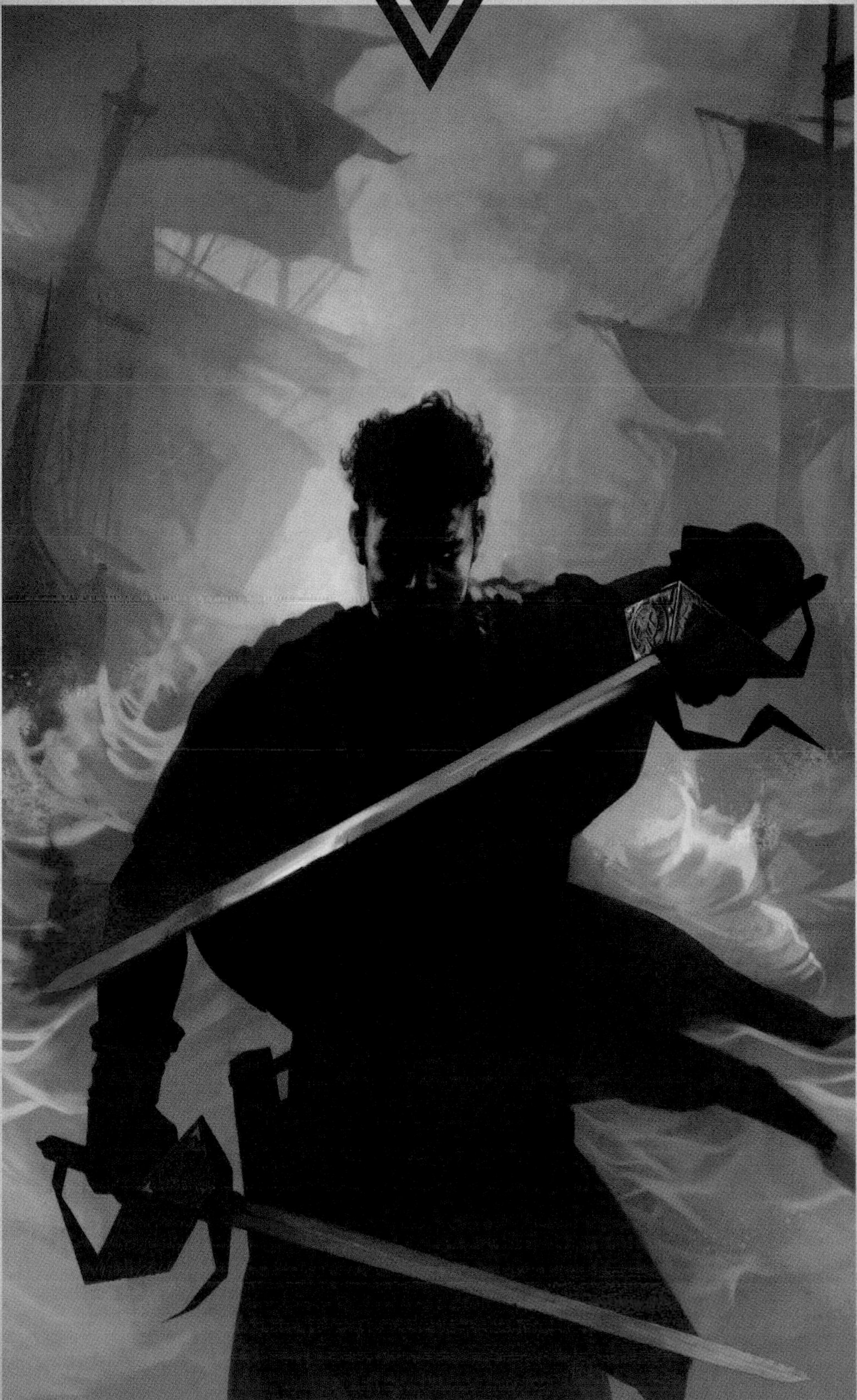

ILLUSTRATION BY CLAUDIA CARANFA

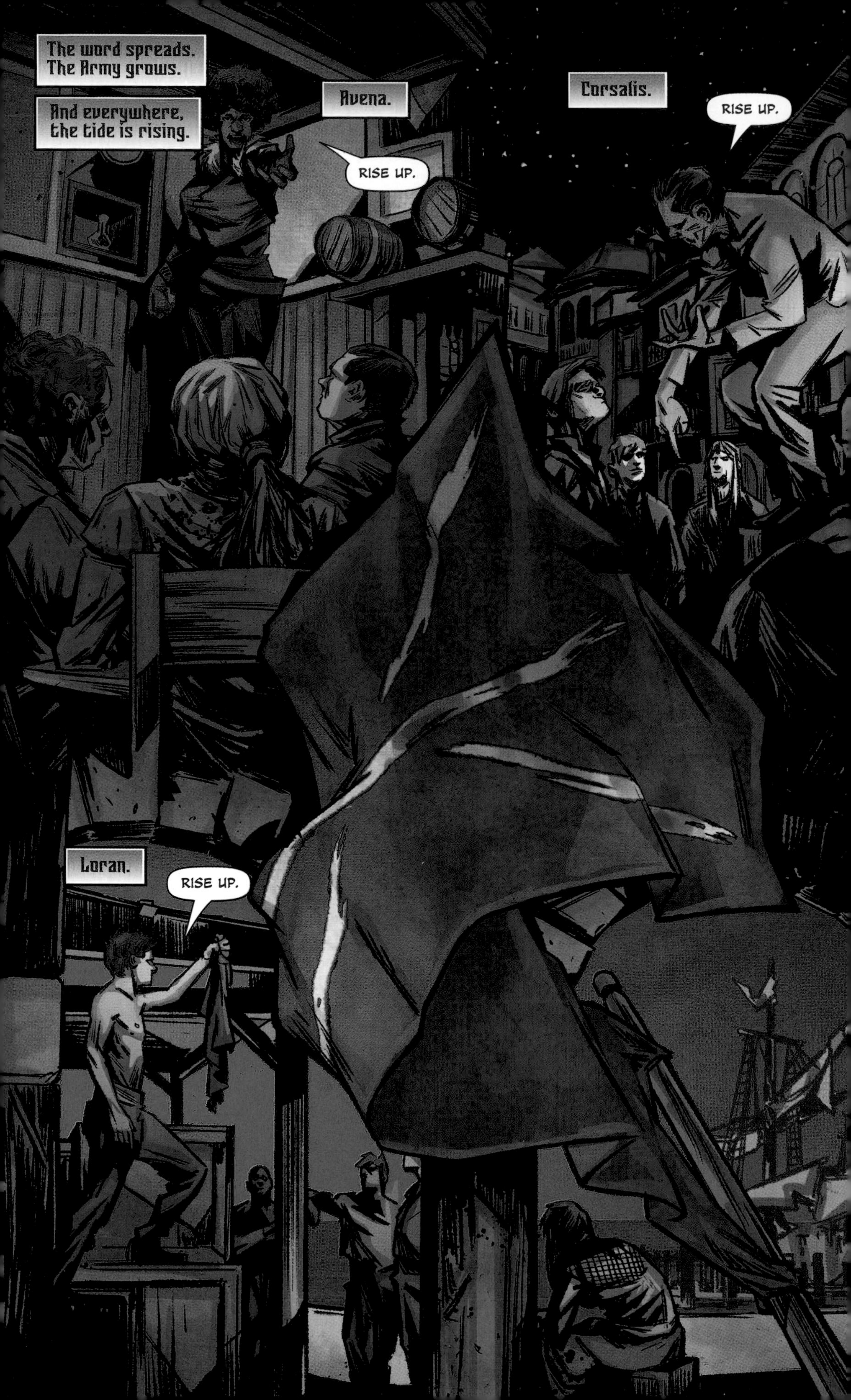
The word spreads.
The Army grows.
And everywhere,
the tide is rising.
Avena.
RISE UP.
Corsalis.
RISE UP.
Loran.
RISE UP.

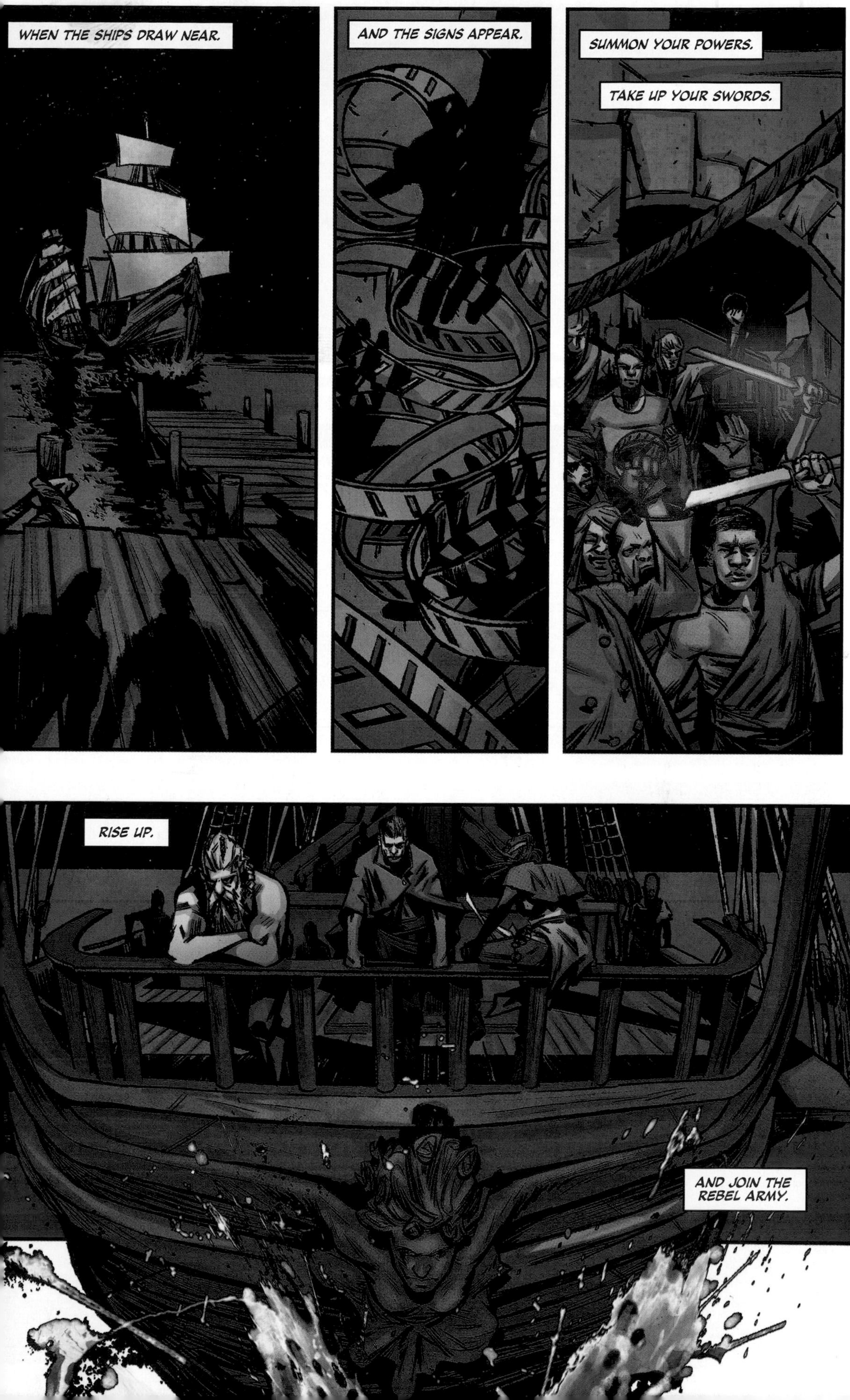
WHEN THE SHIPS DRAW NEAR.
AND THE SIGNS APPEAR.
SUMMON YOUR POWERS.
TAKE UP YOUR SWORDS.
RISE UP.
AND JOIN THE REBEL ARMY.

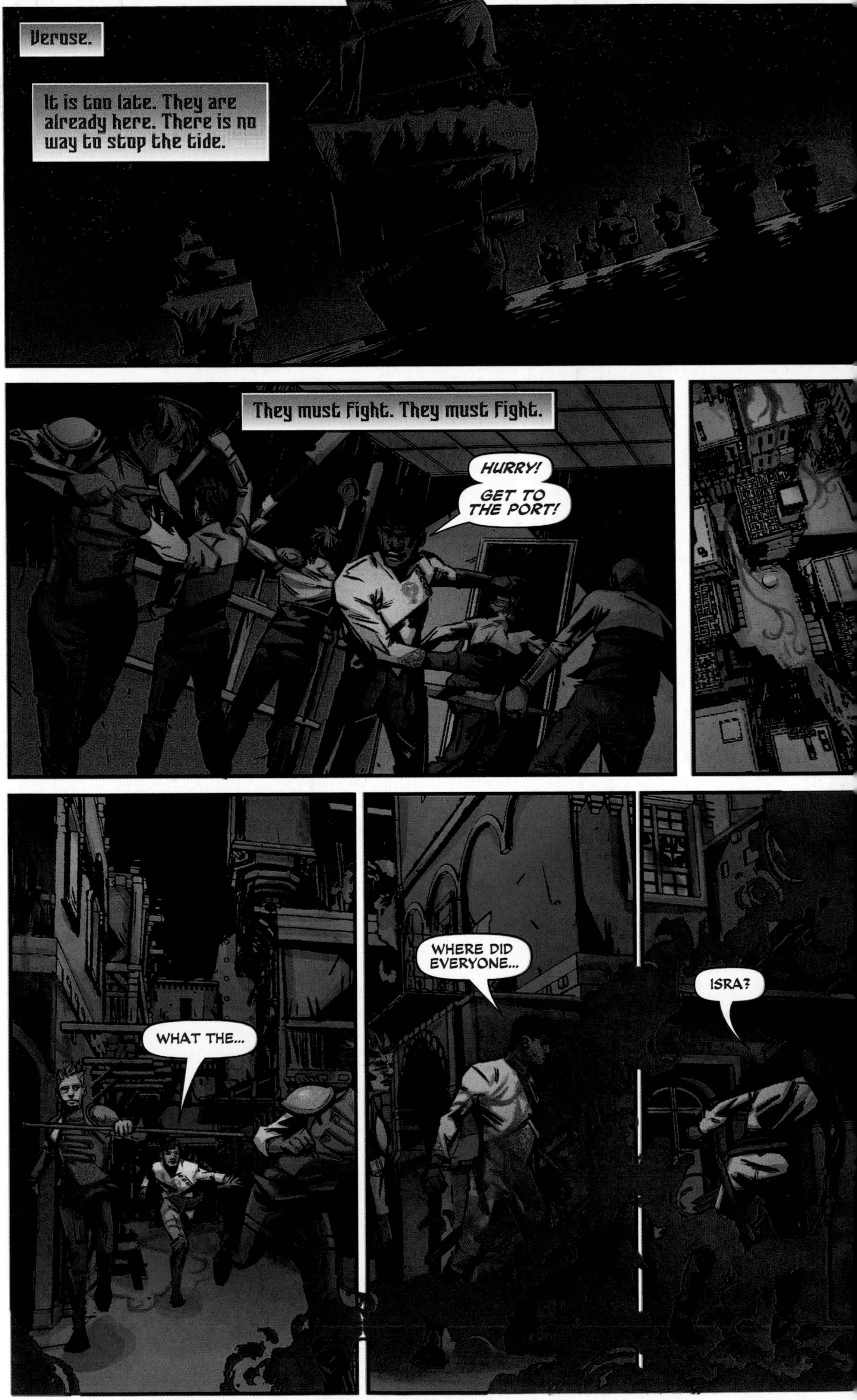
Verose.
It is too late. They are already here. There is no way to stop the tide.
They must fight. They must fight.
HURRY!
GET TO THE PORT!
WHAT THE...
WHERE DID EVERYONE...
ISRA?

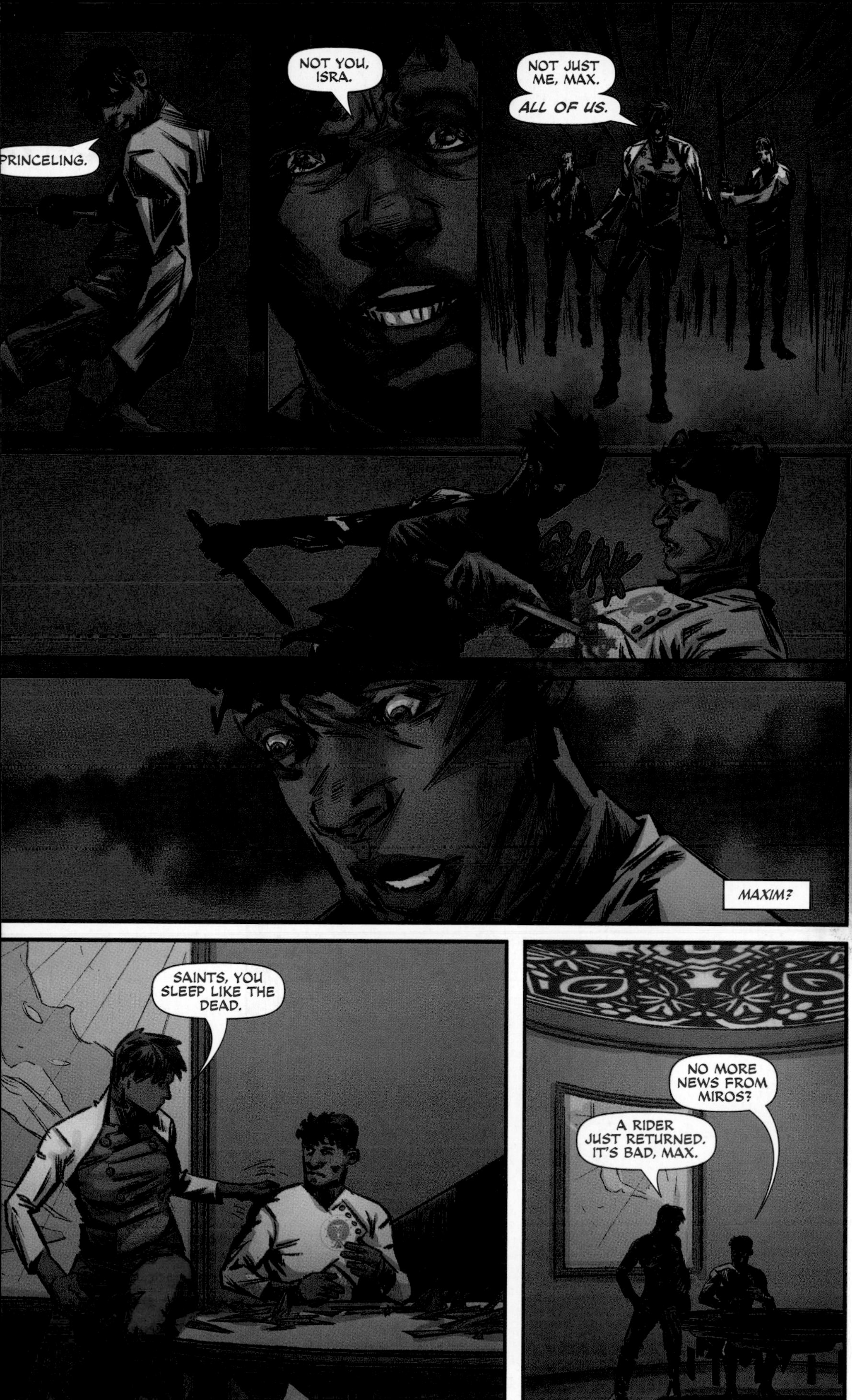
PRINCELING.
NOT YOU, ISRA.
NOT JUST ME, MAX.
ALL OF US.
MAXIM?
SAINTS, YOU SLEEP LIKE THE DEAD.
NO MORE NEWS FROM MIROS?
A RIDER JUST RETURNED. IT'S BAD, MAX.

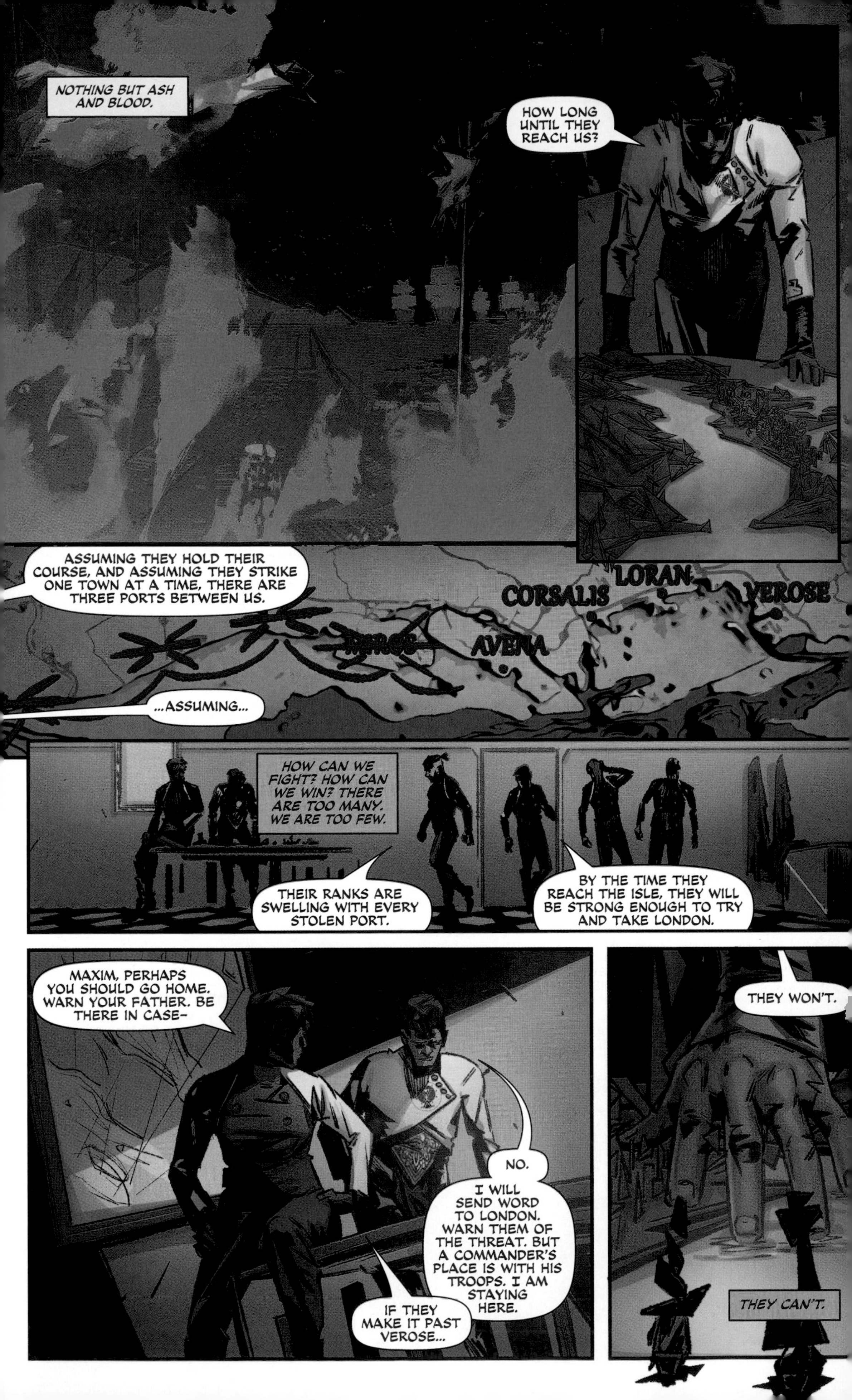
NOTHING BUT ASH AND BLOOD.
HOW LONG UNTIL THEY REACH US?
ASSUMING THEY HOLD THEIR COURSE, AND ASSUMING THEY STRIKE ONE TOWN AT A TIME, THERE ARE THREE PORTS BETWEEN US.
CORSALIS
LORAN
VEROSE
AVENA
...ASSUMING...
HOW CAN WE FIGHT? HOW CAN WE WIN? THERE ARE TOO MANY. WE ARE TOO FEW.
THEIR RANKS ARE SWELLING WITH EVERY STOLEN PORT.
BY THE TIME THEY REACH THE ISLE, THEY WILL BE STRONG ENOUGH TO TRY AND TAKE LONDON.
MAXIM, PERHAPS YOU SHOULD GO HOME. WARN YOUR FATHER. BE THERE IN CASE–
NO.
I WILL SEND WORD TO LONDON. WARN THEM OF THE THREAT. BUT A COMMANDER'S PLACE IS WITH HIS TROOPS. I AM STAYING HERE.
IF THEY MAKE IT PAST VEROSE...
THEY WON'T.
THEY CAN'T.

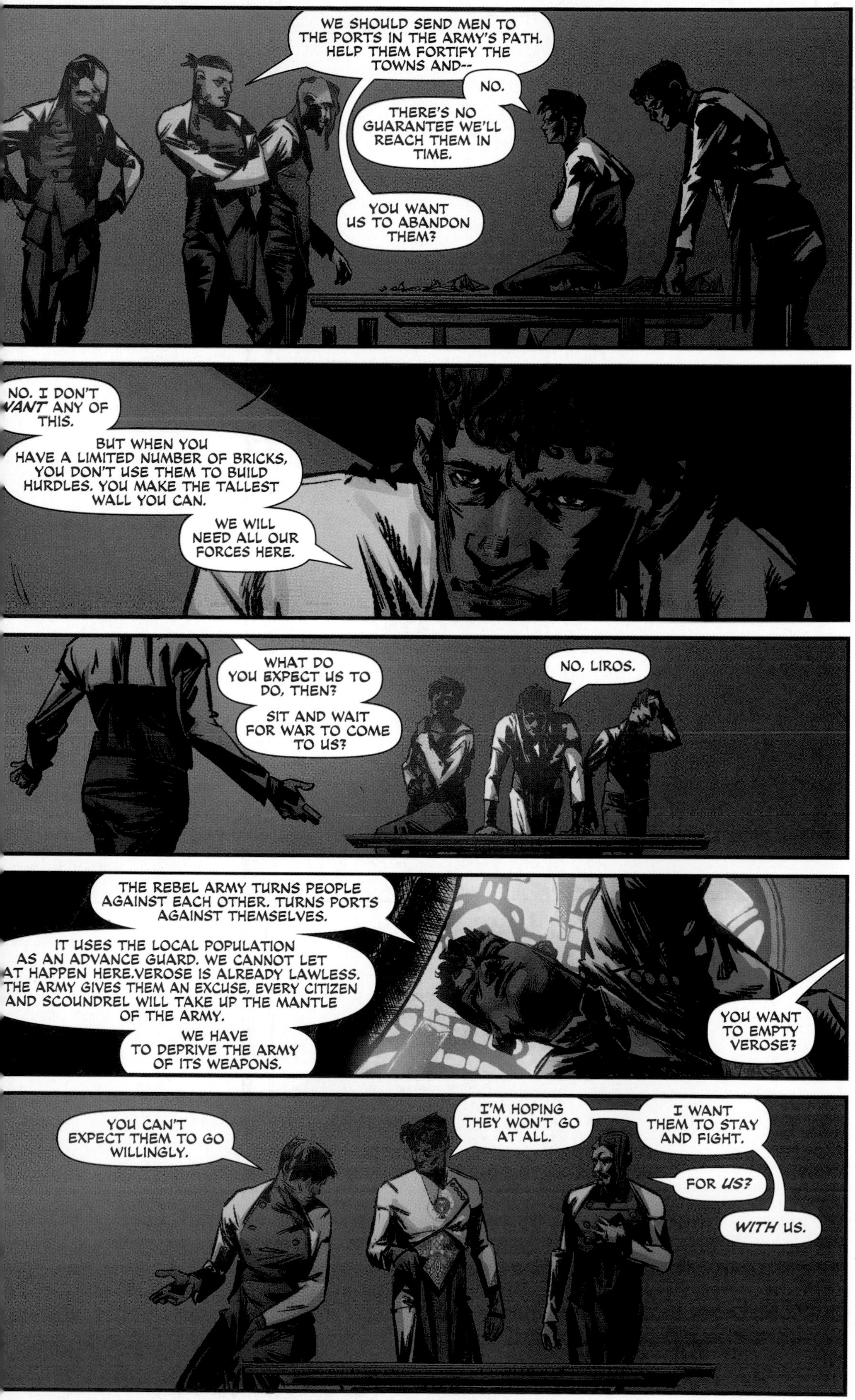
WE SHOULD SEND MEN TO THE PORTS IN THE ARMY'S PATH. HELP THEM FORTIFY THE TOWNS AND--
NO.
THERE'S NO GUARANTEE WE'LL REACH THEM IN TIME.
YOU WANT US TO ABANDON THEM?
NO. I DON'T WANT ANY OF THIS.
BUT WHEN YOU HAVE A LIMITED NUMBER OF BRICKS, YOU DON'T USE THEM TO BUILD HURDLES. YOU MAKE THE TALLEST WALL YOU CAN.
WE WILL NEED ALL OUR FORCES HERE.
WHAT DO YOU EXPECT US TO DO, THEN?
SIT AND WAIT FOR WAR TO COME TO US?
NO, LIROS.
THE REBEL ARMY TURNS PEOPLE AGAINST EACH OTHER. TURNS PORTS AGAINST THEMSELVES.
IT USES THE LOCAL POPULATION AS AN ADVANCE GUARD. WE CANNOT LET AT HAPPEN HERE.VEROSE IS ALREADY LAWLESS. THE ARMY GIVES THEM AN EXCUSE, EVERY CITIZEN AND SCOUNDREL WILL TAKE UP THE MANTLE OF THE ARMY.
WE HAVE TO DEPRIVE THE ARMY OF ITS WEAPONS.
YOU WANT TO EMPTY VEROSE?
YOU CAN'T EXPECT THEM TO GO WILLINGLY.
I'M HOPING THEY WON'T GO AT ALL.
I WANT THEM TO STAY AND FIGHT.
FOR US?
WITH US.

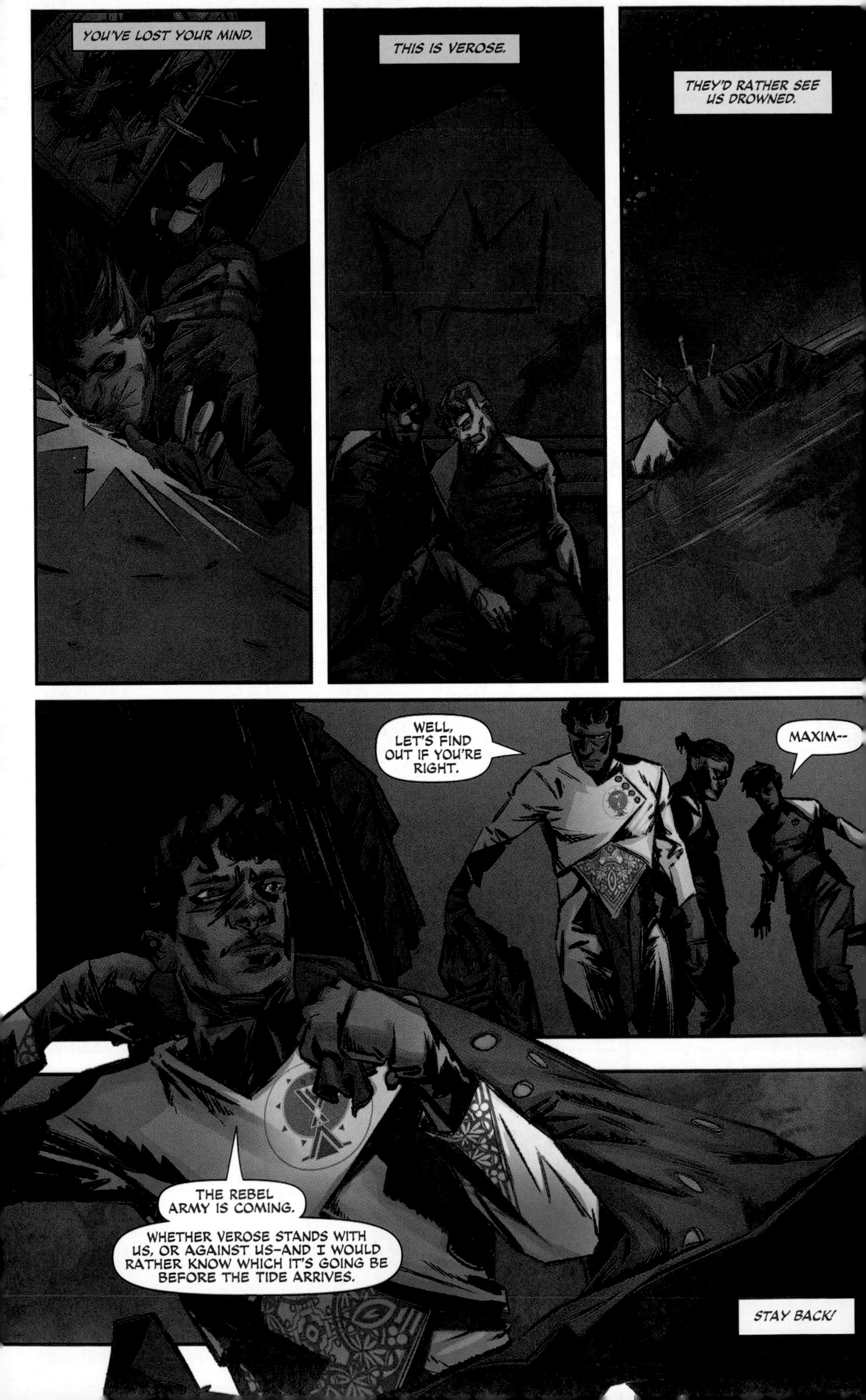
YOU'VE LOST YOUR MIND.
THIS IS VEROSE.
THEY'D RATHER SEE US DROWNED.
WELL, LET'S FIND OUT IF YOU'RE RIGHT.
MAXIM--
THE REBEL ARMY IS COMING.
WHETHER VEROSE STANDS WITH US, OR AGAINST US--AND I WOULD RATHER KNOW WHICH IT'S GOING BE BEFORE THE TIDE ARRIVES.
STAY BACK!

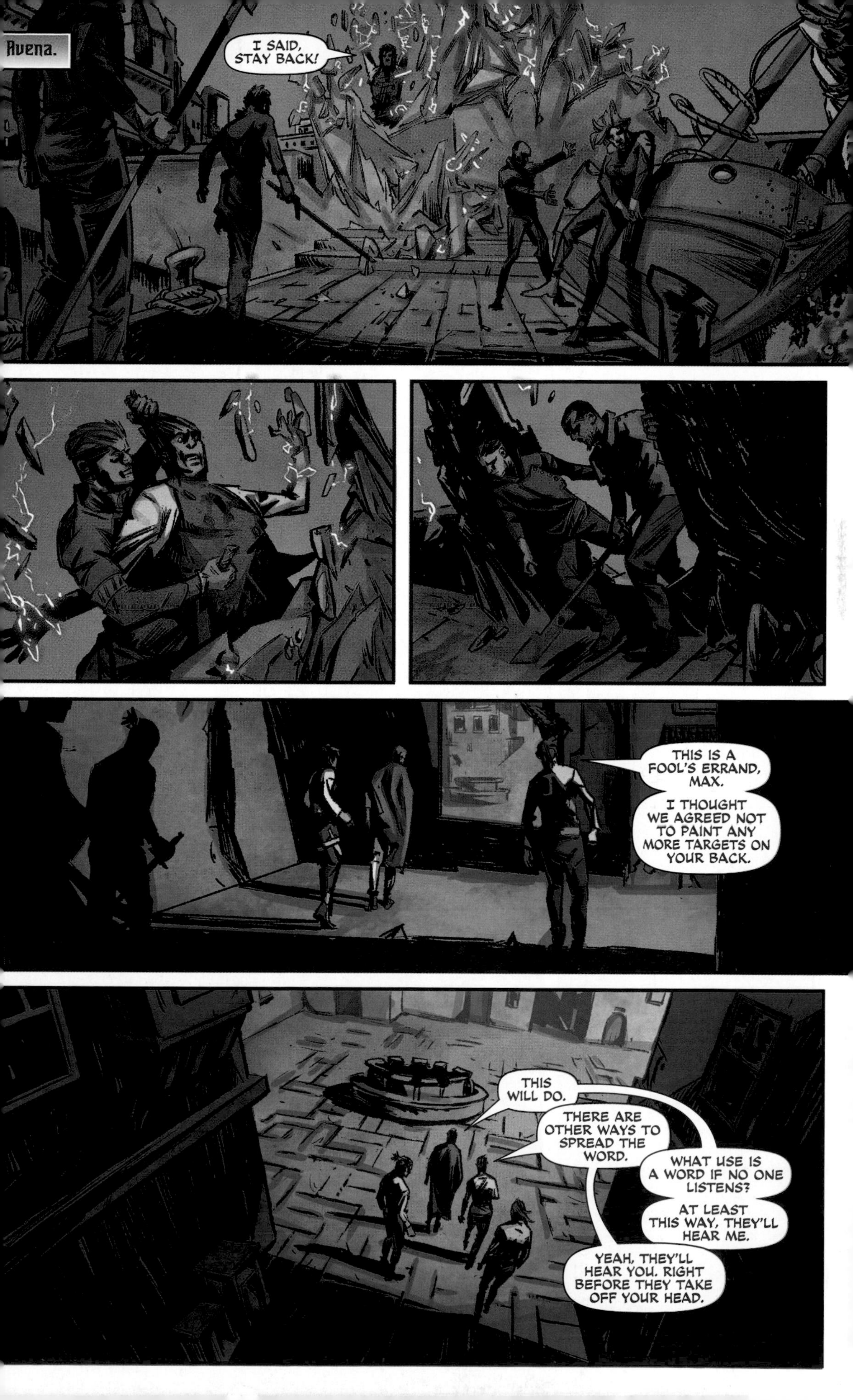
Avena.
I SAID, STAY BACK!
THIS IS A FOOL'S ERRAND, MAX.
I THOUGHT WE AGREED NOT TO PAINT ANY MORE TARGETS ON YOUR BACK.
THIS WILL DO.
THERE ARE OTHER WAYS TO SPREAD THE WORD.
WHAT USE IS A WORD IF NO ONE LISTENS?
AT LEAST THIS WAY, THEY'LL HEAR ME.
YEAH, THEY'LL HEAR YOU. RIGHT BEFORE THEY TAKE OFF YOUR HEAD.

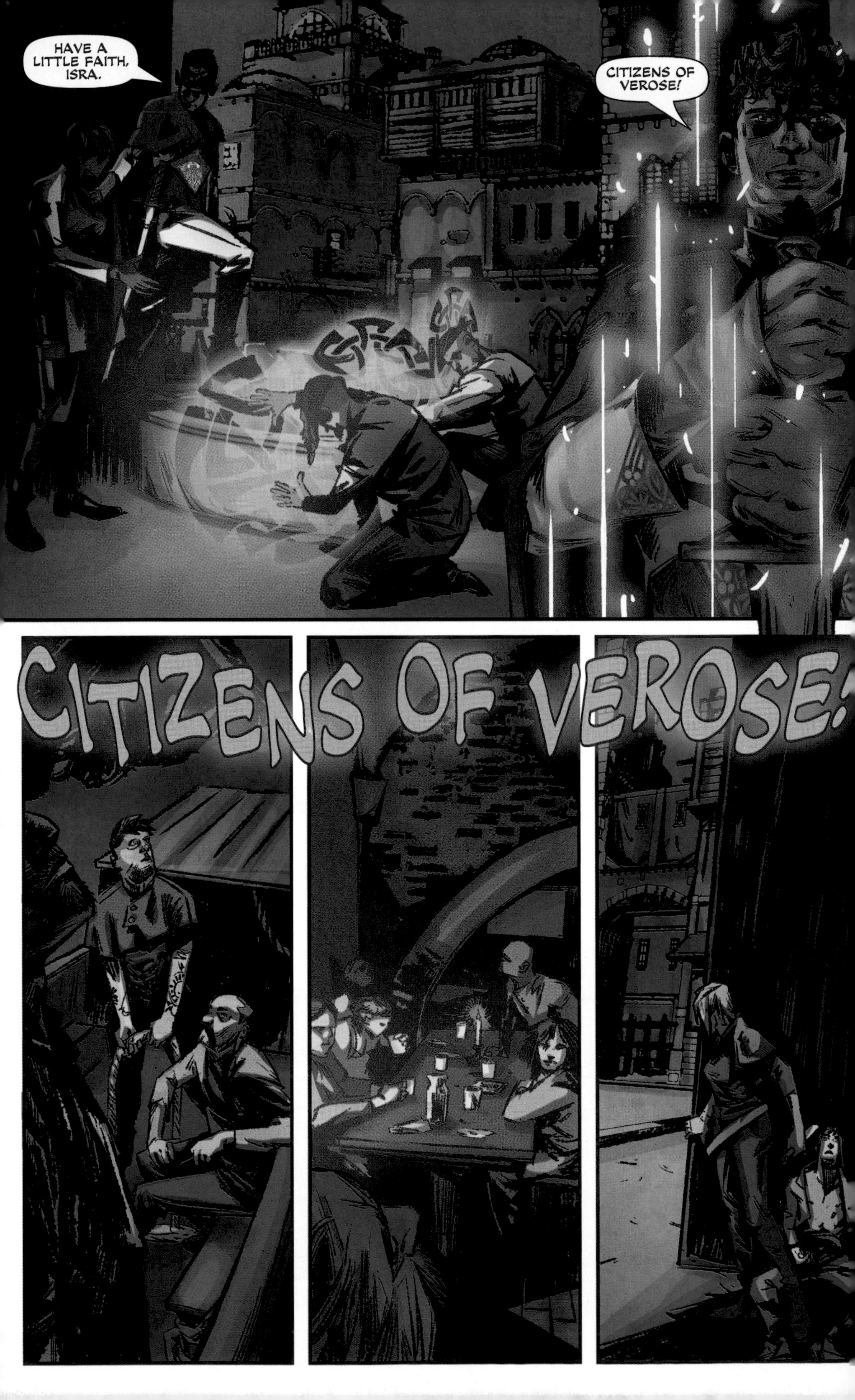
HAVE A LITTLE FAITH, ISRA.
CITIZENS OF VEROSE!
CITIZENS OF VEROSE!

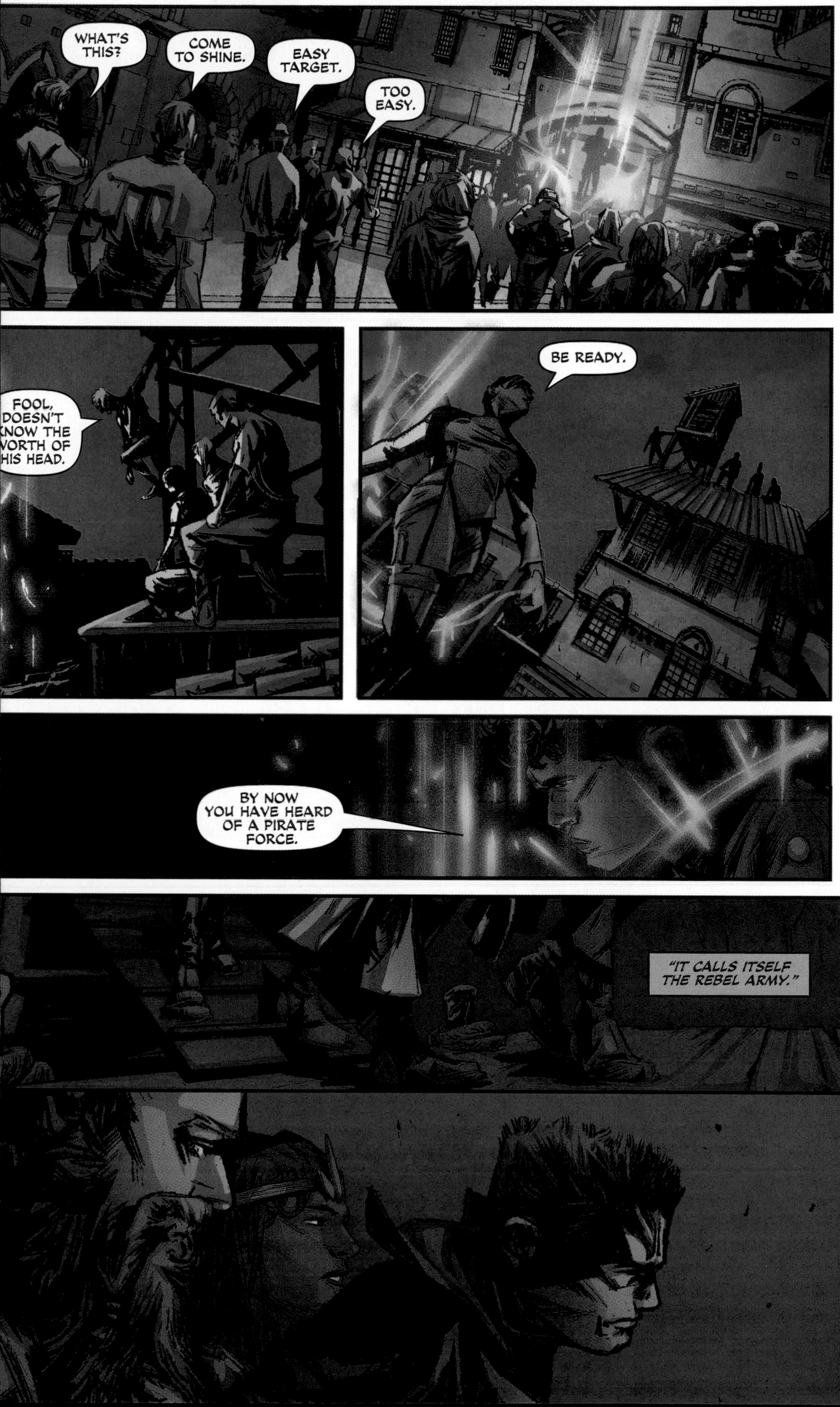
WHAT'S THIS?
COME TO SHINE.
EASY TARGET.
TOO EASY.
FOOL, DOESN'T KNOW THE WORTH OF HIS HEAD.
BE READY.
BY NOW YOU HAVE HEARD OF A PIRATE FORCE.
"IT CALLS ITSELF THE REBEL ARMY."

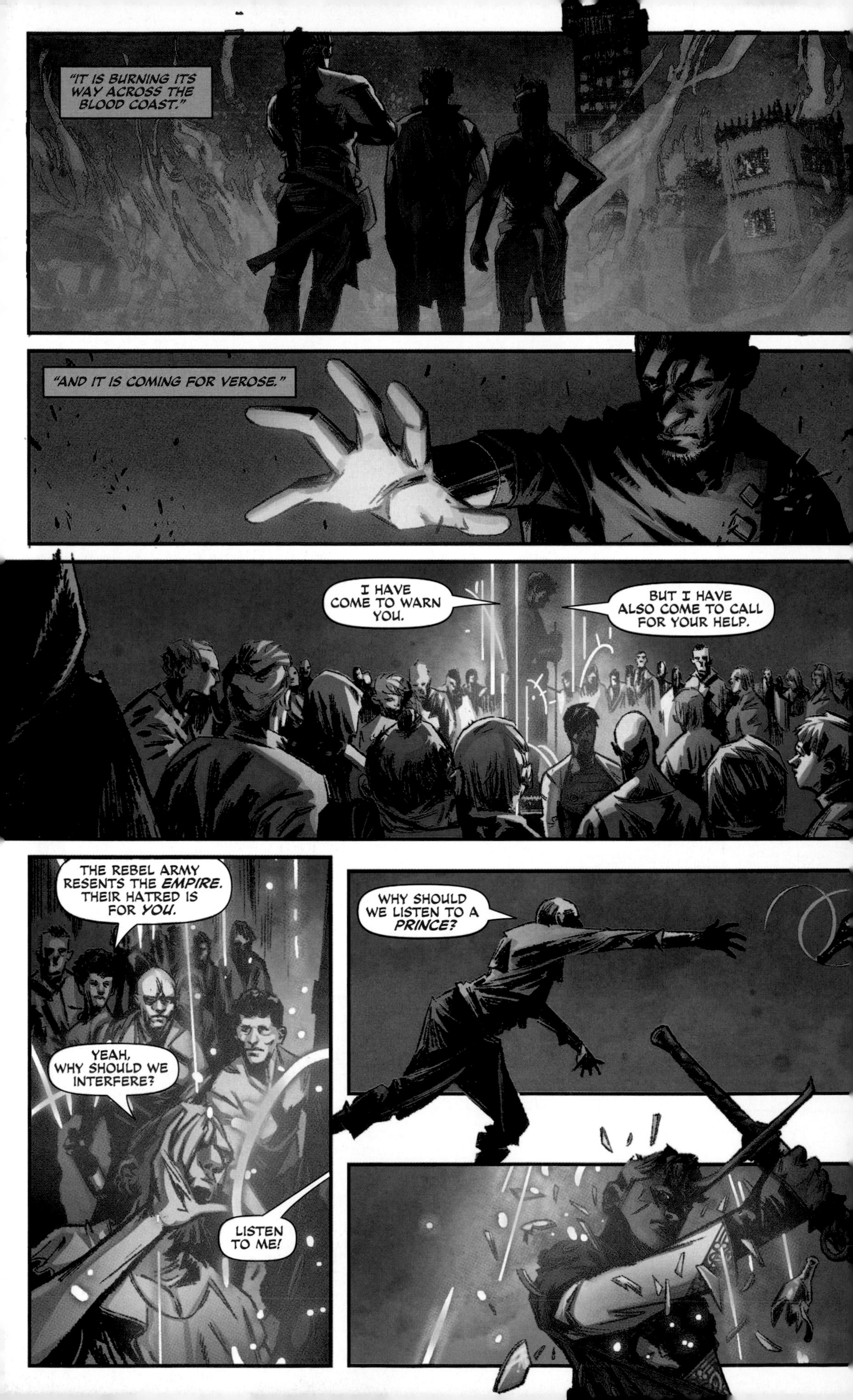
"IT IS BURNING ITS WAY ACROSS THE BLOOD COAST."
"AND IT IS COMING FOR VEROSE."
I HAVE COME TO WARN YOU.
BUT I HAVE ALSO COME TO CALL FOR YOUR HELP.
THE REBEL ARMY RESENTS THE *EMPIRE*. THEIR HATRED IS FOR *YOU*.
YEAH, WHY SHOULD WE INTERFERE?
LISTEN TO ME!
WHY SHOULD WE LISTEN TO A *PRINCE?*

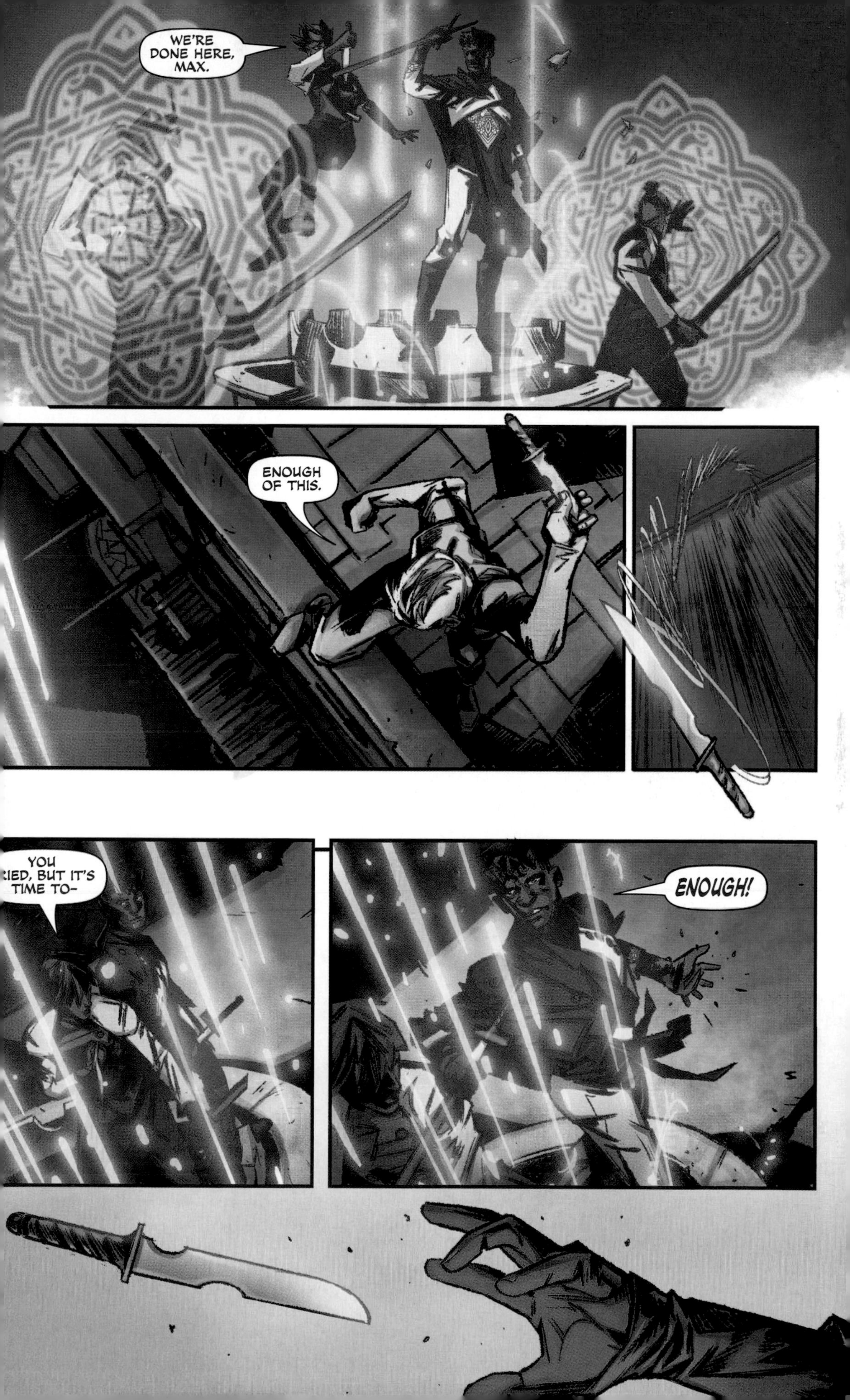
WE'RE DONE HERE, MAX.
ENOUGH OF THIS.
YOU
RIED, BUT IT'S TIME TO-
ENOUGH!

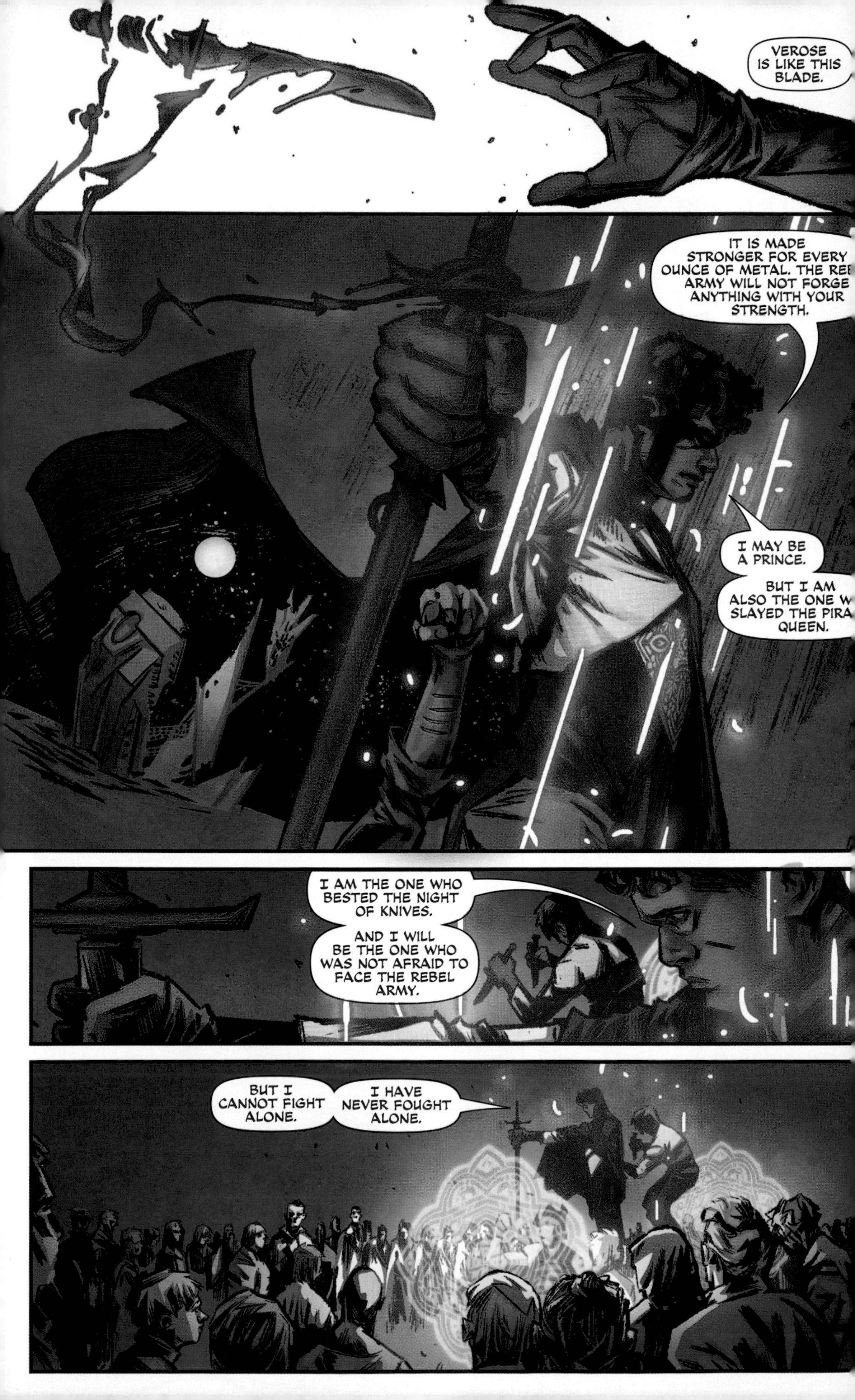
VEROSE IS LIKE THIS BLADE.
IT IS MADE STRONGER FOR EVERY OUNCE OF METAL. THE REB ARMY WILL NOT FORGE ANYTHING WITH YOUR STRENGTH.
I MAY BE A PRINCE.
BUT I AM ALSO THE ONE W SLAYED THE PIRA QUEEN.
I AM THE ONE WHO BESTED THE NIGHT OF KNIVES.
AND I WILL BE THE ONE WHO WAS NOT AFRAID TO FACE THE REBEL ARMY.
BUT I CANNOT FIGHT ALONE.
I HAVE NEVER FOUGHT ALONE.

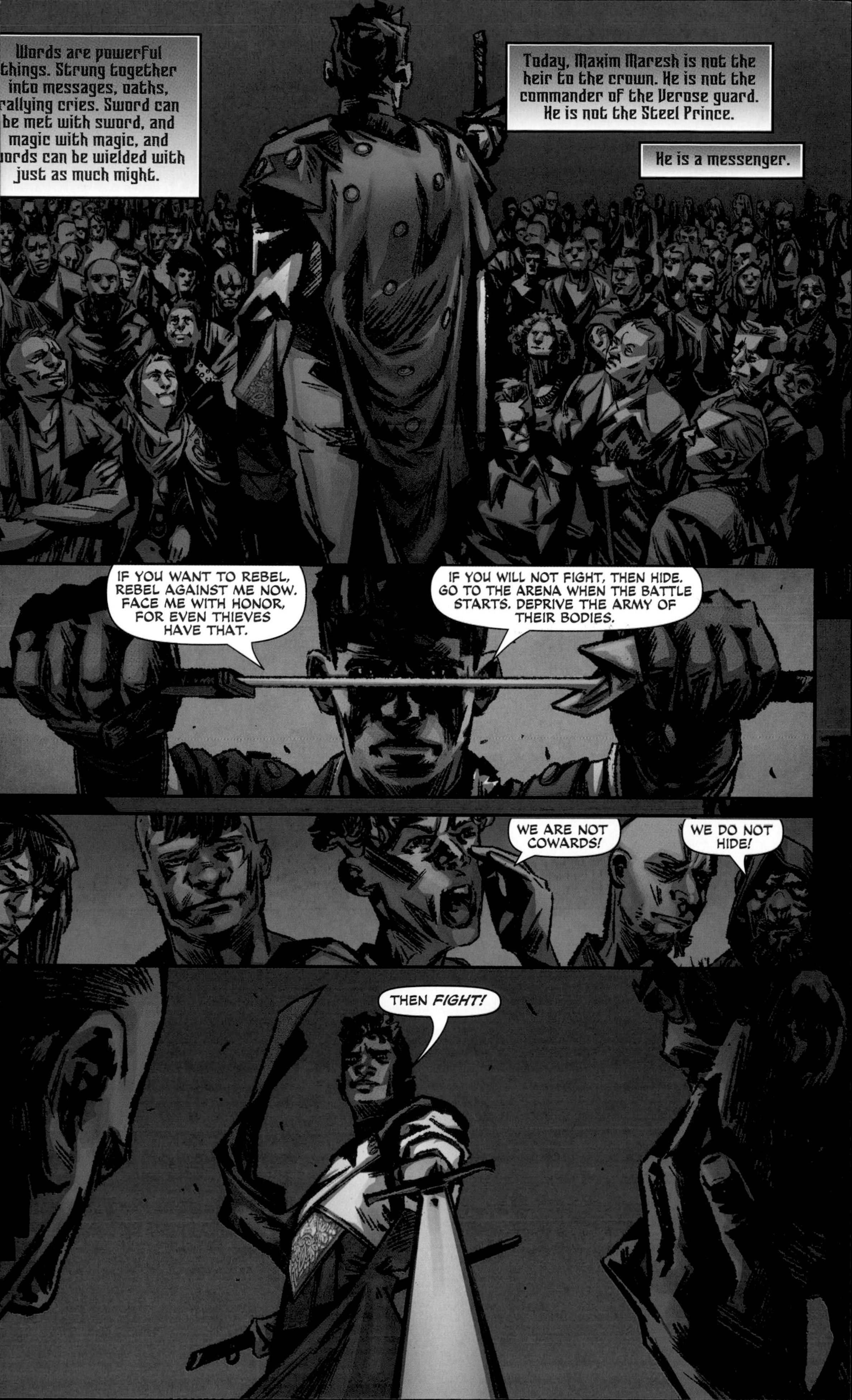
Words are powerful things. Strung together into messages, oaths, rallying cries. Sword can be met with sword, and magic with magic, and words can be wielded with just as much might.
Today, Maxim Maresh is not the heir to the crown. He is not the commander of the Verose guard. He is not the Steel Prince.
He is a messenger.
IF YOU WANT TO REBEL, REBEL AGAINST ME NOW. FACE ME WITH HONOR, FOR EVEN THIEVES HAVE THAT.
IF YOU WILL NOT FIGHT, THEN HIDE. GO TO THE ARENA WHEN THE BATTLE STARTS. DEPRIVE THE ARMY OF THEIR BODIES.
WE ARE NOT COWARDS!
WE DO NOT HIDE!
THEN FIGHT!

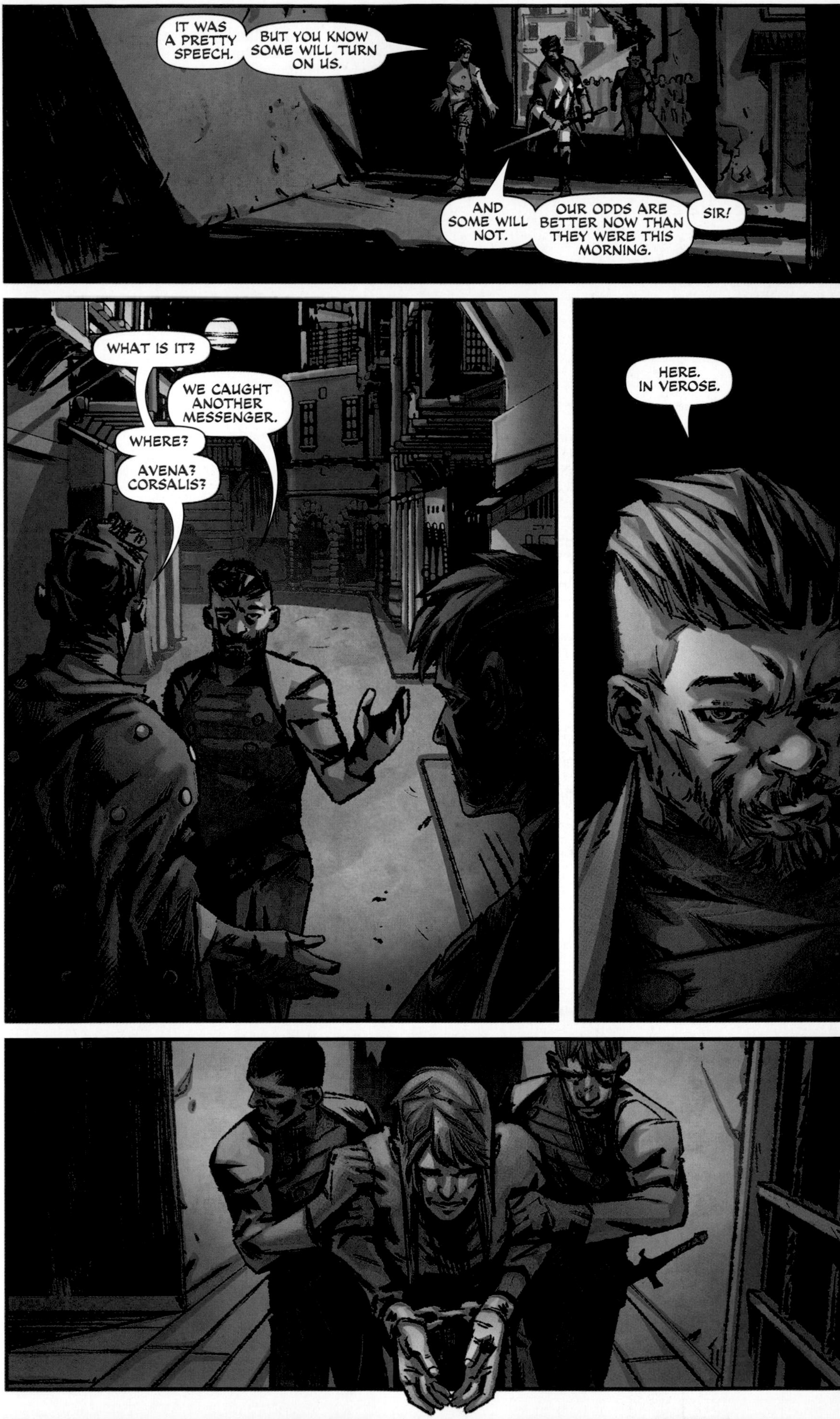
IT WAS A PRETTY SPEECH.
BUT YOU KNOW SOME WILL TURN ON US.
AND SOME WILL NOT.
OUR ODDS ARE BETTER NOW THAN THEY WERE THIS MORNING.
SIR!
WHAT IS IT?
WE CAUGHT ANOTHER MESSENGER.
WHERE?
AVENA? CORSALIS?
HERE. IN VEROSE.

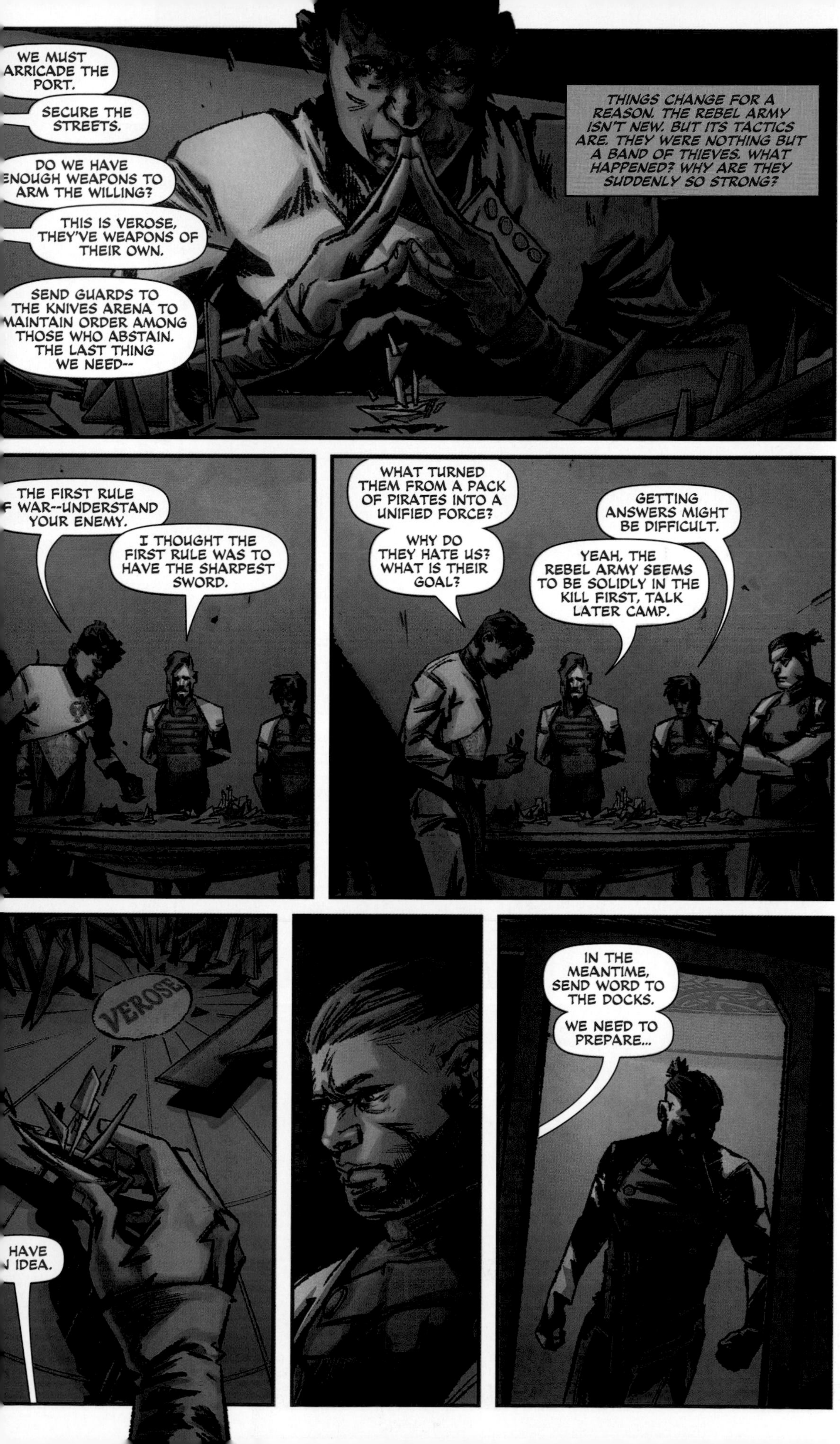
WE MUST ARRICADE THE PORT.
SECURE THE STREETS.
DO WE HAVE ENOUGH WEAPONS TO ARM THE WILLING?
THIS IS VEROSE, THEY'VE WEAPONS OF THEIR OWN.
SEND GUARDS TO THE KNIVES ARENA TO MAINTAIN ORDER AMONG THOSE WHO ABSTAIN. THE LAST THING WE NEED--
THINGS CHANGE FOR A REASON. THE REBEL ARMY ISN'T NEW. BUT ITS TACTICS ARE. THEY WERE NOTHING BUT A BAND OF THIEVES. WHAT HAPPENED? WHY ARE THEY SUDDENLY SO STRONG?
THE FIRST RULE F WAR--UNDERSTAND YOUR ENEMY.
I THOUGHT THE FIRST RULE WAS TO HAVE THE SHARPEST SWORD.
WHAT TURNED THEM FROM A PACK OF PIRATES INTO A UNIFIED FORCE?
WHY DO THEY HATE US? WHAT IS THEIR GOAL?
GETTING ANSWERS MIGHT BE DIFFICULT.
YEAH, THE REBEL ARMY SEEMS TO BE SOLIDLY IN THE KILL FIRST, TALK LATER CAMP.
VEROSE
HAVE N IDEA.
IN THE MEANTIME, SEND WORD TO THE DOCKS.
WE NEED TO PREPARE...

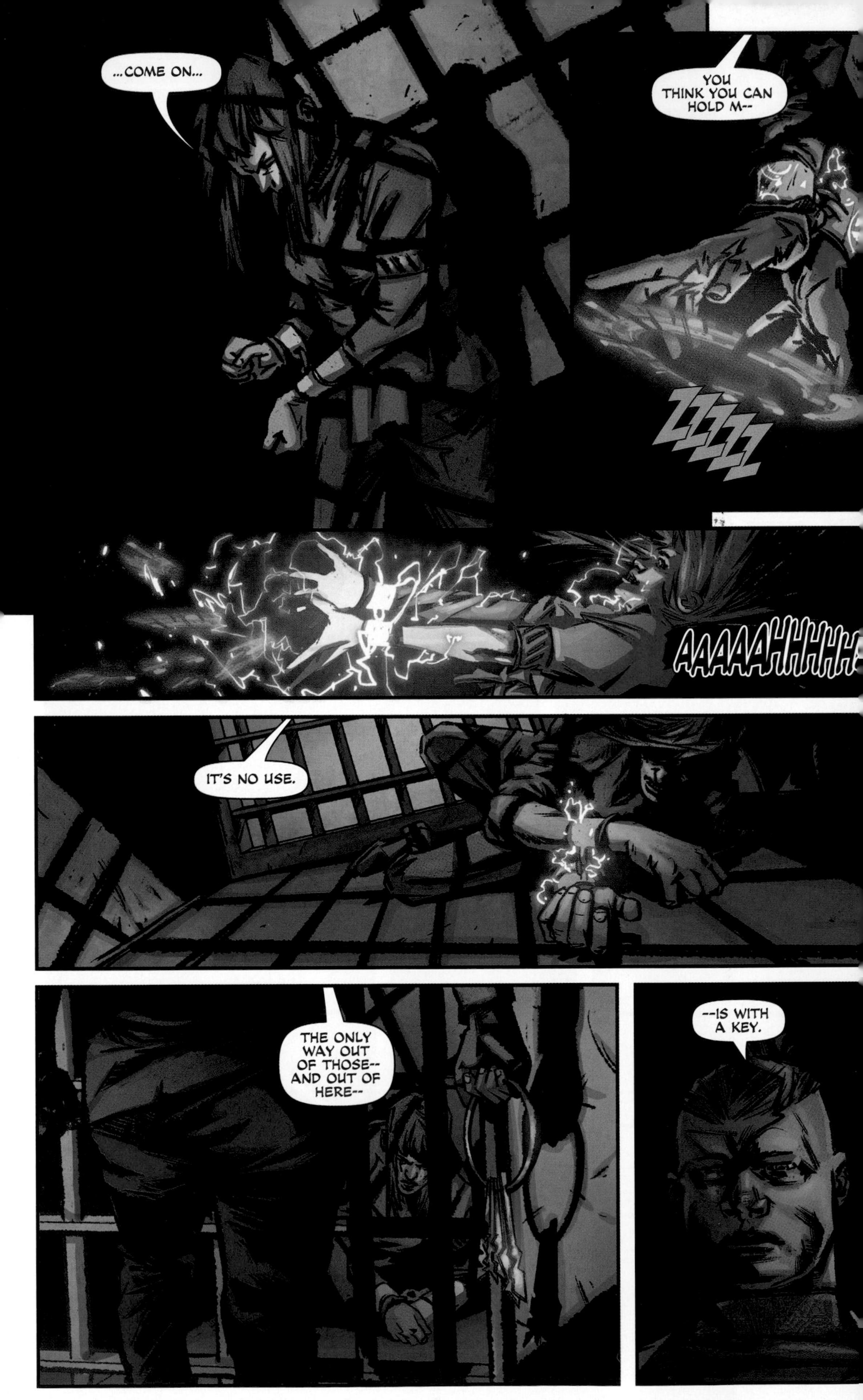
...COME ON...
YOU THINK YOU CAN HOLD M--
ZZZZZ
AAAAAHHHHH
IT'S NO USE.
THE ONLY WAY OUT OF THOSE-- AND OUT OF HERE--
--IS WITH A KEY.

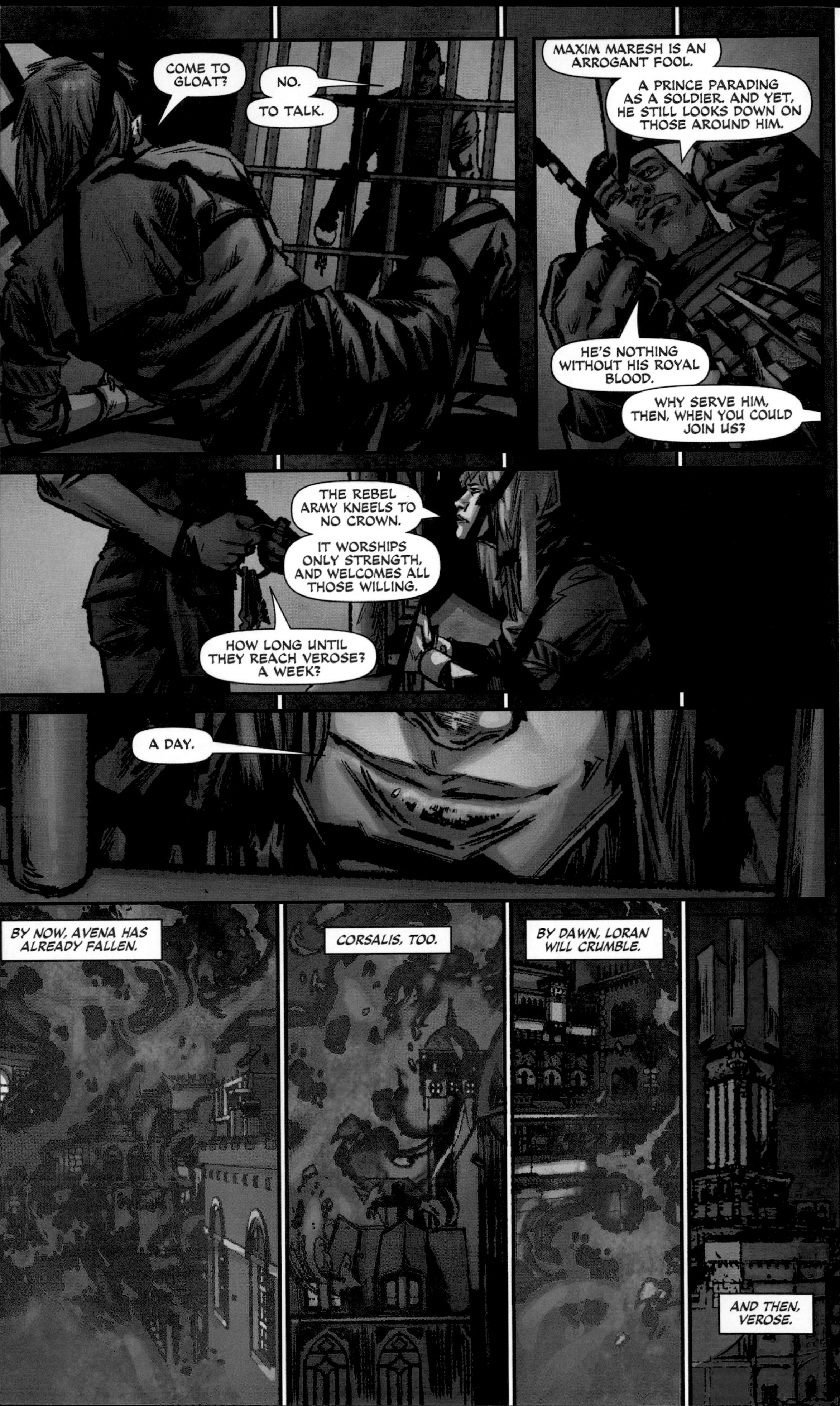
COME TO GLOAT?
NO.
TO TALK.
MAXIM MARESH IS AN ARROGANT FOOL.
A PRINCE PARADING AS A SOLDIER. AND YET, HE STILL LOOKS DOWN ON THOSE AROUND HIM.
HE'S NOTHING WITHOUT HIS ROYAL BLOOD.
WHY SERVE HIM, THEN, WHEN YOU COULD JOIN US?
THE REBEL ARMY KNEELS TO NO CROWN.
IT WORSHIPS ONLY STRENGTH, AND WELCOMES ALL THOSE WILLING.
HOW LONG UNTIL THEY REACH VEROSE? A WEEK?
A DAY.
BY NOW, AVENA HAS ALREADY FALLEN.
CORSALIS, TOO.
BY DAWN, LORAN WILL CRUMBLE.
AND THEN, VEROSE.

THE REBEL ARMY
IS A TIDE.

AND IT IS RISING.

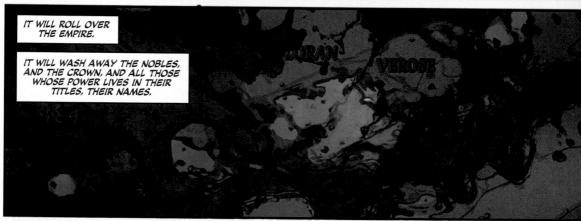

IT WILL ROLL OVER
THE EMPIRE.

IT WILL WASH AWAY THE NOBLES,
AND THE CROWN, AND ALL THOSE
WHOSE POWER LIVES IN THEIR
TITLES, THEIR NAMES.

JOIN US.

HURRY.

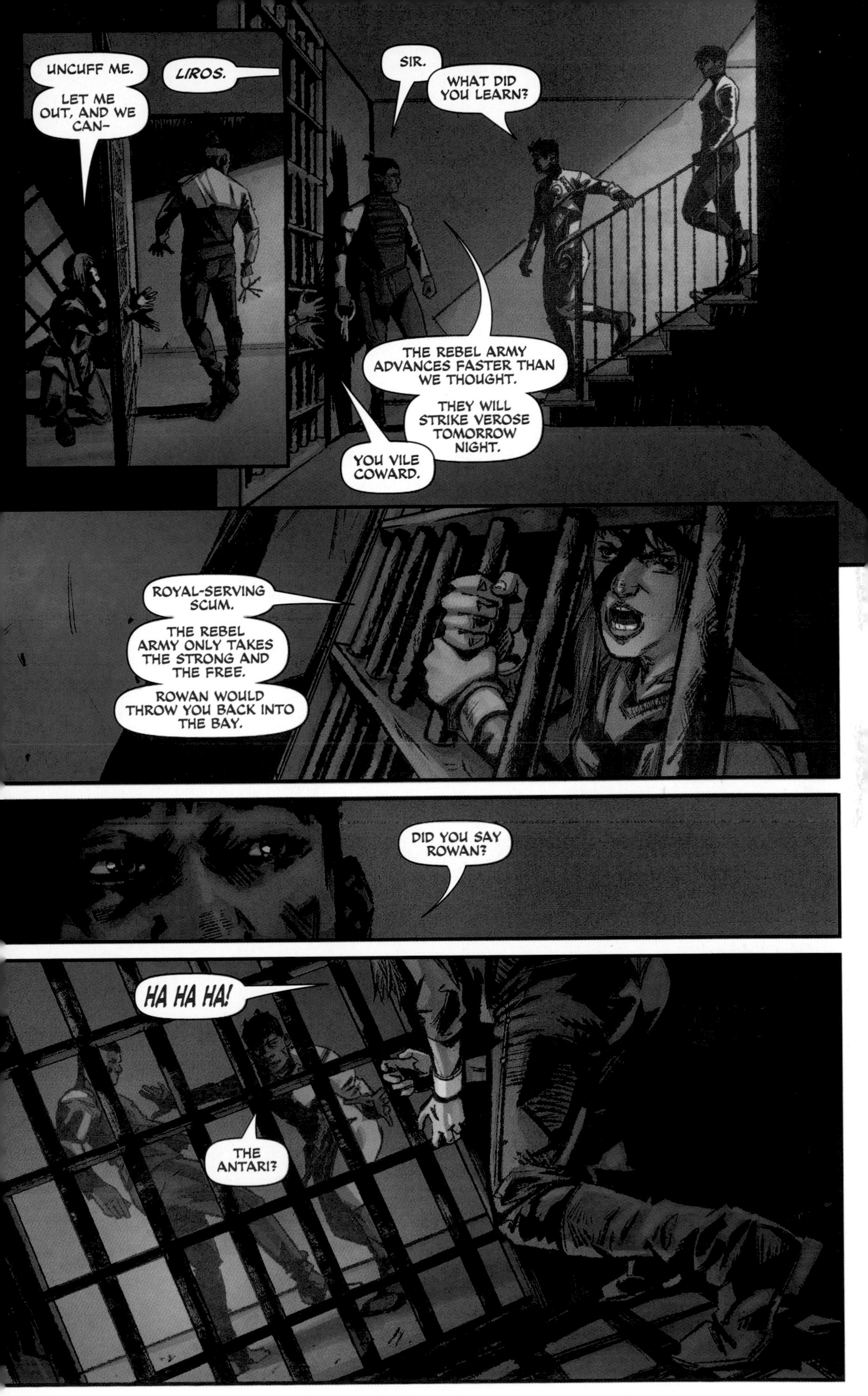
UNCUFF ME.
LET ME OUT, AND WE CAN-
LIROS.
SIR.
WHAT DID YOU LEARN?
THE REBEL ARMY ADVANCES FASTER THAN WE THOUGHT.
THEY WILL STRIKE VEROSE TOMORROW NIGHT.
YOU VILE COWARD.
ROYAL-SERVING SCUM.
THE REBEL ARMY ONLY TAKES THE STRONG AND THE FREE.
ROWAN WOULD THROW YOU BACK INTO THE BAY.
DID YOU SAY ROWAN?
HA HA HA!
THE ANTARI?

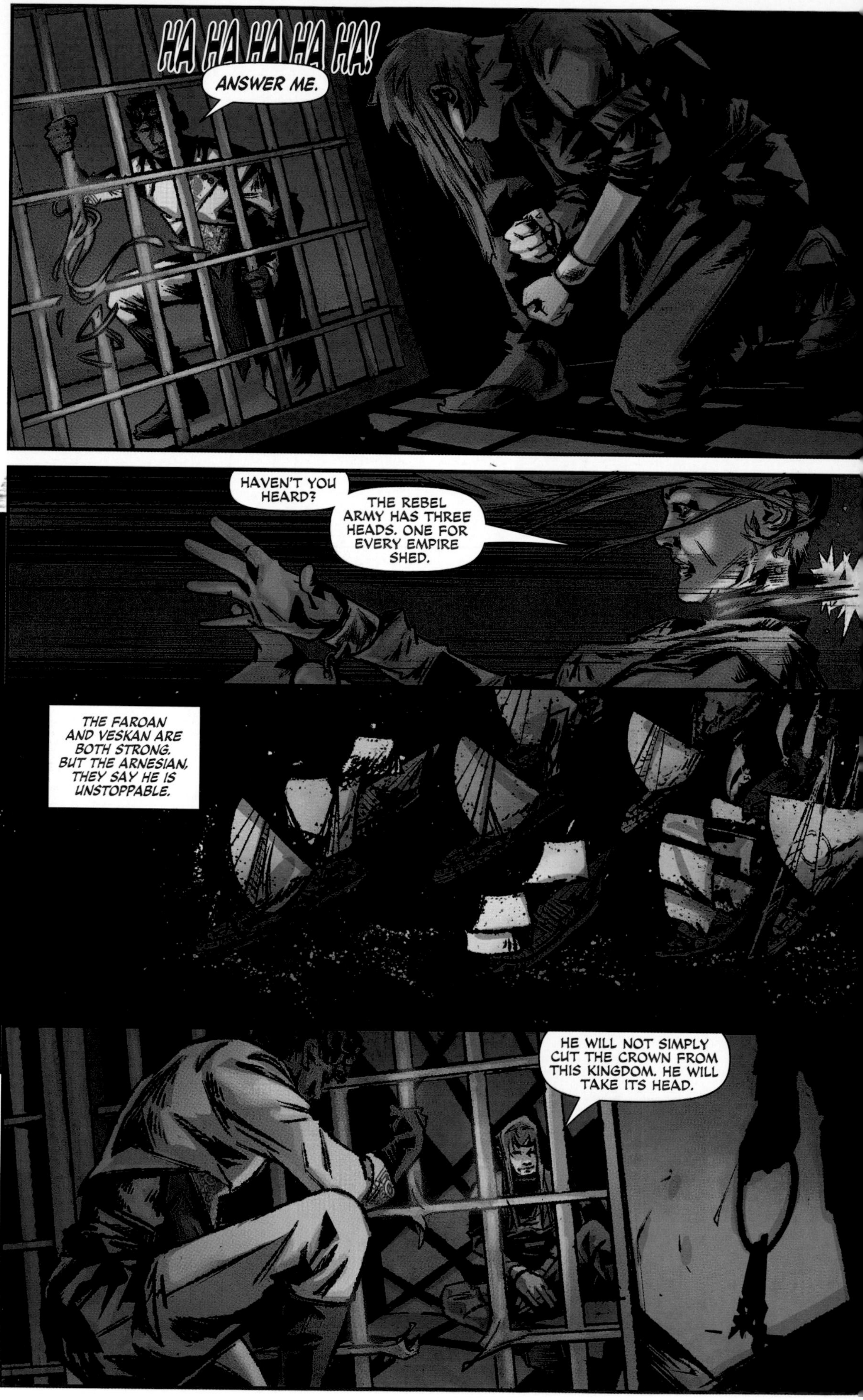
HA HA HA HA HA!
ANSWER ME.
HAVEN'T YOU HEARD?
THE REBEL ARMY HAS THREE HEADS. ONE FOR EVERY EMPIRE SHED.
THE FAROAN AND VESKAN ARE BOTH STRONG. BUT THE ARNESIAN, THEY SAY HE IS UNSTOPPABLE.
HE WILL NOT SIMPLY CUT THE CROWN FROM THIS KINGDOM. HE WILL TAKE ITS HEAD.

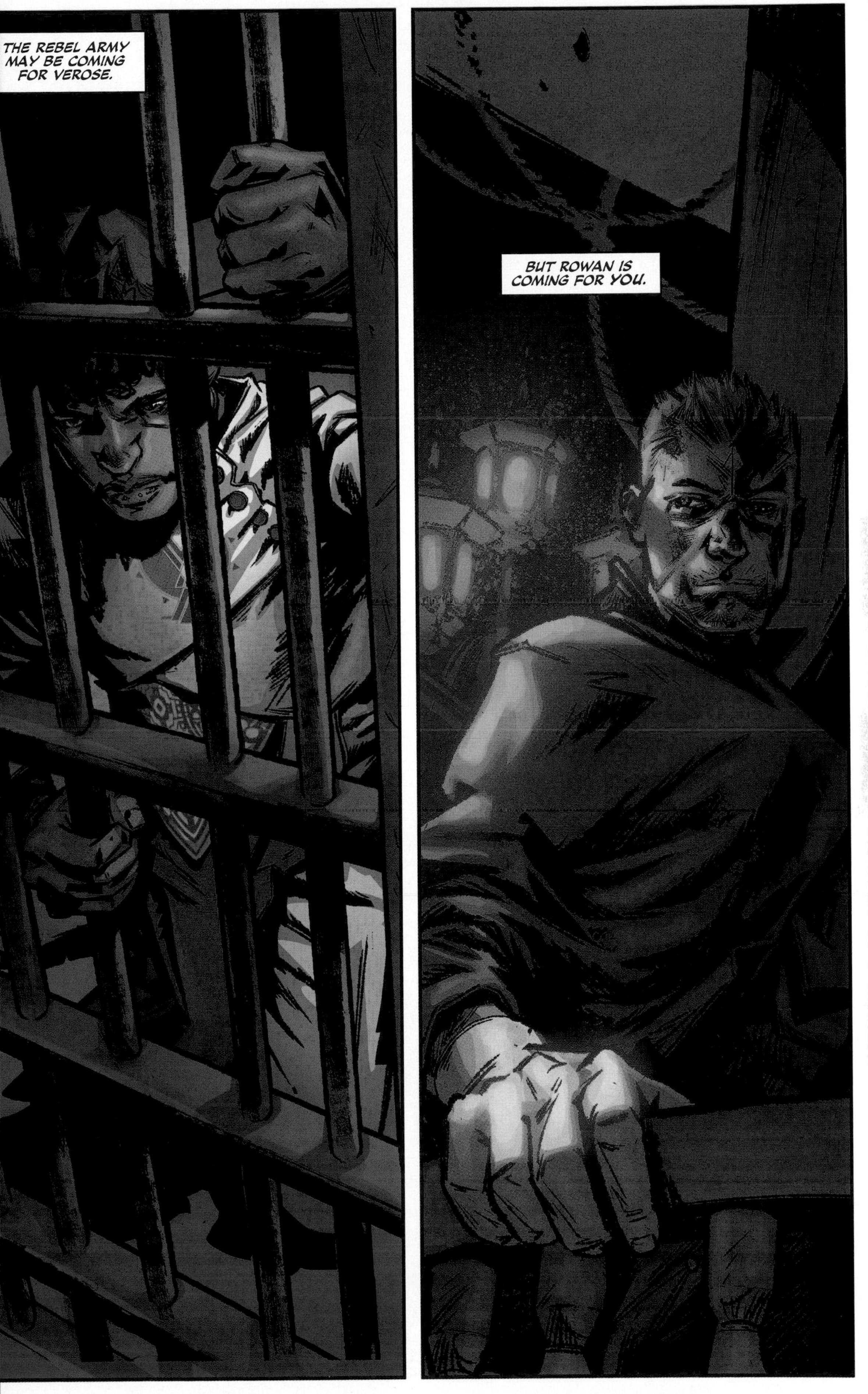
THE REBEL ARMY MAY BE COMING FOR VEROSE.
BUT ROWAN IS COMING FOR YOU.

#3

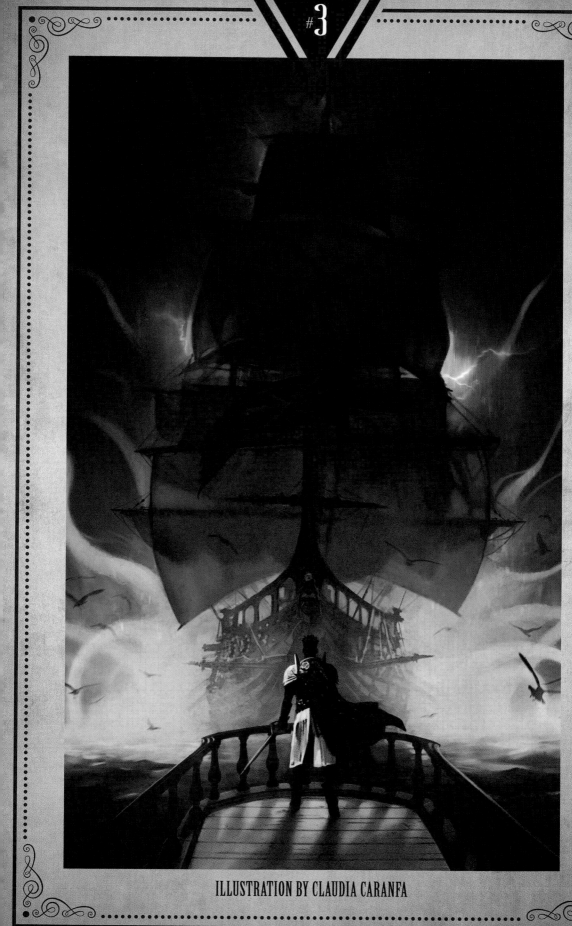

ILLUSTRATION BY CLAUDIA CARANFA

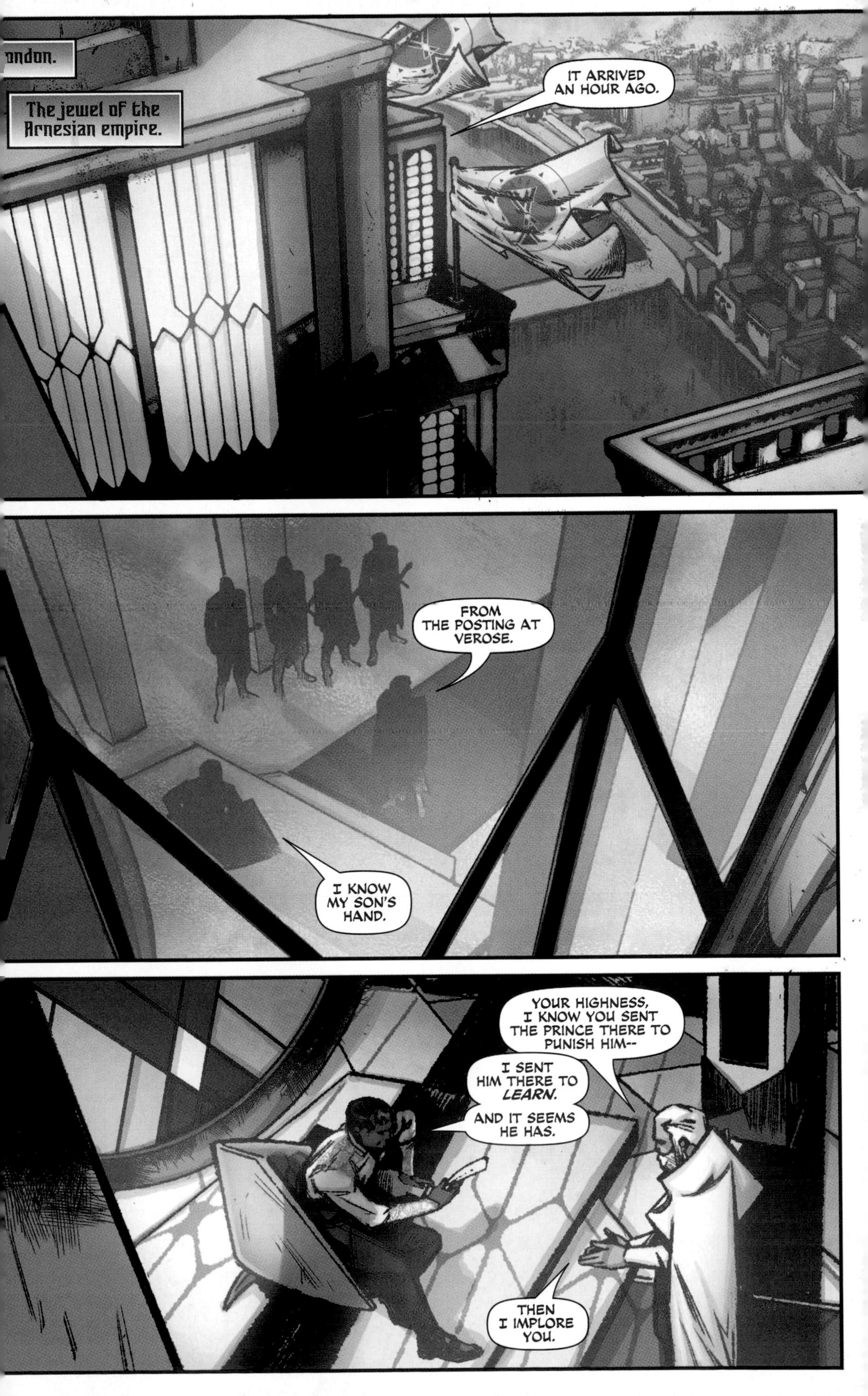

ondon.
The jewel of the Arnesian empire.
IT ARRIVED AN HOUR AGO.
FROM THE POSTING AT VEROSE.
I KNOW MY SON'S HAND.
YOUR HIGHNESS, I KNOW YOU SENT THE PRINCE THERE TO PUNISH HIM--
I SENT HIM THERE TO *LEARN*.
AND IT SEEMS HE HAS.
THEN I IMPLORE YOU.

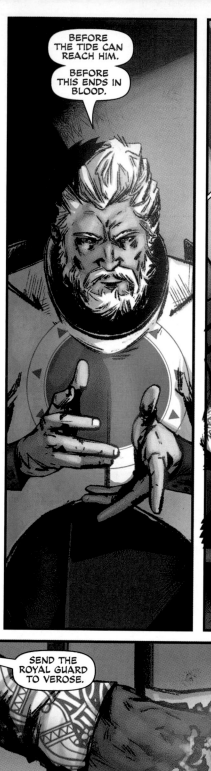

BEFORE THE TIDE CAN REACH HIM.

BEFORE THIS ENDS IN BLOOD.

CALL YOUR SON HOME.

NO.

NOKIL--

MY SON WISHES TO STAND AND FIGHT.

THE CROWN WILL STAND WITH HIM.

SEND THE ROYAL GUARD TO VEROSE.

the Rebel Army, is coming, Maxim

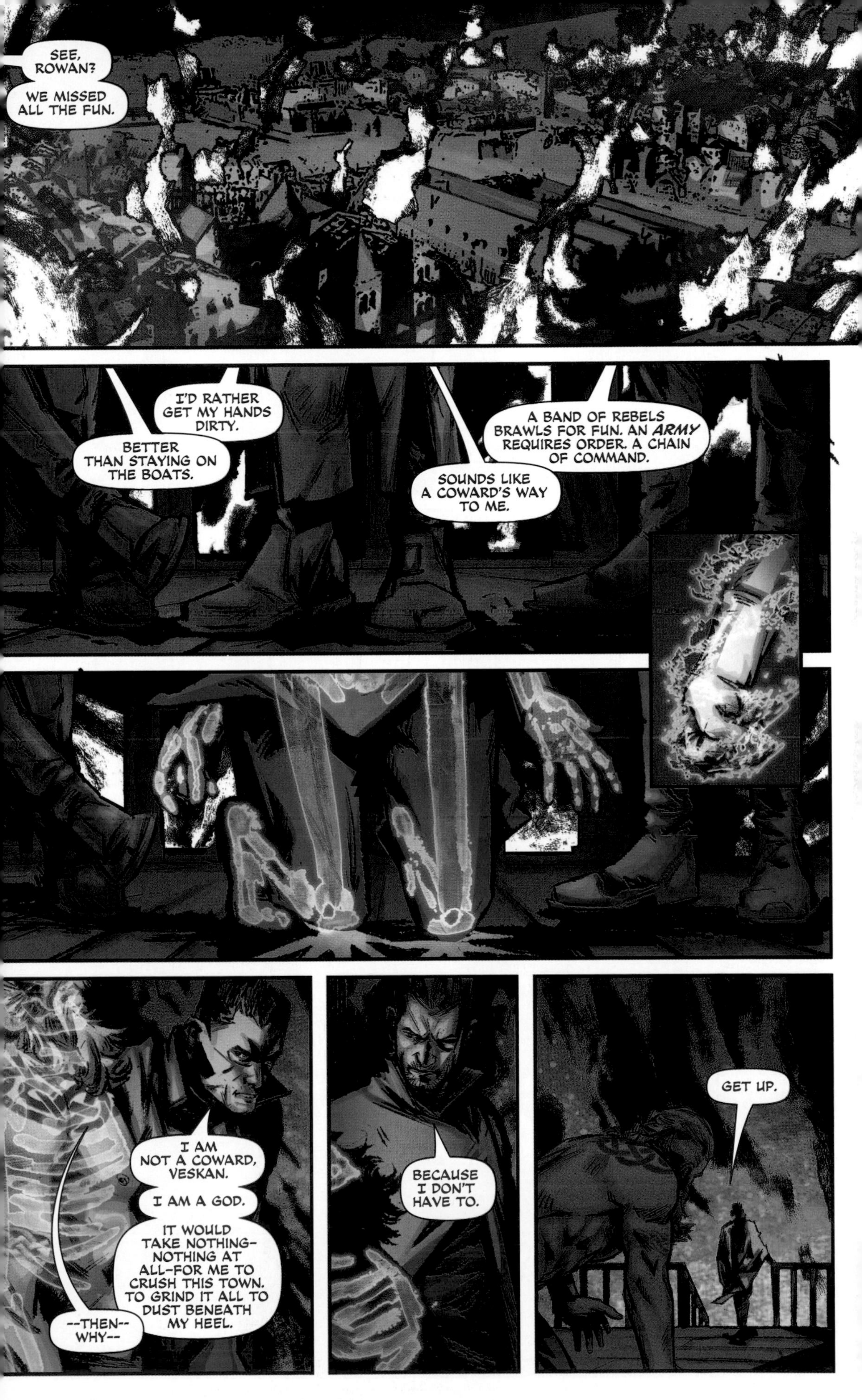
SEE, ROWAN?
WE MISSED ALL THE FUN.
I'D RATHER GET MY HANDS DIRTY.
BETTER THAN STAYING ON THE BOATS.
A BAND OF REBELS BRAWLS FOR FUN. AN ARMY REQUIRES ORDER. A CHAIN OF COMMAND.
SOUNDS LIKE A COWARD'S WAY TO ME.
I AM NOT A COWARD, VESKAN.
I AM A GOD.
IT WOULD TAKE NOTHING-NOTHING AT ALL-FOR ME TO CRUSH THIS TOWN. TO GRIND IT ALL TO DUST BENEATH MY HEEL.
--THEN--WHY--
BECAUSE I DON'T HAVE TO.
GET UP.

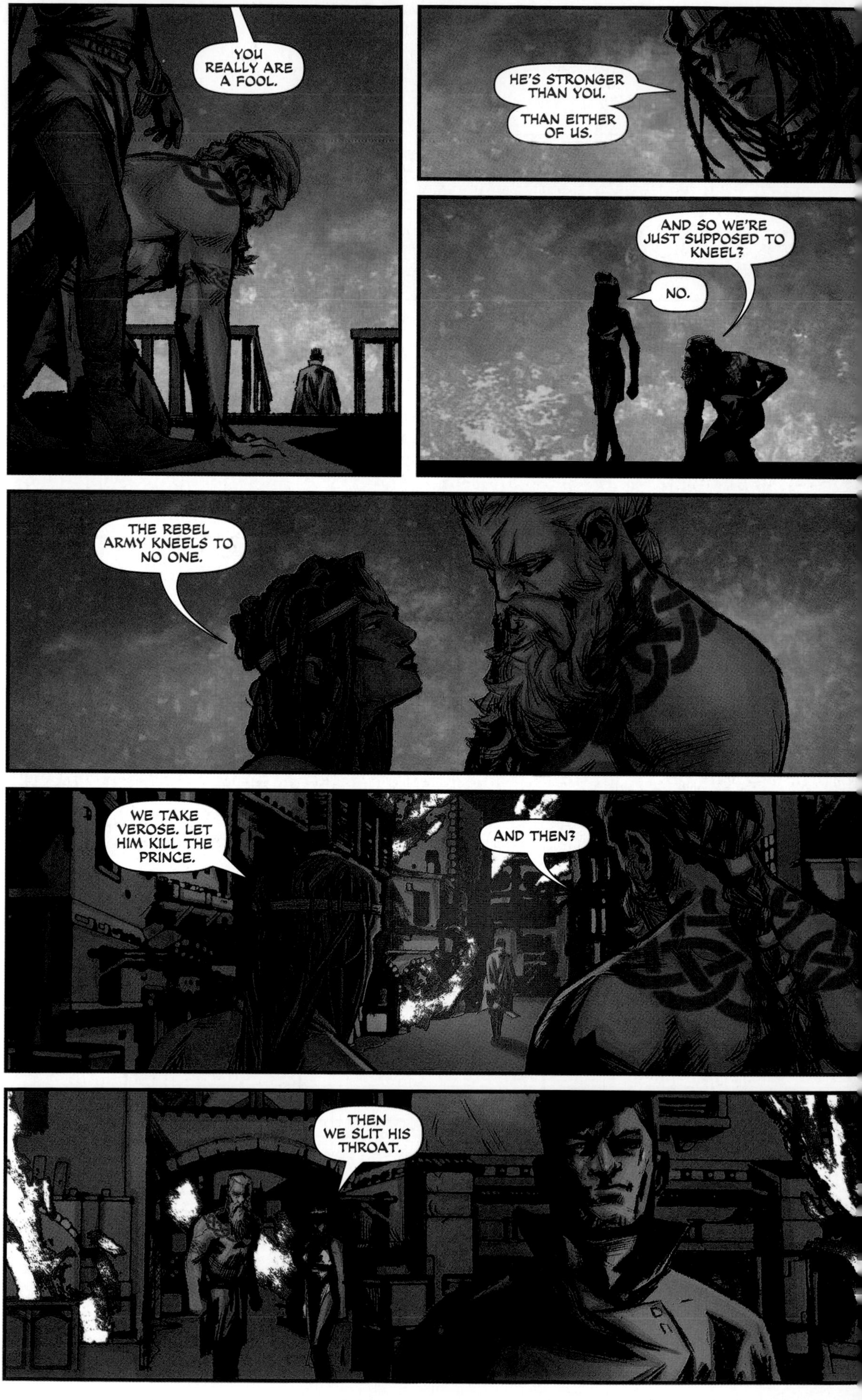
YOU REALLY ARE A FOOL.
HE'S STRONGER THAN YOU.
THAN EITHER OF US.
AND SO WE'RE JUST SUPPOSED TO KNEEL?
NO.
THE REBEL ARMY KNEELS TO NO ONE.
WE TAKE VEROSE. LET HIM KILL THE PRINCE.
AND THEN?
THEN WE SLIT HIS THROAT.

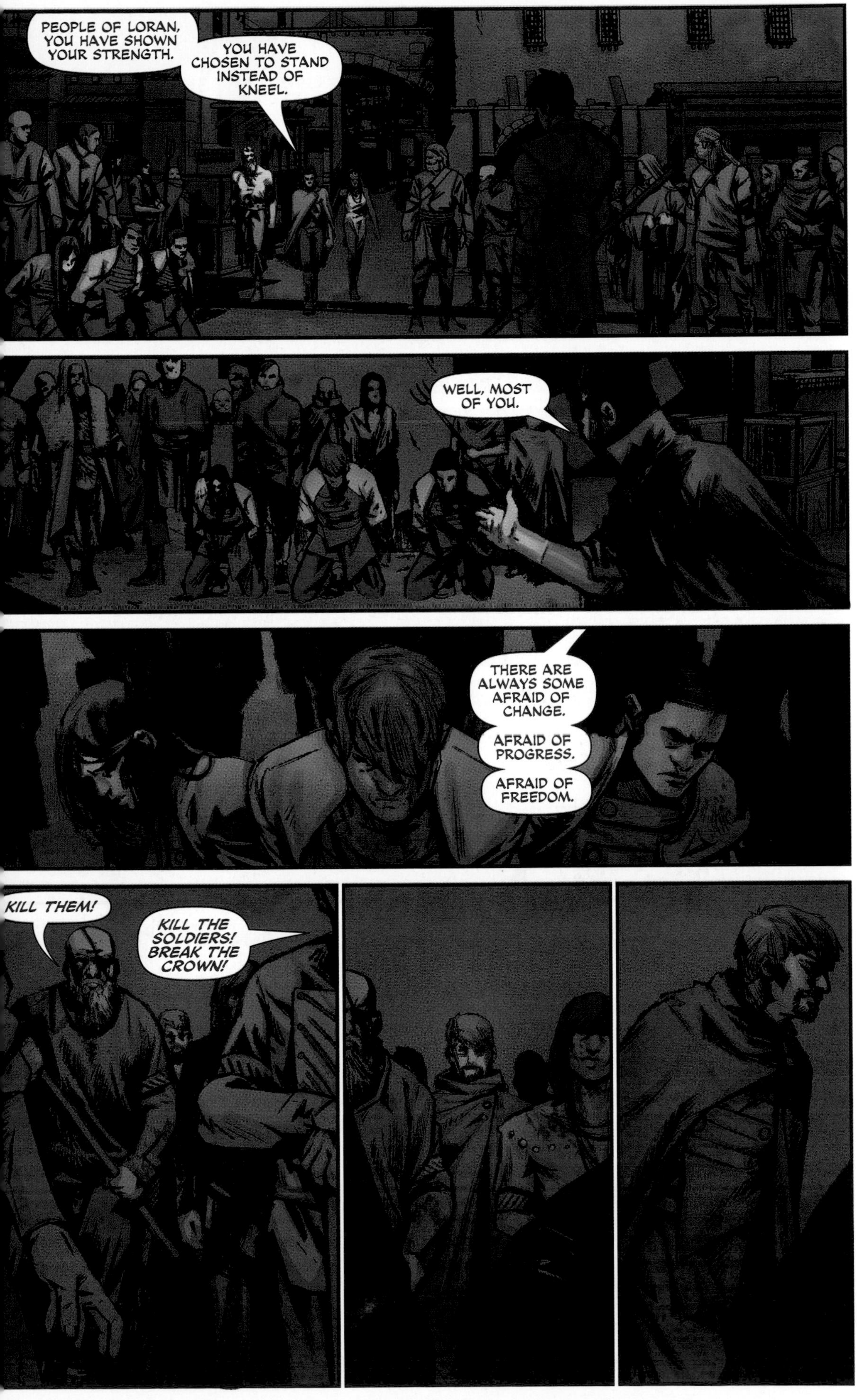
PEOPLE OF LORAN, YOU HAVE SHOWN YOUR STRENGTH.
YOU HAVE CHOSEN TO STAND INSTEAD OF KNEEL.
WELL, MOST OF YOU.
THERE ARE ALWAYS SOME AFRAID OF CHANGE.
AFRAID OF PROGRESS.
AFRAID OF FREEDOM.
KILL THEM!
KILL THE SOLDIERS! BREAK THE CROWN!

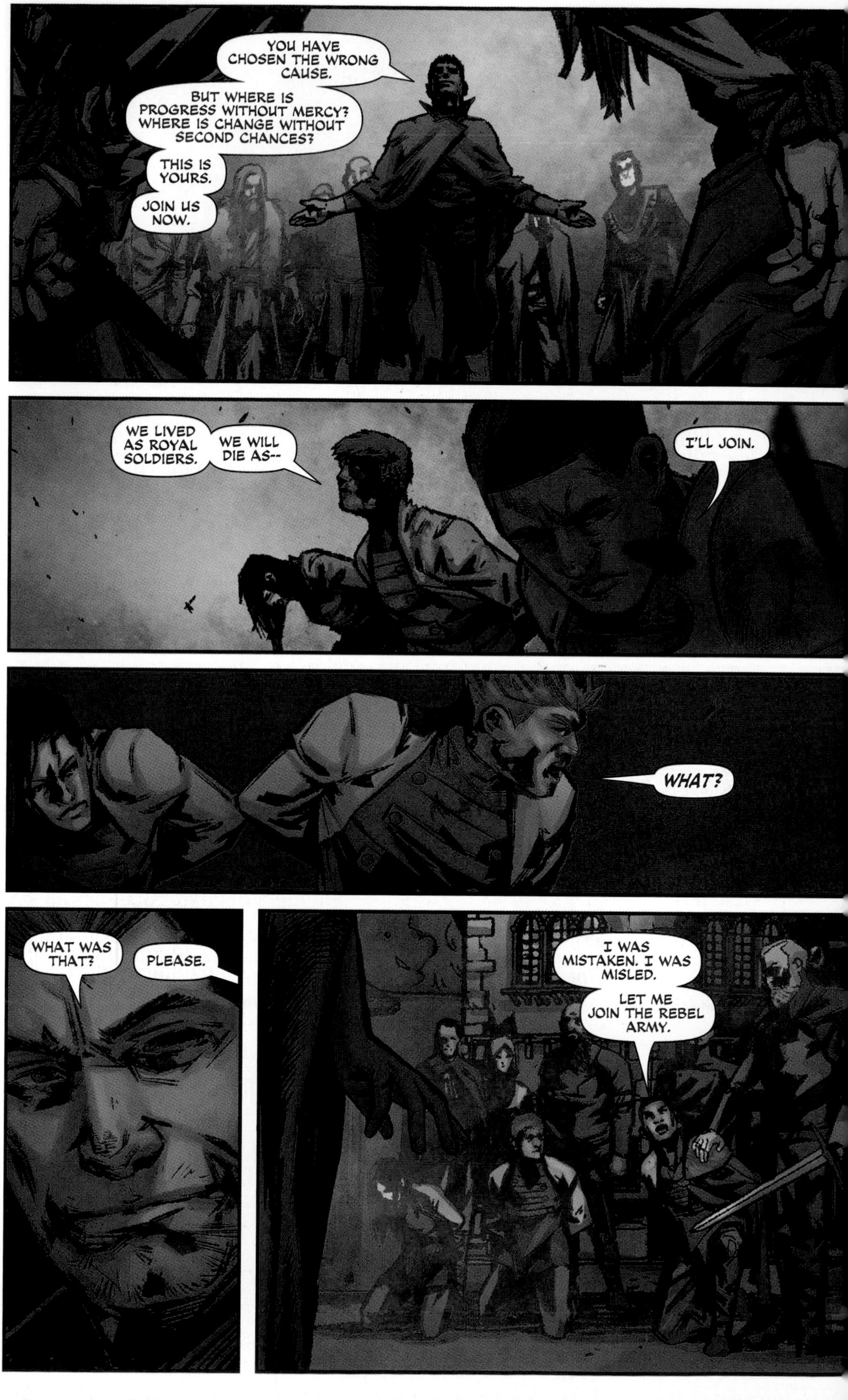
YOU HAVE CHOSEN THE WRONG CAUSE.
BUT WHERE IS PROGRESS WITHOUT MERCY? WHERE IS CHANGE WITHOUT SECOND CHANCES?
THIS IS YOURS.
JOIN US NOW.
WE LIVED AS ROYAL SOLDIERS.
WE WILL DIE AS--
I'LL JOIN.
WHAT?
WHAT WAS THAT?
PLEASE.
I WAS MISTAKEN. I WAS MISLED.
LET ME JOIN THE REBEL ARMY.

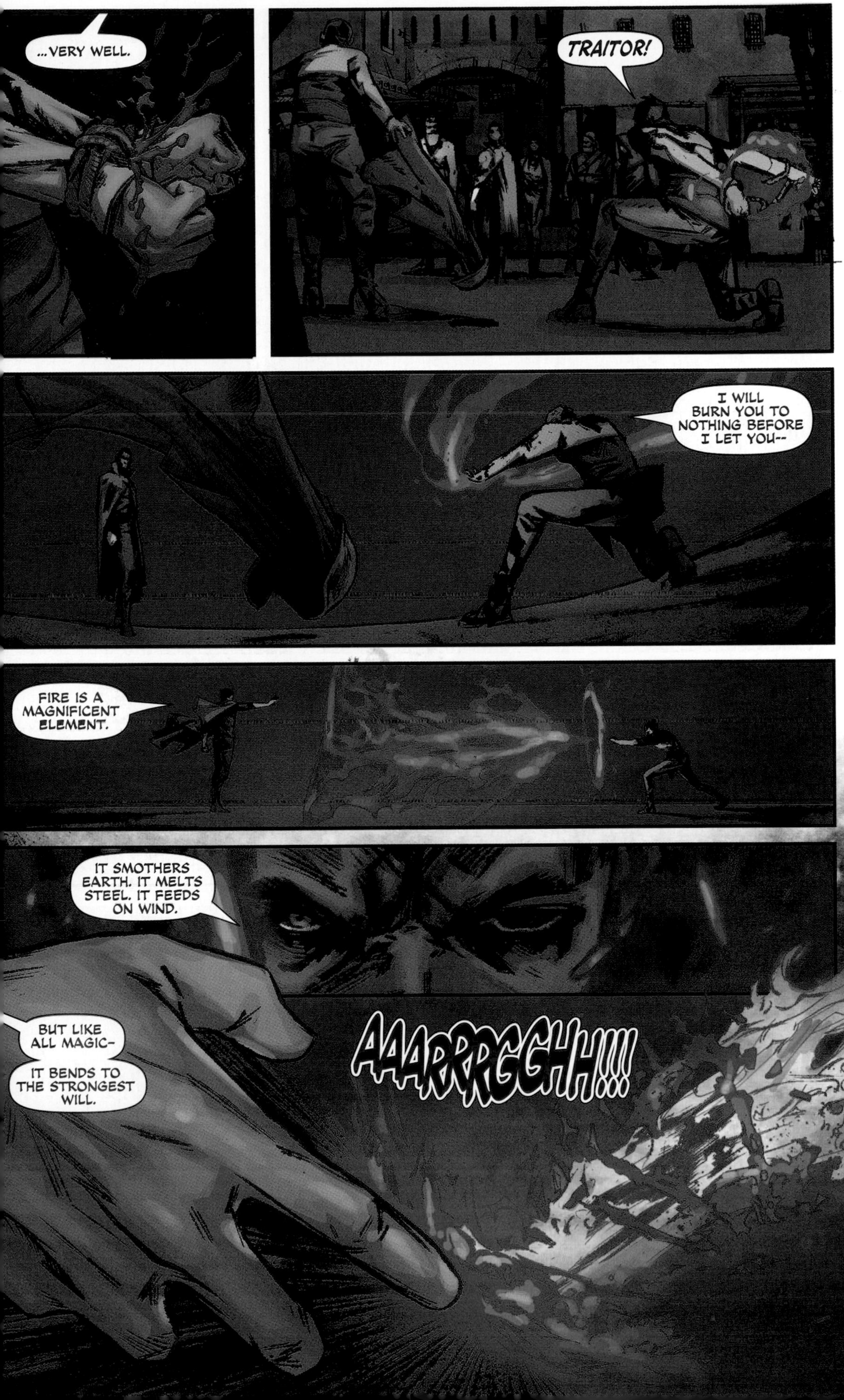

...VERY WELL.
TRAITOR!
I WILL BURN YOU TO NOTHING BEFORE I LET YOU--
FIRE IS A MAGNIFICENT ELEMENT.
IT SMOTHERS EARTH. IT MELTS STEEL. IT FEEDS ON WIND.
BUT LIKE ALL MAGIC-
IT BENDS TO THE STRONGEST WILL.
AAARRRGGHH!!!

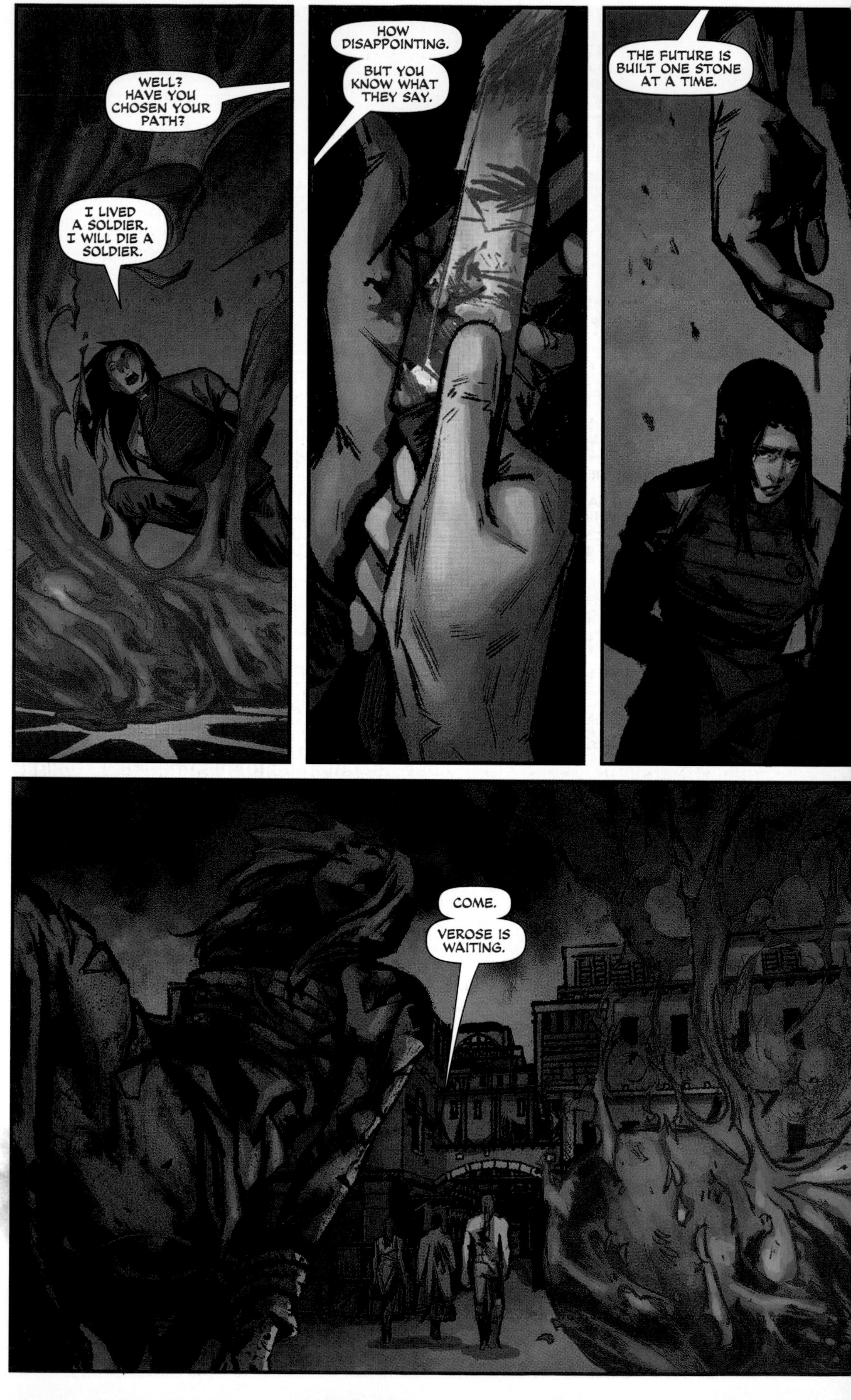
WELL? HAVE YOU CHOSEN YOUR PATH?
I LIVED A SOLDIER. I WILL DIE A SOLDIER.
HOW DISAPPOINTING.
BUT YOU KNOW WHAT THEY SAY.
THE FUTURE IS BUILT ONE STONE AT A TIME.
COME.
VEROSE IS WAITING.

erose.

WE NEED TO FORTIFY THE NORTHERN SIDE OF THE CITY.

FIND A WAY TO RESTRICT THE FIGHTING TO THE PORT AND SURROUNDING BLOCKS SO WE CAN DICTATE THE--

SIR. WE HAVE A MESSENGER FROM LORAN.

ANOTHER ONE?

NO, THIS ONE'S OURS.

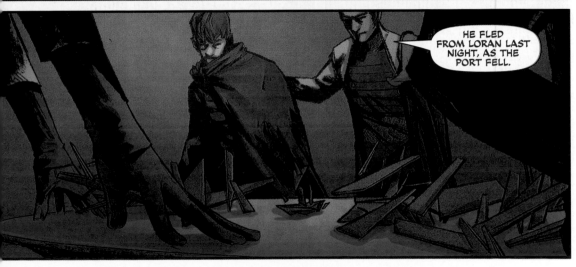

HE FLED FROM LORAN LAST NIGHT, AS THE PORT FELL.

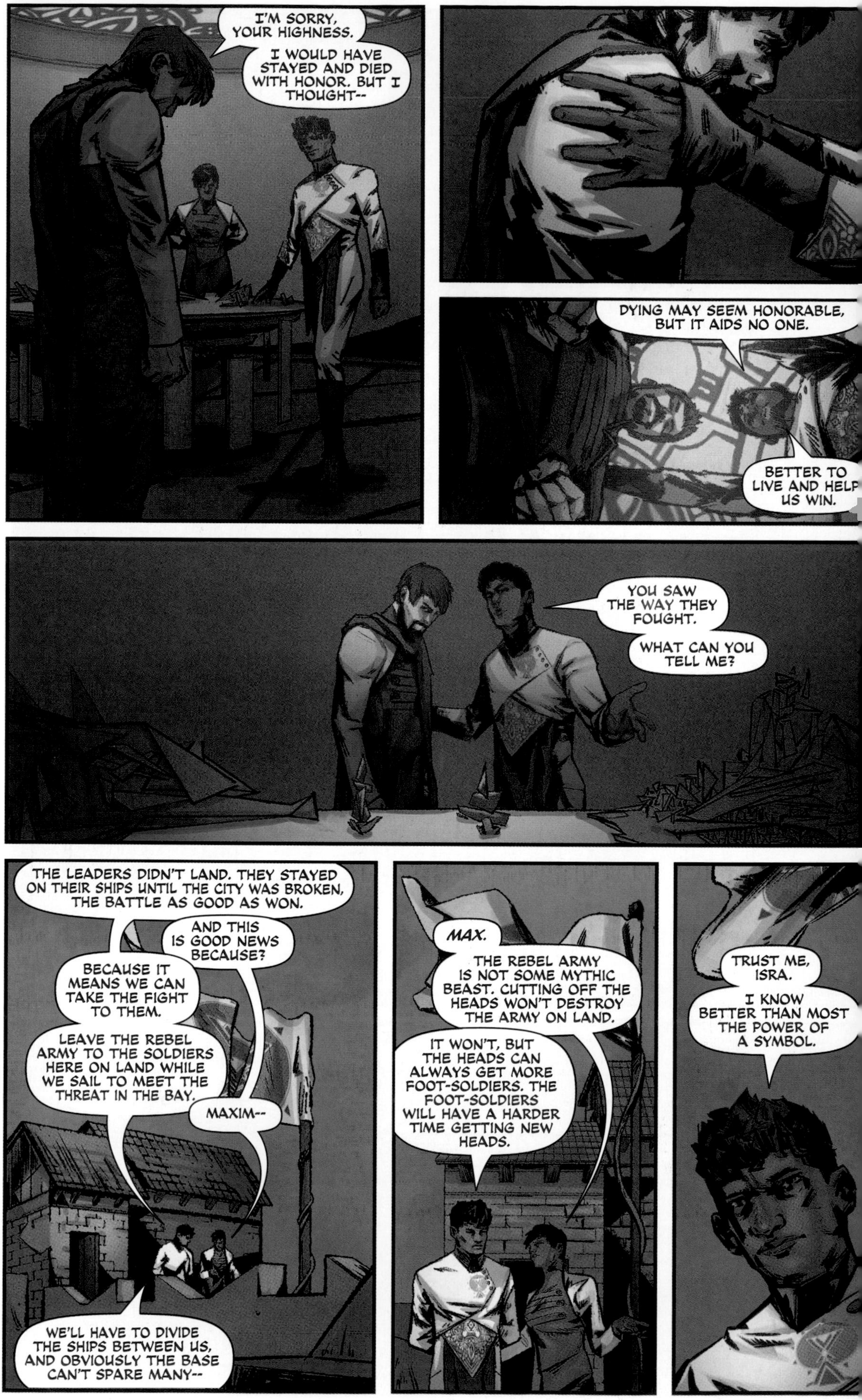

I'M SORRY, YOUR HIGHNESS.
I WOULD HAVE STAYED AND DIED WITH HONOR. BUT I THOUGHT--
DYING MAY SEEM HONORABLE, BUT IT AIDS NO ONE.
BETTER TO LIVE AND HELP US WIN.
YOU SAW THE WAY THEY FOUGHT.
WHAT CAN YOU TELL ME?
THE LEADERS DIDN'T LAND. THEY STAYED ON THEIR SHIPS UNTIL THE CITY WAS BROKEN, THE BATTLE AS GOOD AS WON.
AND THIS IS GOOD NEWS BECAUSE?
BECAUSE IT MEANS WE CAN TAKE THE FIGHT TO THEM.
LEAVE THE REBEL ARMY TO THE SOLDIERS HERE ON LAND WHILE WE SAIL TO MEET THE THREAT IN THE BAY.
MAXIM--
WE'LL HAVE TO DIVIDE THE SHIPS BETWEEN US, AND OBVIOUSLY THE BASE CAN'T SPARE MANY--
MAX.
THE REBEL ARMY IS NOT SOME MYTHIC BEAST. CUTTING OFF THE HEADS WON'T DESTROY THE ARMY ON LAND.
IT WON'T, BUT THE HEADS CAN ALWAYS GET MORE FOOT-SOLDIERS. THE FOOT-SOLDIERS WILL HAVE A HARDER TIME GETTING NEW HEADS.
TRUST ME, ISRA.
I KNOW BETTER THAN MOST THE POWER OF A SYMBOL.

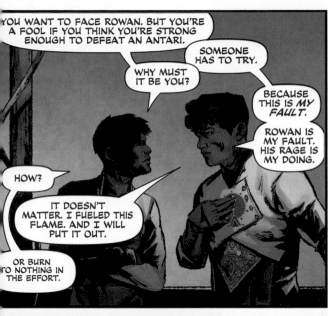

YOU WANT TO FACE ROWAN. BUT YOU'RE A FOOL IF YOU THINK YOU'RE STRONG ENOUGH TO DEFEAT AN ANTARI.

SOMEONE HAS TO TRY.

WHY MUST IT BE YOU?

BECAUSE THIS IS *MY FAULT*.

ROWAN IS MY FAULT. HIS RAGE IS MY DOING.

HOW?

IT DOESN'T MATTER. I FUELED THIS FLAME. AND I WILL PUT IT OUT.

OR BURN TO NOTHING IN THE EFFORT.

EVEN IF WE *WERE* TO ATTACK THE SHIPS, IT WOULD MEAN LEAVING THE REST OF VEROSE TO FIGHT THE REBEL ARMY ON LAND.

OUR OWN SOLDIERS ARE STRONG. YOU AND I HAVE TRAINED THEM WELL.

AND NOW, WE HAVE NEW RECRUITS.

ARE WE SURE IT'S A GOOD IDEA TO ARM THEM?

THIS IS VEROSE.

THEY'RE ALREADY ARMED.

MINE'S BETTER.

THE ROYAL STEEL IS JUST A BRIBE.

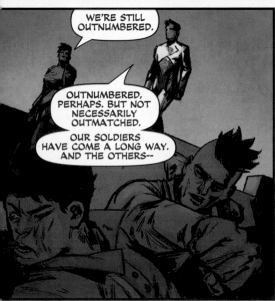

WE'RE STILL OUTNUMBERED.

OUTNUMBERED, PERHAPS. BUT NOT NECESSARILY OUTMATCHED.

OUR SOLDIERS HAVE COME A LONG WAY. AND THE OTHERS--

AT LEAST THEY FIGHT DIRTY.

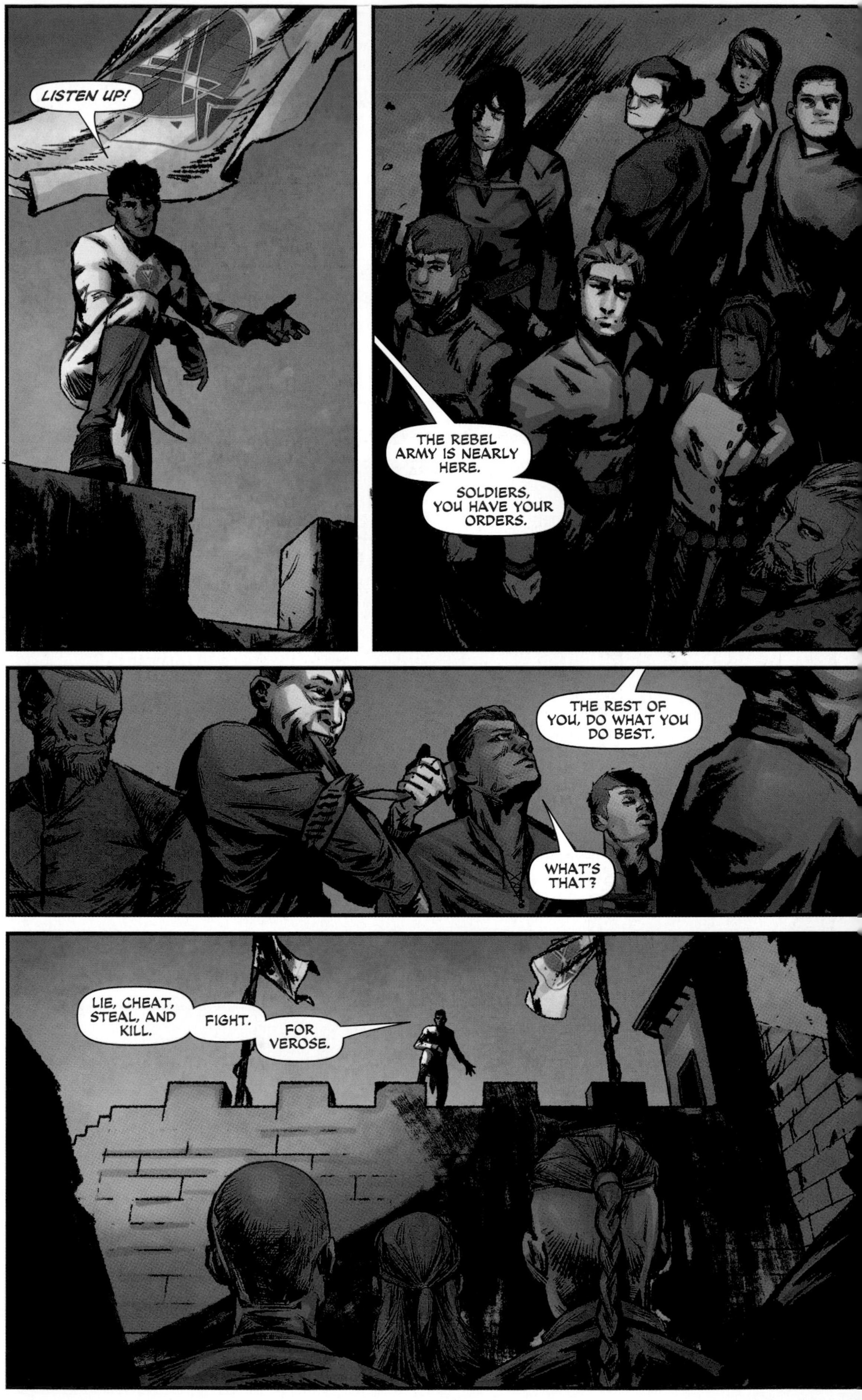
LISTEN UP!
THE REBEL ARMY IS NEARLY HERE.
SOLDIERS, YOU HAVE YOUR ORDERS.
THE REST OF YOU, DO WHAT YOU DO BEST.
WHAT'S THAT?
LIE, CHEAT, STEAL, AND KILL.
FIGHT.
FOR VEROSE.

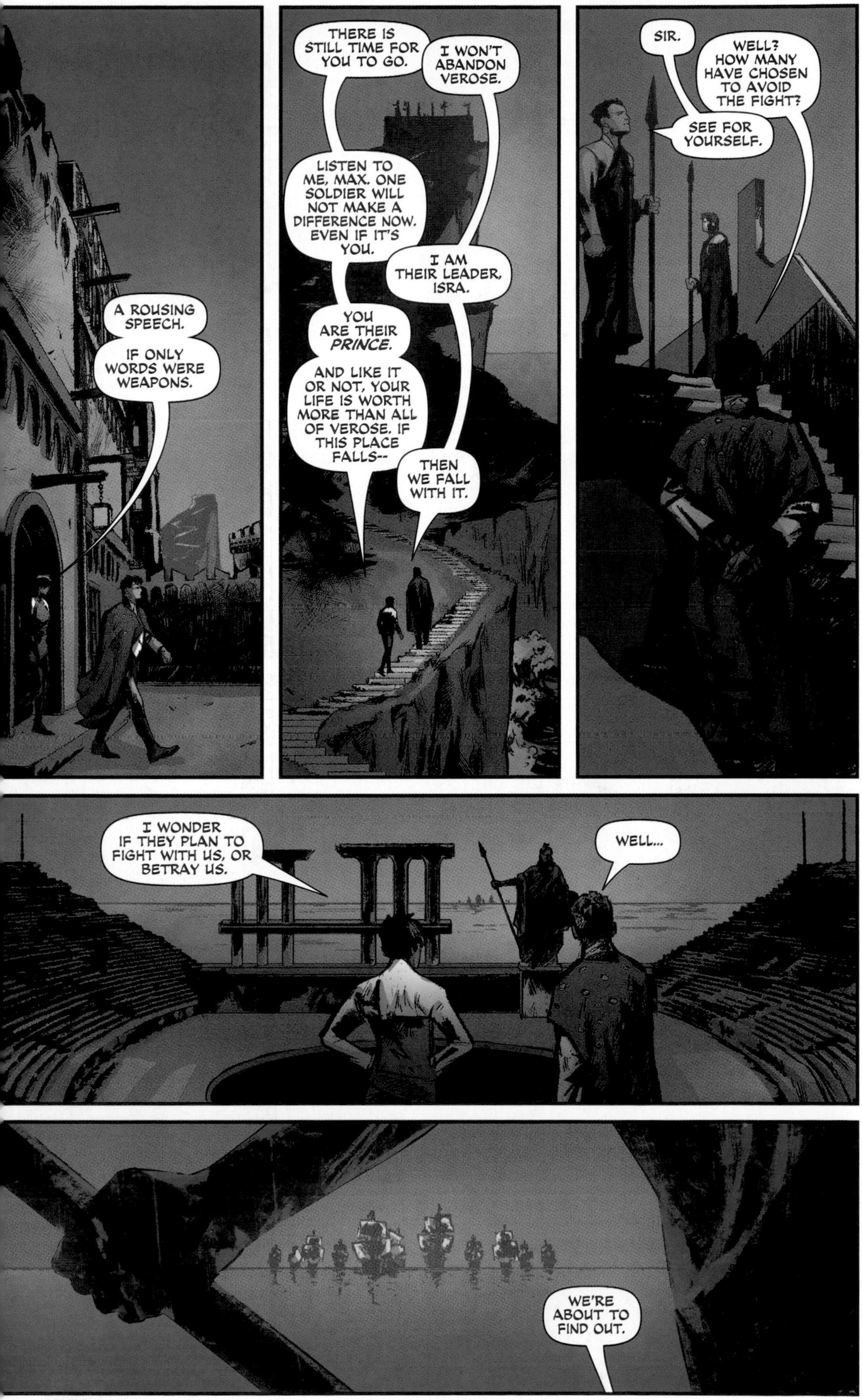
A ROUSING SPEECH.
IF ONLY WORDS WERE WEAPONS.
THERE IS STILL TIME FOR YOU TO GO.
I WON'T ABANDON VEROSE.
LISTEN TO ME, MAX. ONE SOLDIER WILL NOT MAKE A DIFFERENCE NOW. EVEN IF IT'S YOU.
I AM THEIR LEADER, ISRA.
YOU ARE THEIR *PRINCE.*
AND LIKE IT OR NOT, YOUR LIFE IS WORTH MORE THAN ALL OF VEROSE. IF THIS PLACE FALLS--
THEN WE FALL WITH IT.
SIR.
WELL? HOW MANY HAVE CHOSEN TO AVOID THE FIGHT?
SEE FOR YOURSELF.
I WONDER IF THEY PLAN TO FIGHT WITH US, OR BETRAY US.
WELL...
WE'RE ABOUT TO FIND OUT.

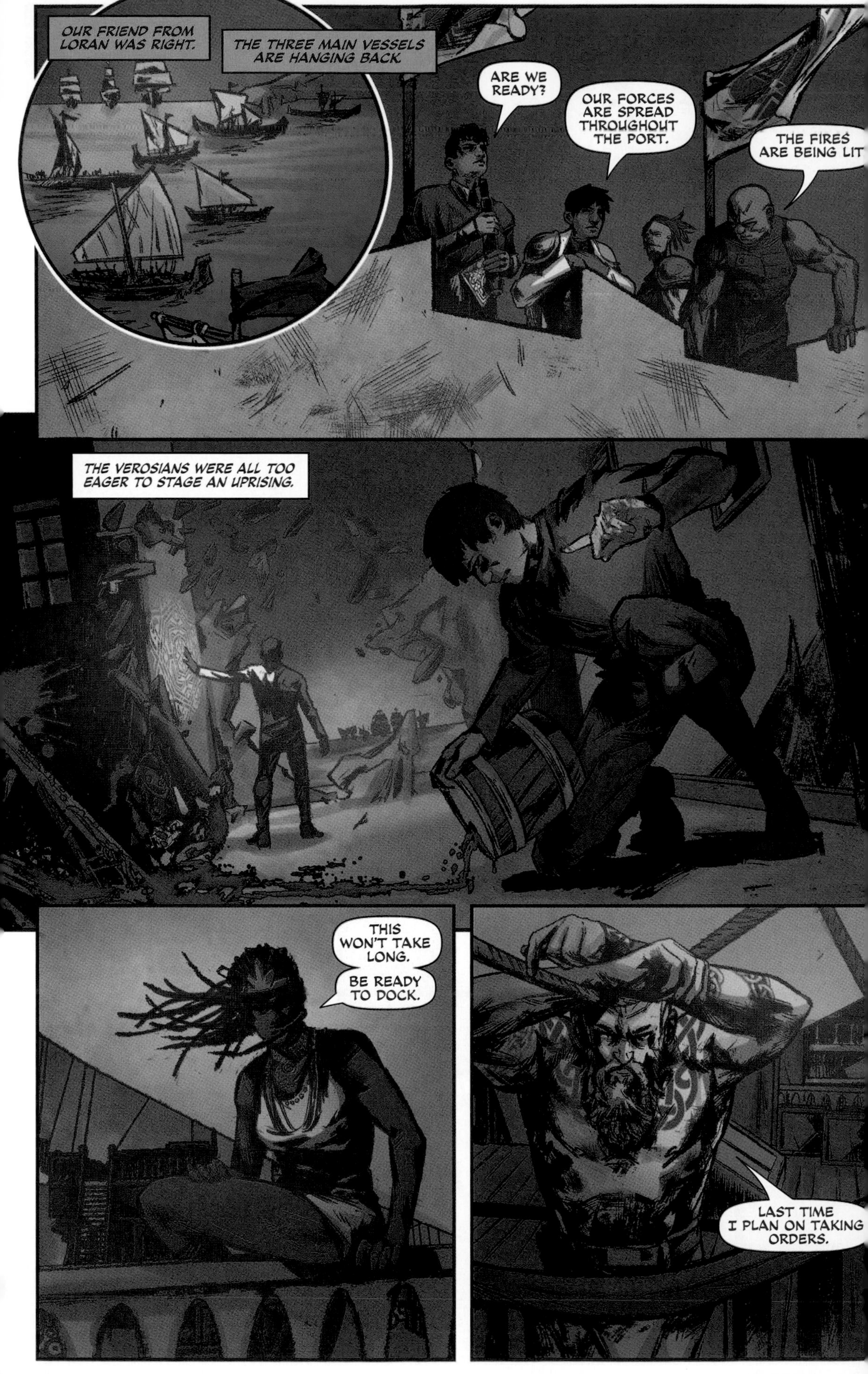
OUR FRIEND FROM LORAN WAS RIGHT.
THE THREE MAIN VESSELS ARE HANGING BACK.
ARE WE READY?
OUR FORCES ARE SPREAD THROUGHOUT THE PORT.
THE FIRES ARE BEING LIT
THE VEROSIANS WERE ALL TOO EAGER TO STAGE AN UPRISING.
THIS WON'T TAKE LONG.
BE READY TO DOCK.
LAST TIME I PLAN ON TAKING ORDERS.

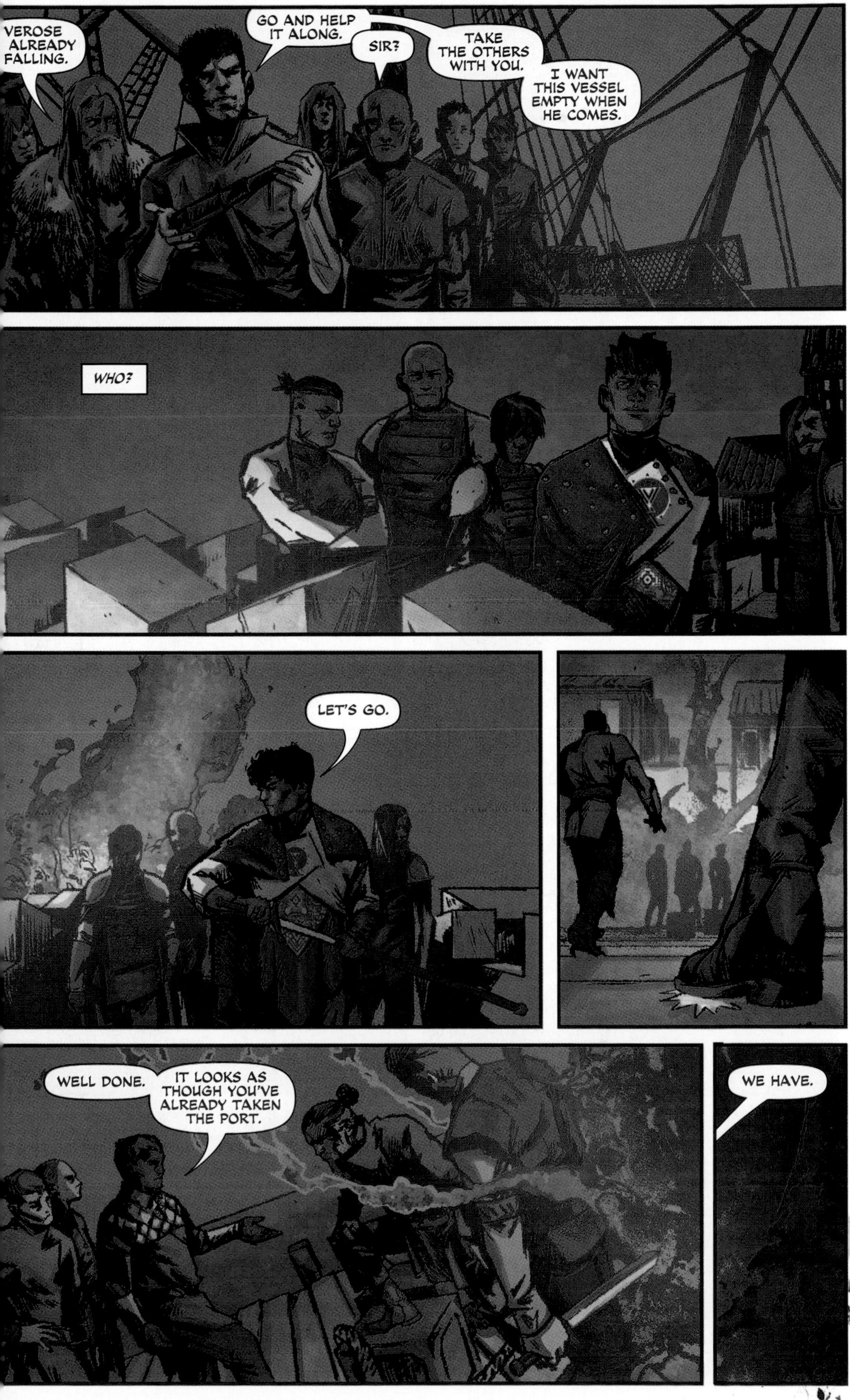
VEROSE ALREADY FALLING.
GO AND HELP IT ALONG.
SIR?
TAKE THE OTHERS WITH YOU.
I WANT THIS VESSEL EMPTY WHEN HE COMES.
WHO?
LET'S GO.
WELL DONE.
IT LOOKS AS THOUGH YOU'VE ALREADY TAKEN THE PORT.
WE HAVE.

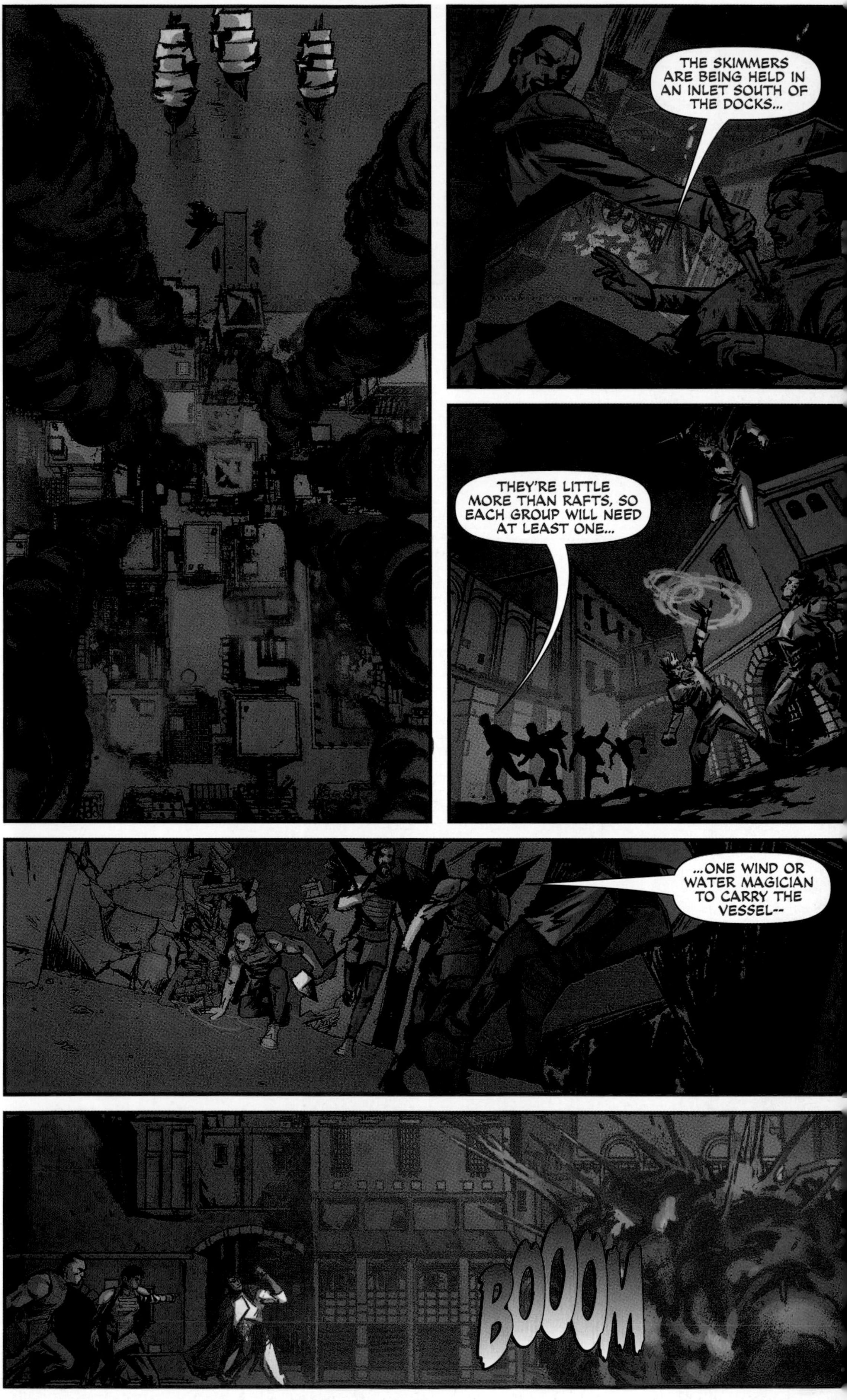
THE SKIMMERS ARE BEING HELD IN AN INLET SOUTH OF THE DOCKS...
THEY'RE LITTLE MORE THAN RAFTS, SO EACH GROUP WILL NEED AT LEAST ONE...
...ONE WIND OR WATER MAGICIAN TO CARRY THE VESSEL--
BOOOM

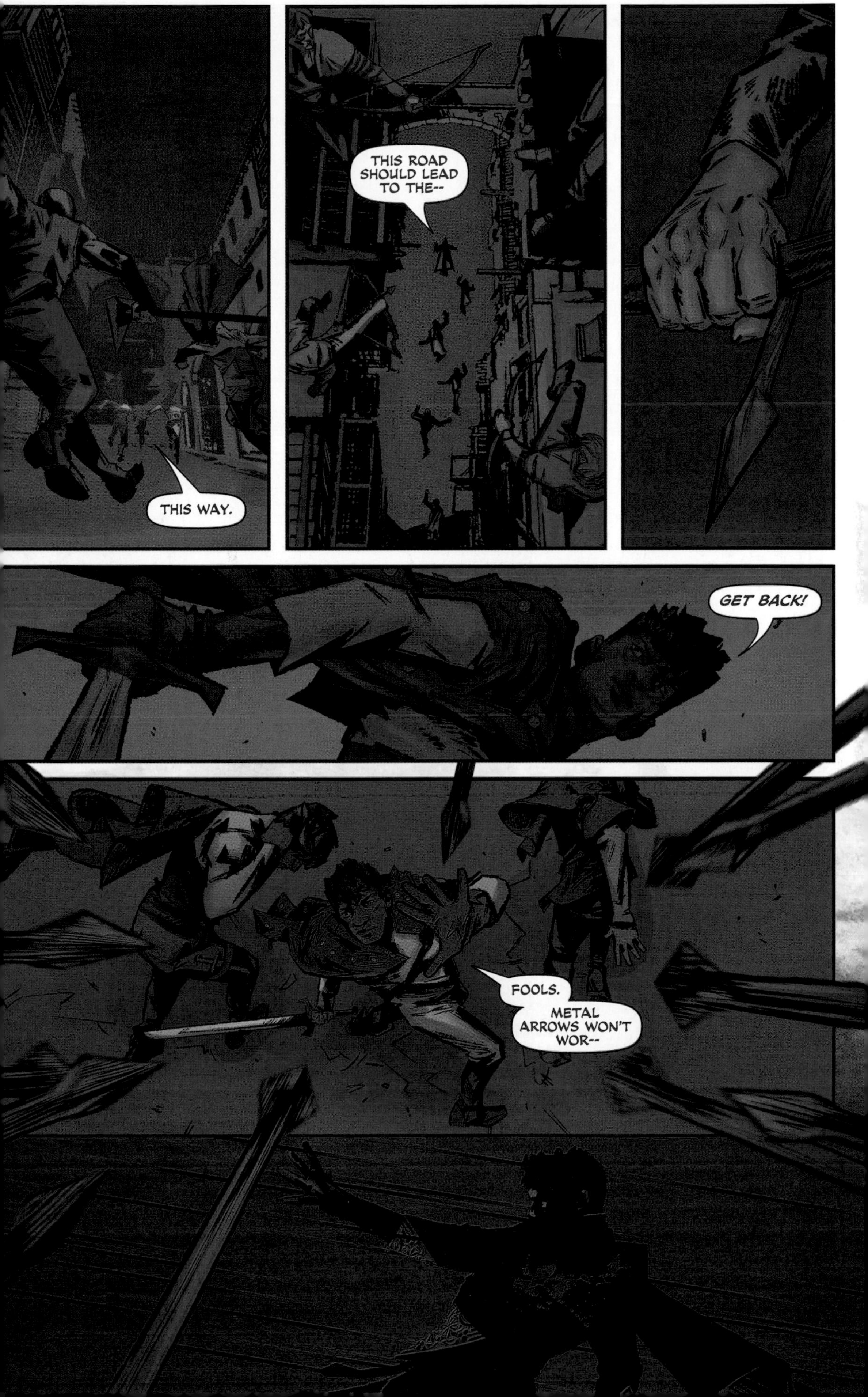
THIS WAY.
THIS ROAD SHOULD LEAD TO THE--
GET BACK!
FOOLS.
METAL ARROWS WON'T WOR--

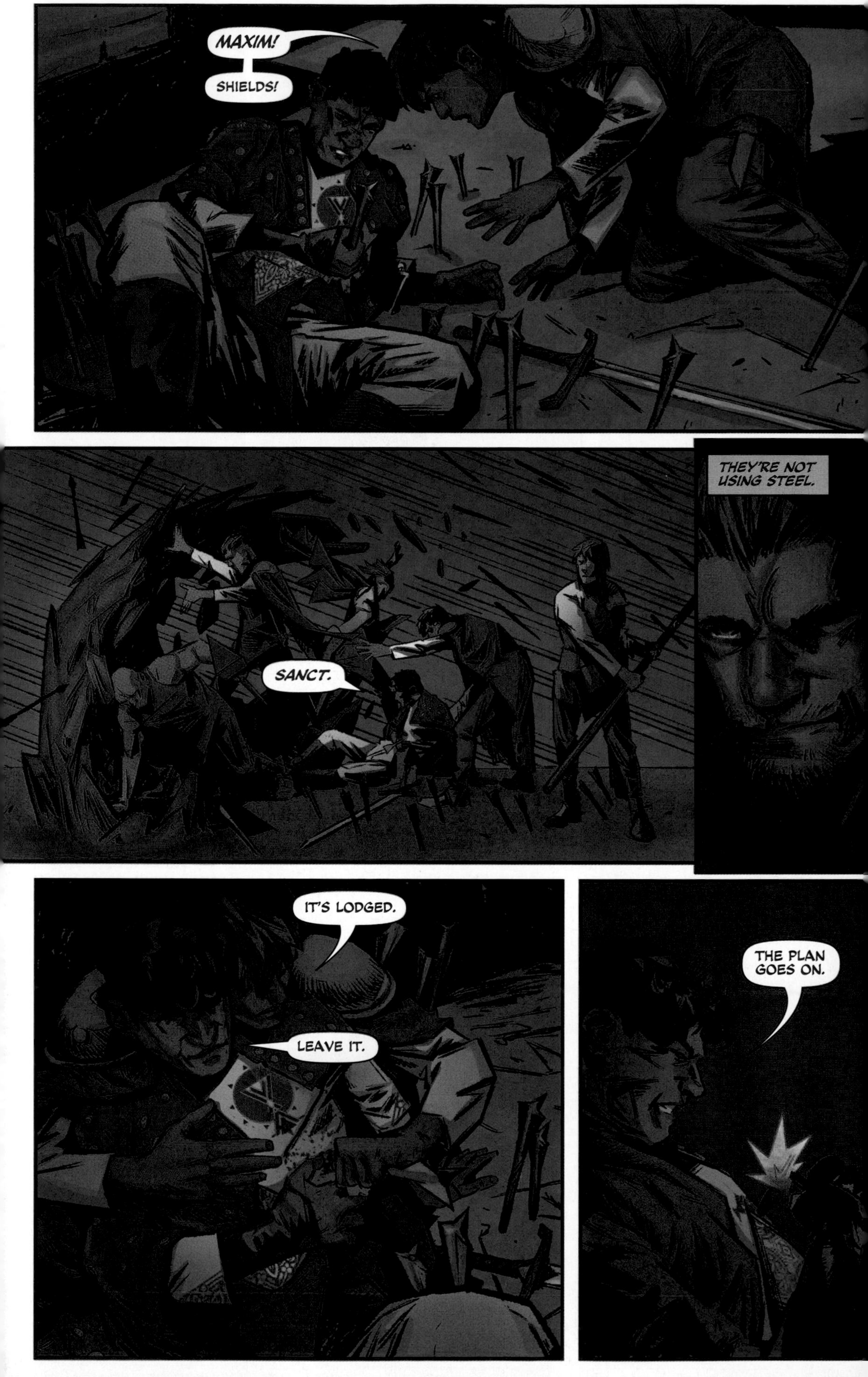
MAXIM!
SHIELDS!
THEY'RE NOT USING STEEL.
SANCT.
IT'S LODGED.
LEAVE IT.
THE PLAN GOES ON.

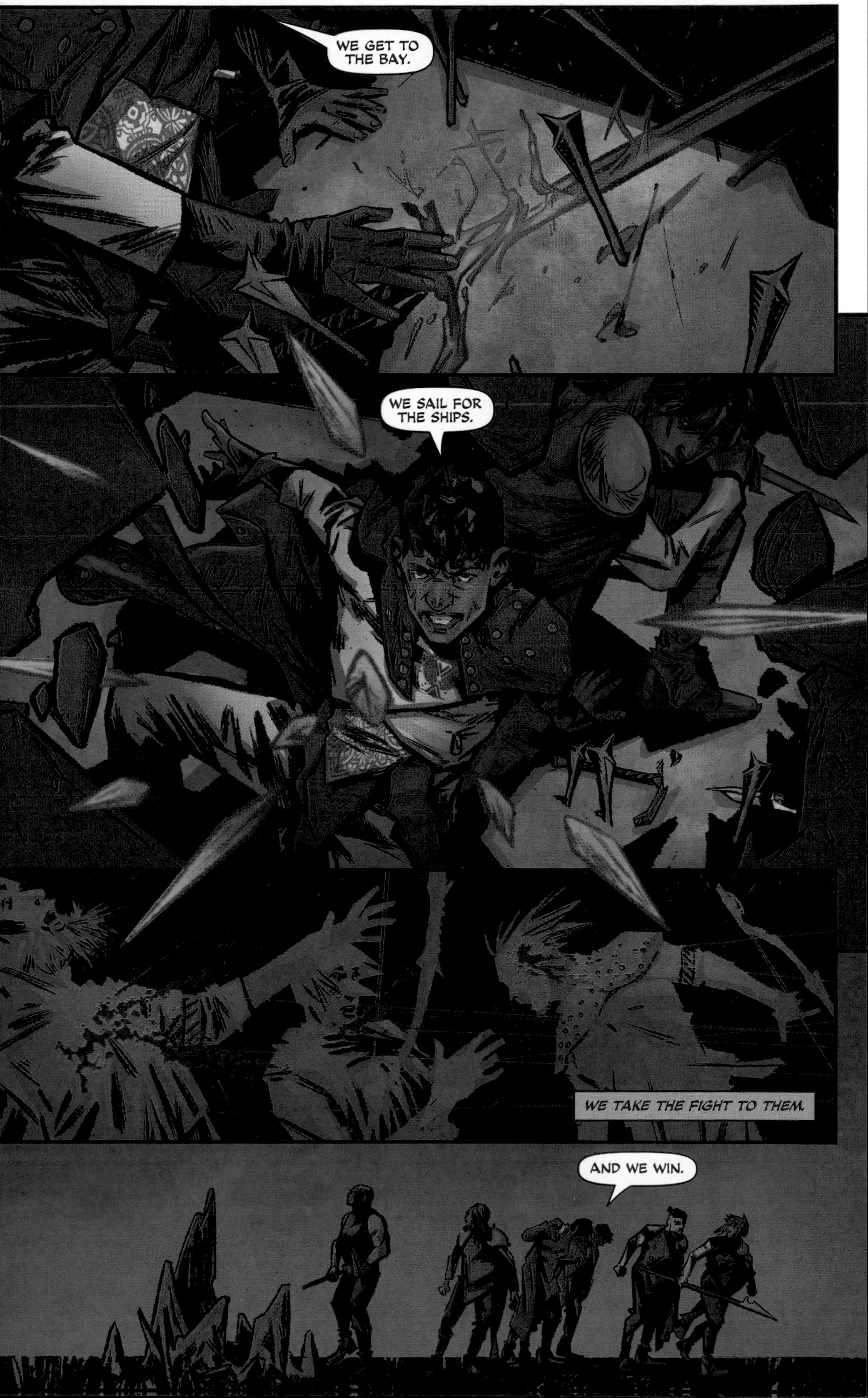
WE GET TO THE BAY.
WE SAIL FOR THE SHIPS.
WE TAKE THE FIGHT TO THEM.
AND WE WIN.

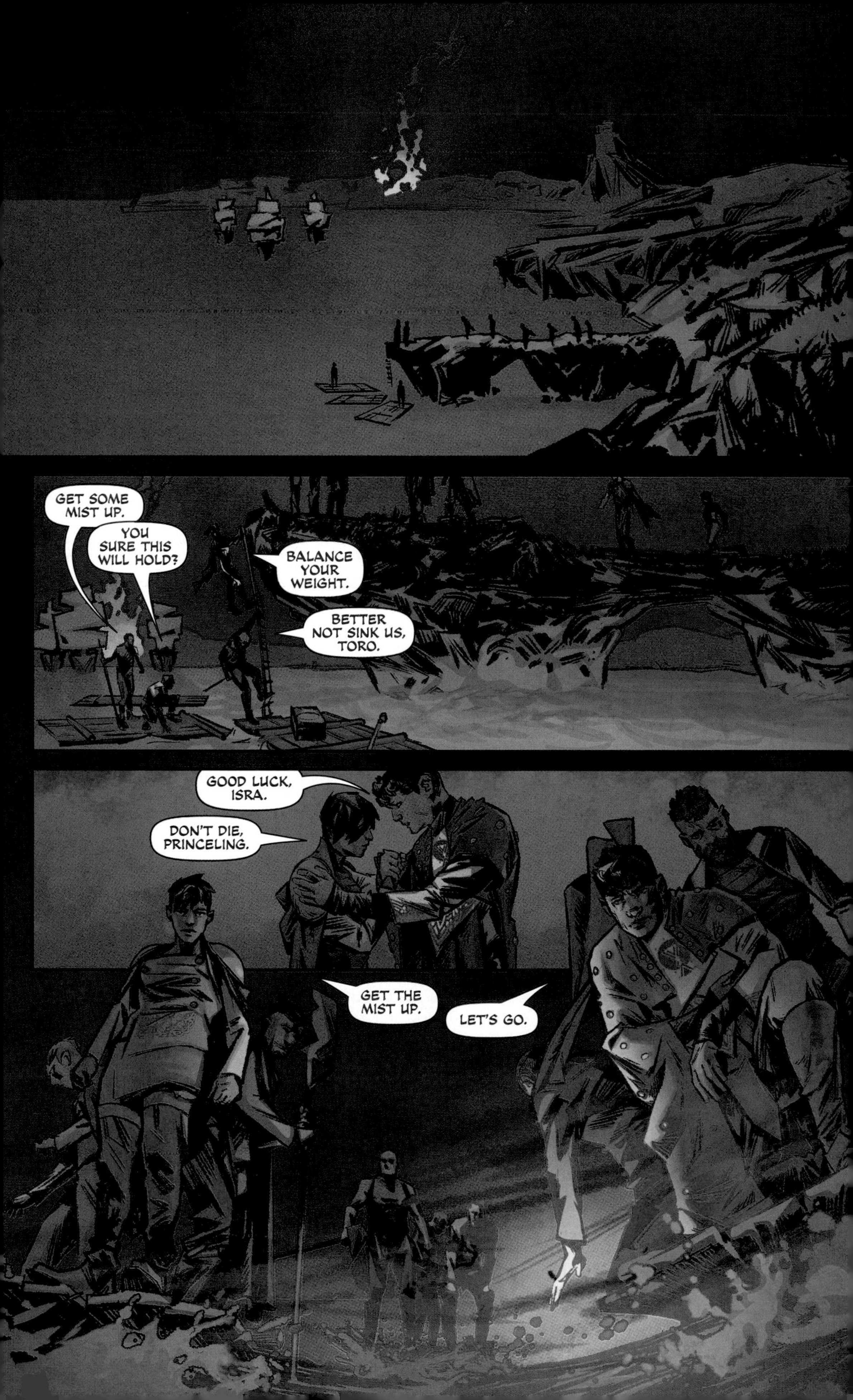
GET SOME MIST UP.
YOU SURE THIS WILL HOLD?
BALANCE YOUR WEIGHT.
BETTER NOT SINK US, TORO.
GOOD LUCK, ISRA.
DON'T DIE, PRINCELING.
GET THE MIST UP.
LET'S GO.

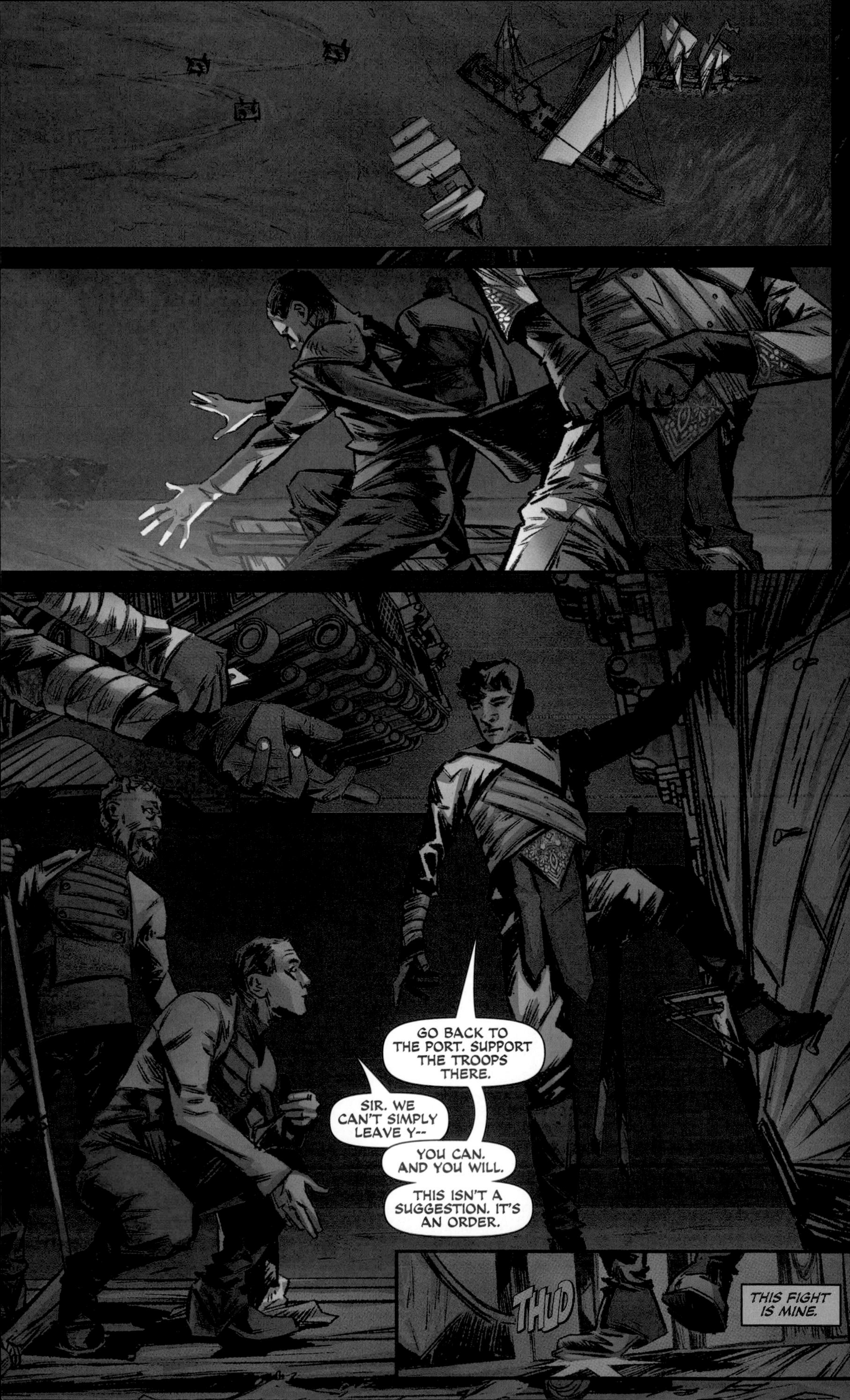
GO BACK TO THE PORT. SUPPORT THE TROOPS THERE.
SIR. WE CAN'T SIMPLY LEAVE Y--
YOU CAN. AND YOU WILL.
THIS ISN'T A SUGGESTION. IT'S AN ORDER.
THUD
THIS FIGHT IS MINE.

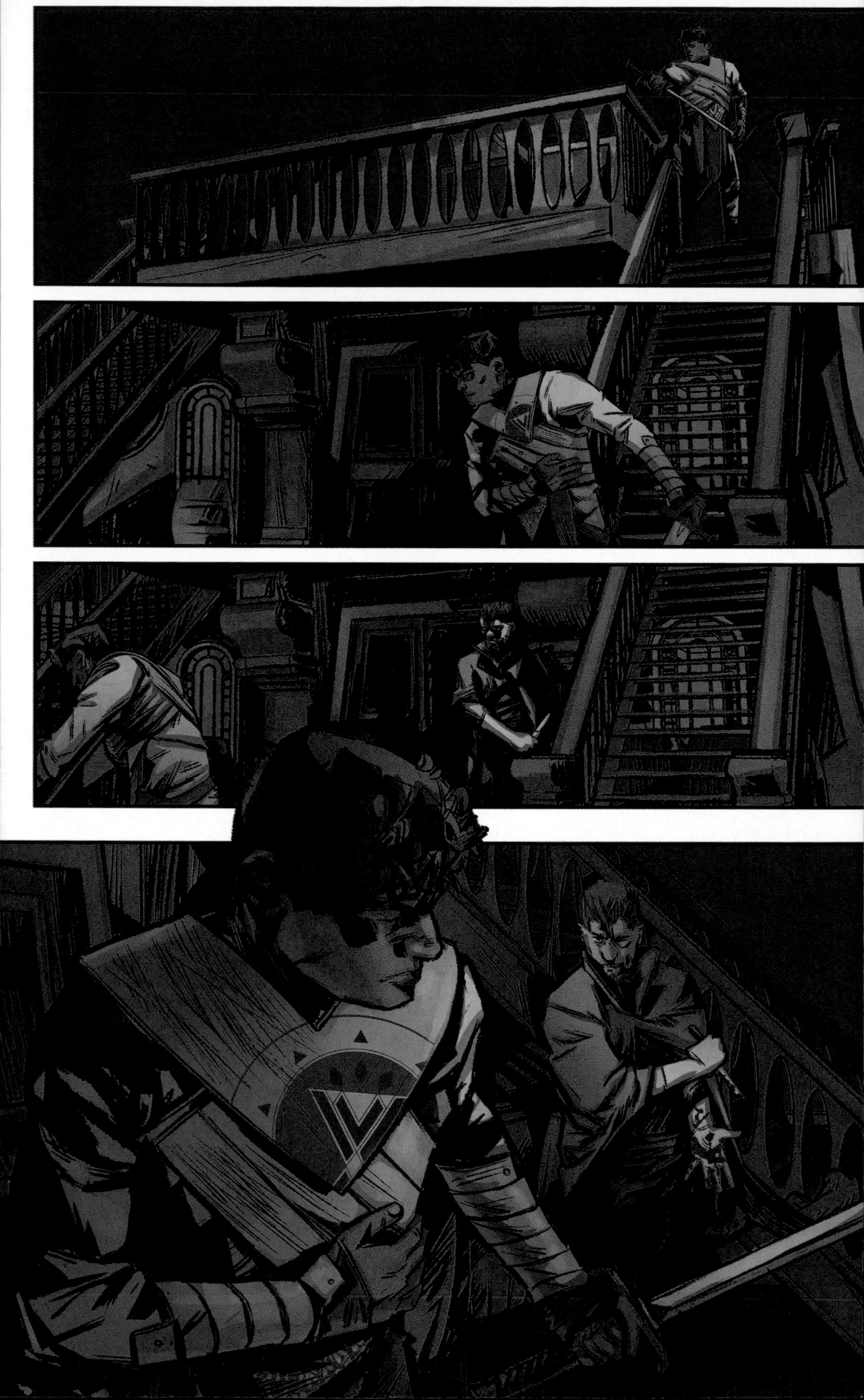

#4

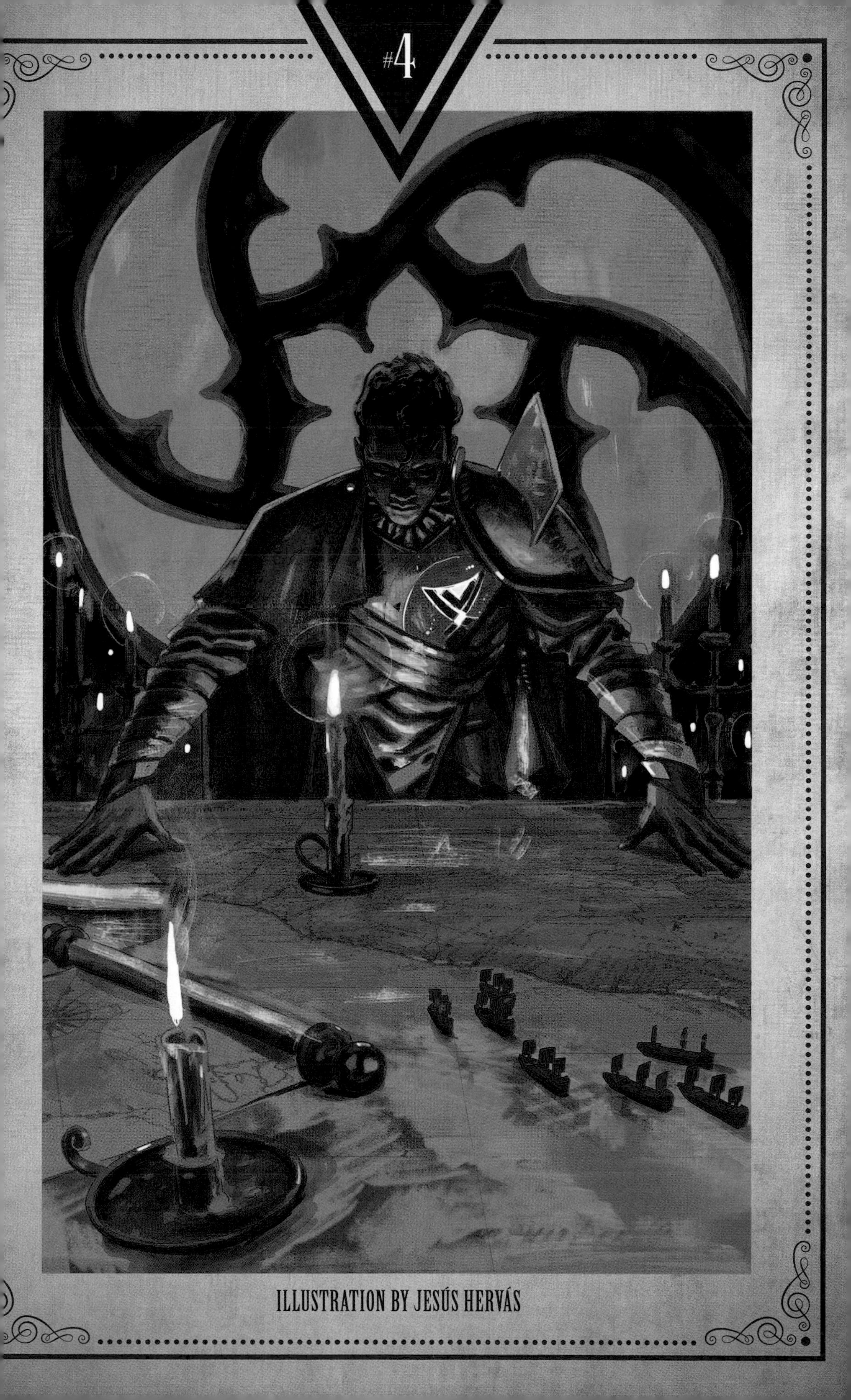

ILLUSTRATION BY JESÚS HERVÁS

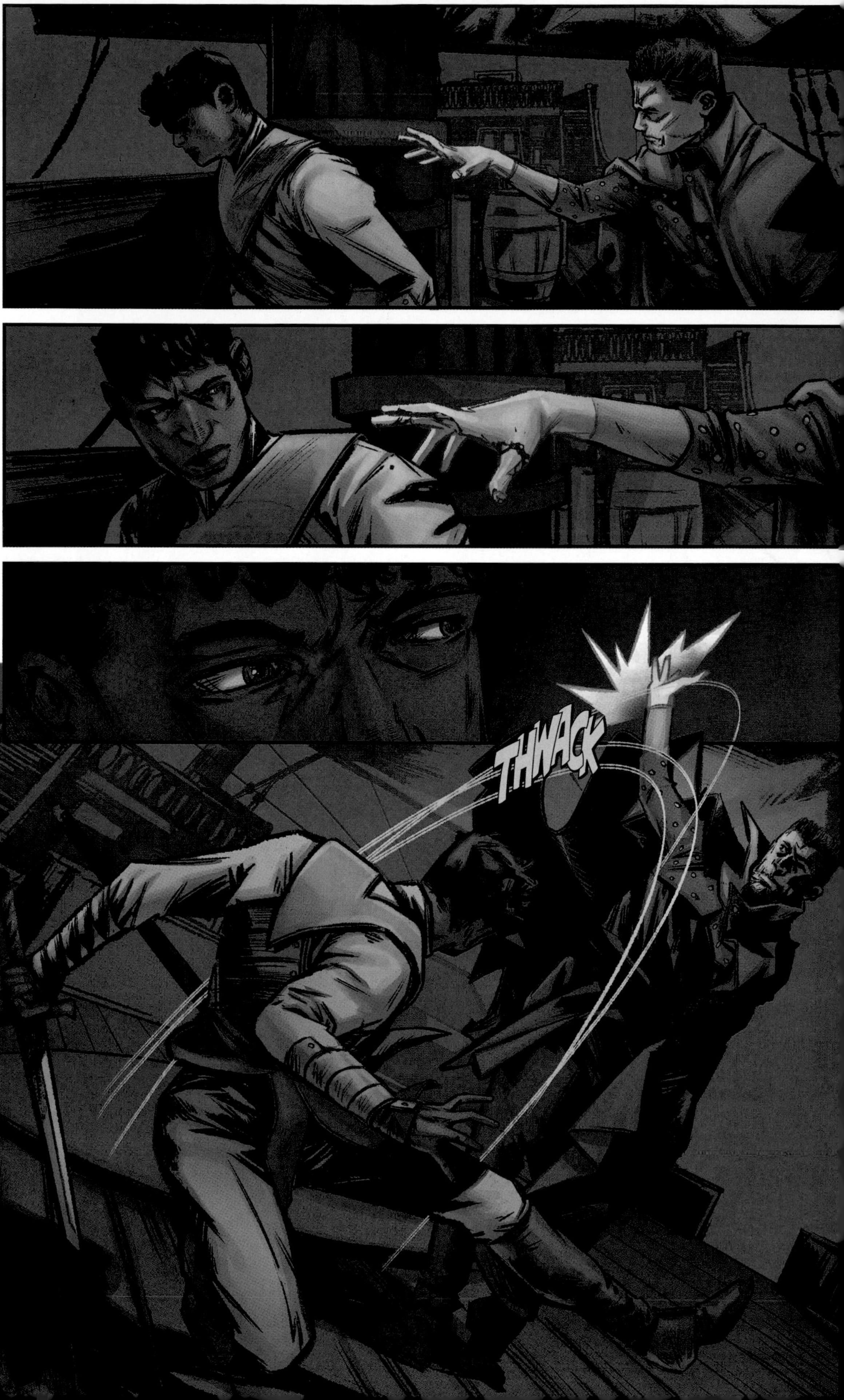
THWACK

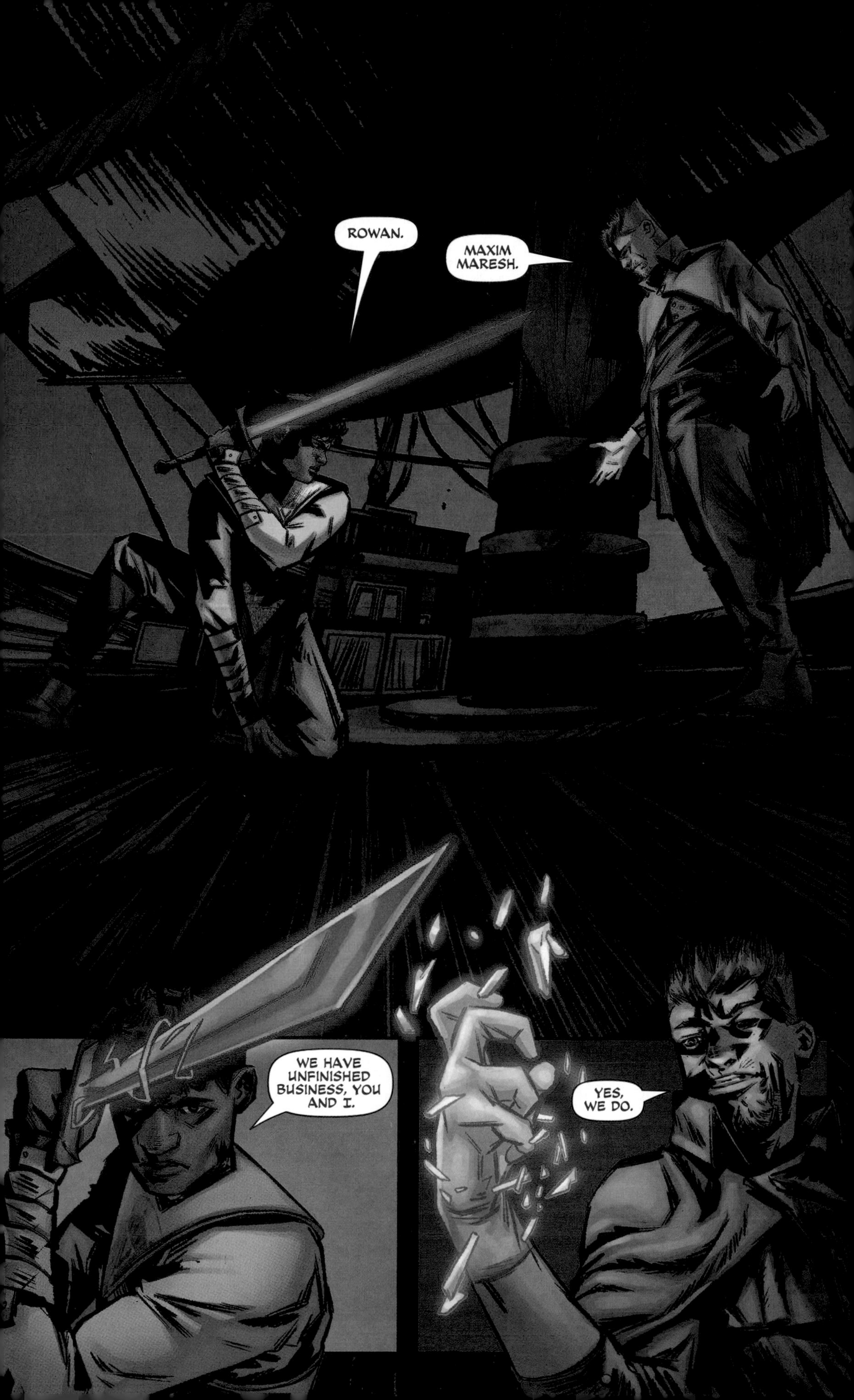
ROWAN.
MAXIM MARESH.
WE HAVE UNFINISHED BUSINESS, YOU AND I.
YES, WE DO.

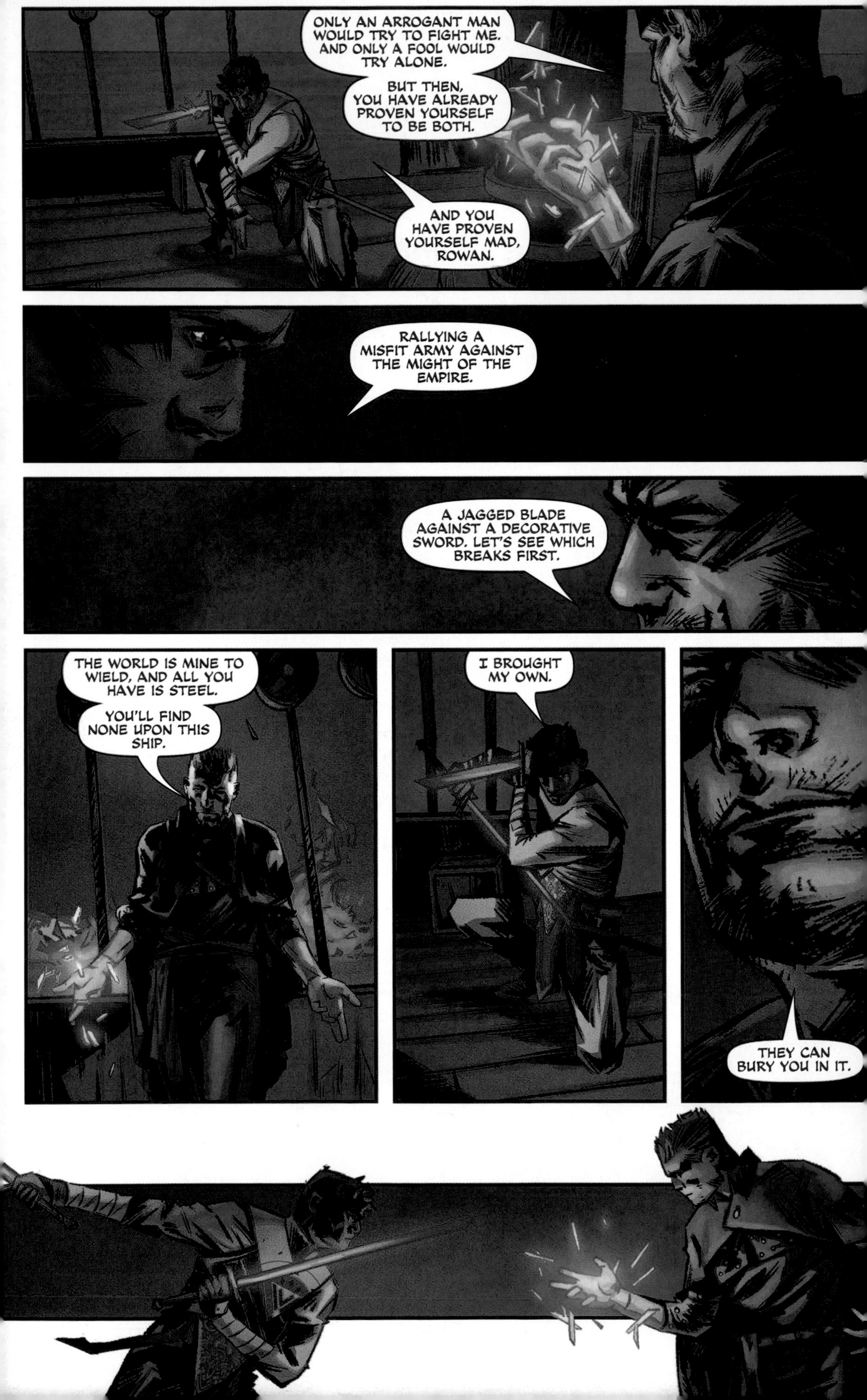
ONLY AN ARROGANT MAN WOULD TRY TO FIGHT ME. AND ONLY A FOOL WOULD TRY ALONE.
BUT THEN, YOU HAVE ALREADY PROVEN YOURSELF TO BE BOTH.
AND YOU HAVE PROVEN YOURSELF MAD, ROWAN.
RALLYING A MISFIT ARMY AGAINST THE MIGHT OF THE EMPIRE.
A JAGGED BLADE AGAINST A DECORATIVE SWORD. LET'S SEE WHICH BREAKS FIRST.
THE WORLD IS MINE TO WIELD, AND ALL YOU HAVE IS STEEL.
YOU'LL FIND NONE UPON THIS SHIP.
I BROUGHT MY OWN.
THEY CAN BURY YOU IN IT.

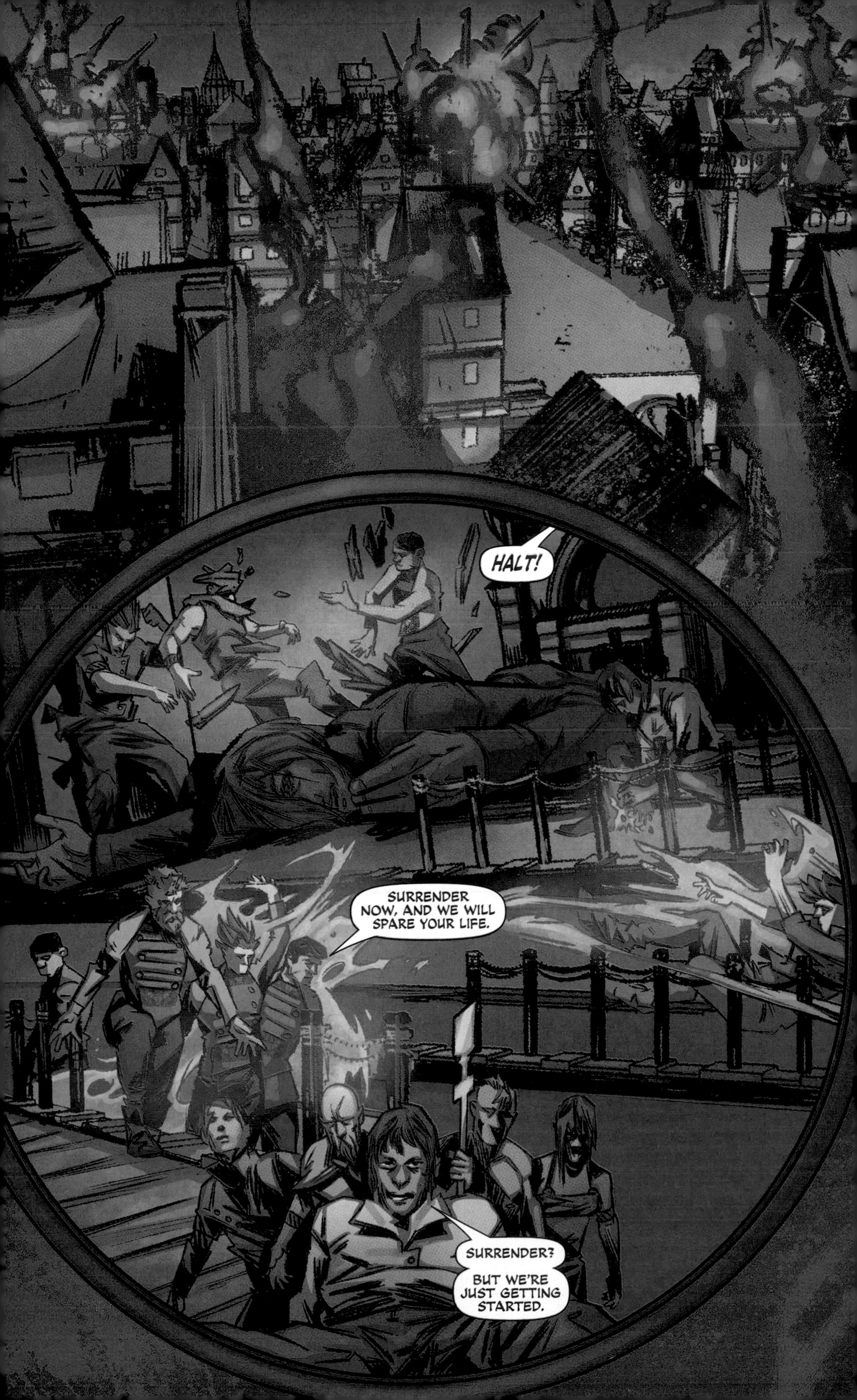
HALT!
SURRENDER NOW, AND WE WILL SPARE YOUR LIFE.
SURRENDER?
BUT WE'RE JUST GETTING STARTED.

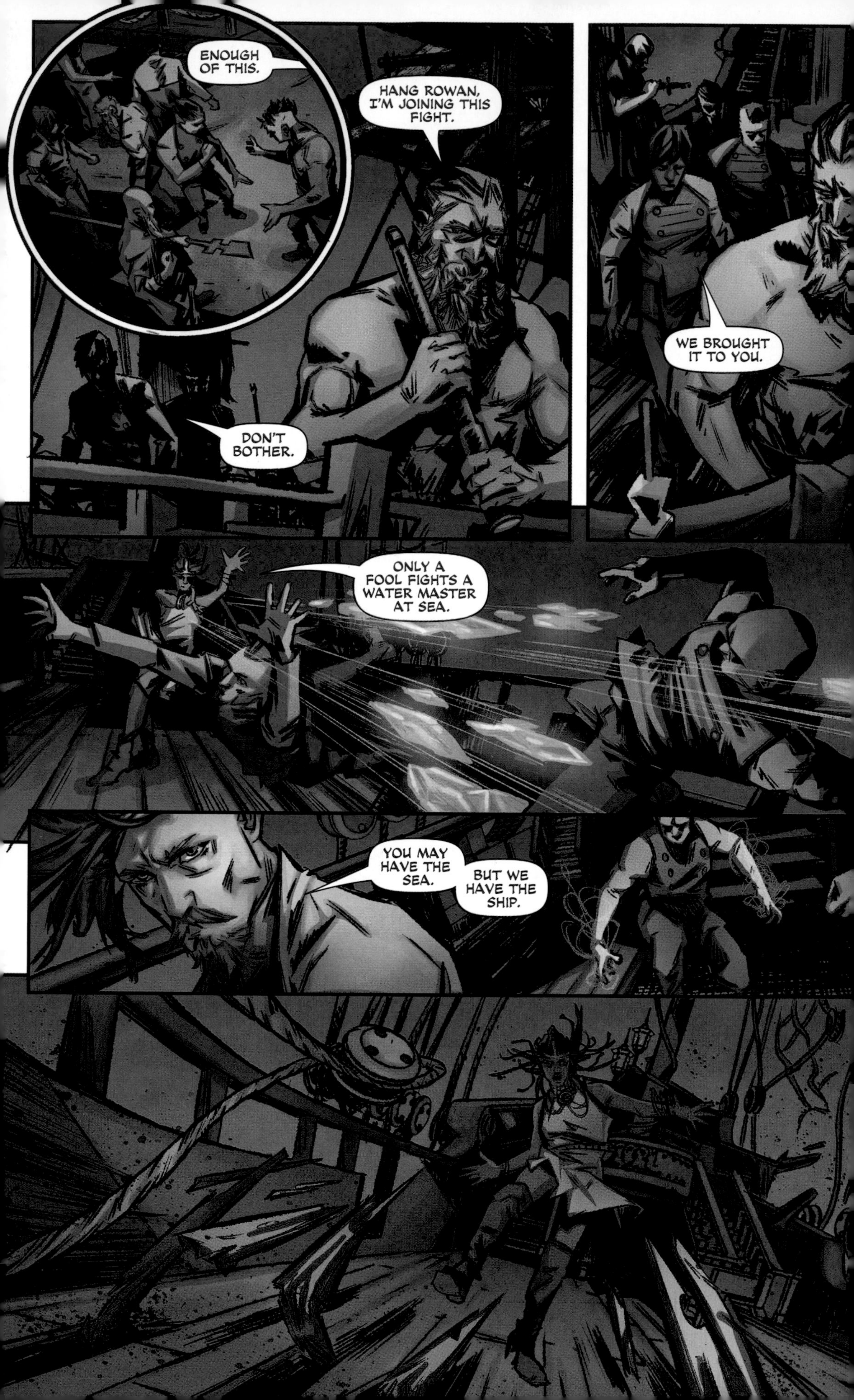
ENOUGH OF THIS.
HANG ROWAN, I'M JOINING THIS FIGHT.
DON'T BOTHER.
WE BROUGHT IT TO YOU.
ONLY A FOOL FIGHTS A WATER MASTER AT SEA.
YOU MAY HAVE THE SEA.
BUT WE HAVE THE SHIP.

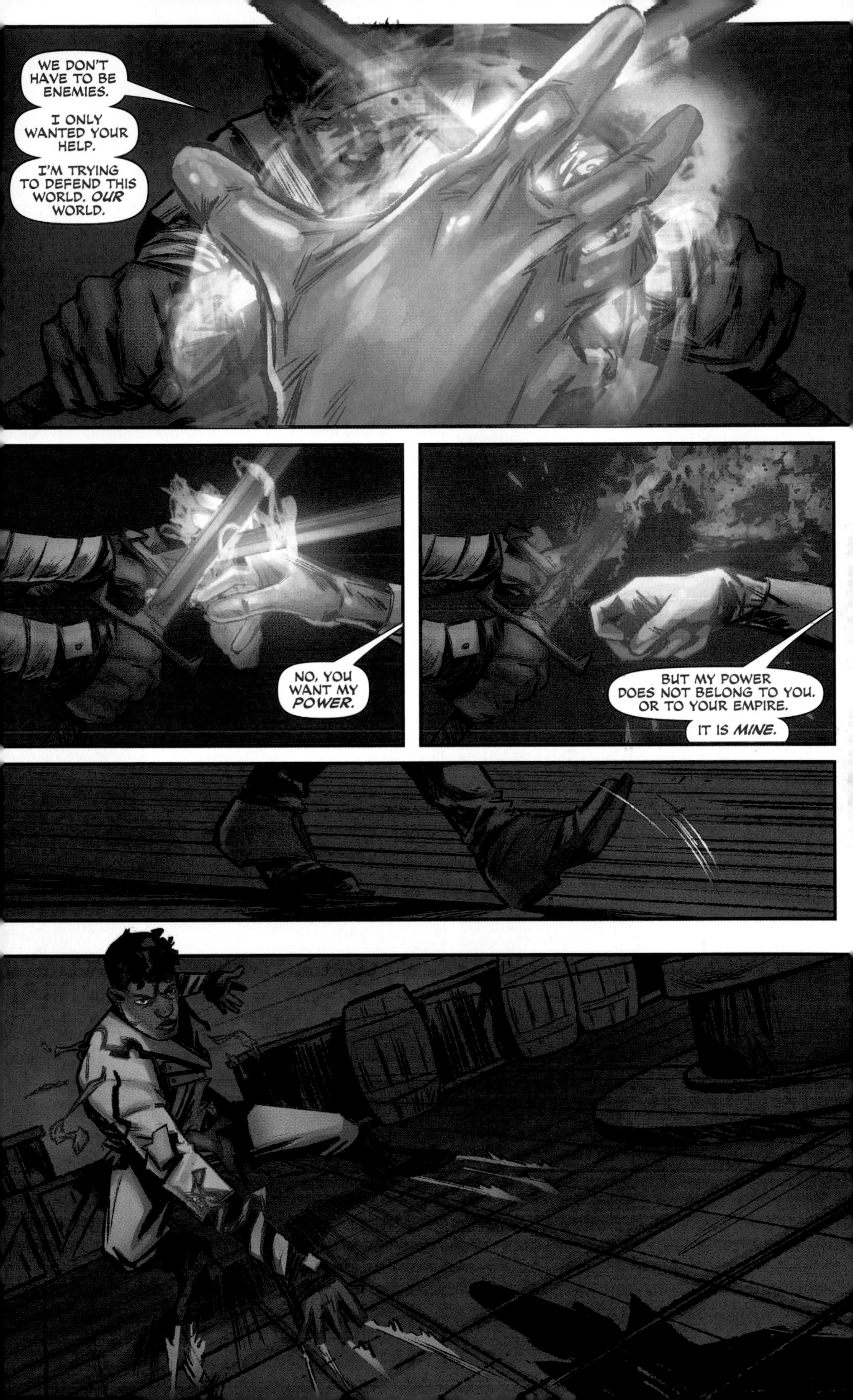
WE DON'T HAVE TO BE ENEMIES.
I ONLY WANTED YOUR HELP.
I'M TRYING TO DEFEND THIS WORLD. *OUR* WORLD.
NO, YOU WANT MY *POWER*.
BUT MY POWER DOES NOT BELONG TO YOU. OR TO YOUR EMPIRE.
IT IS *MINE*.

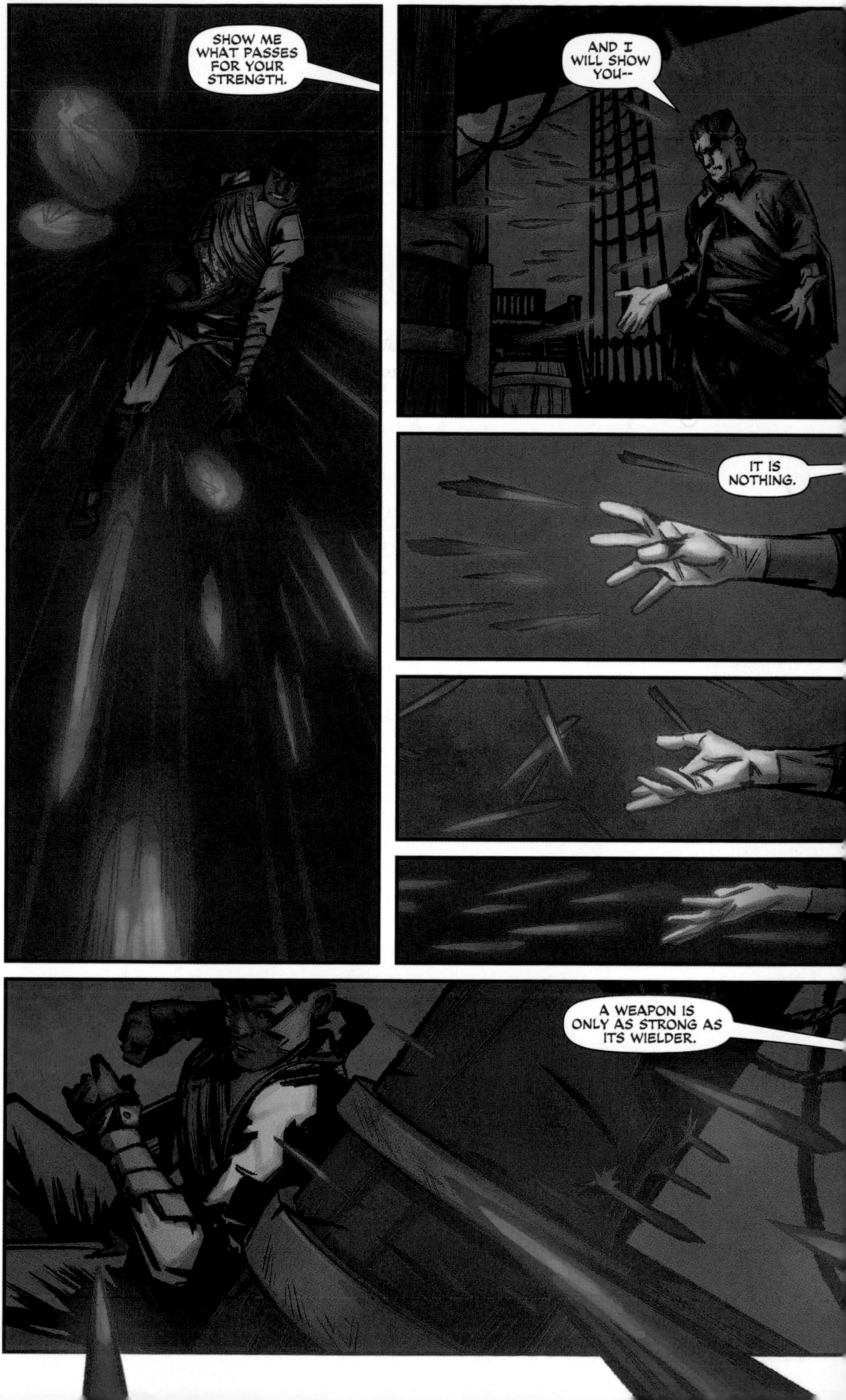
SHOW ME WHAT PASSES FOR YOUR STRENGTH.
AND I WILL SHOW YOU--
IT IS NOTHING.
A WEAPON IS ONLY AS STRONG AS ITS WIELDER.

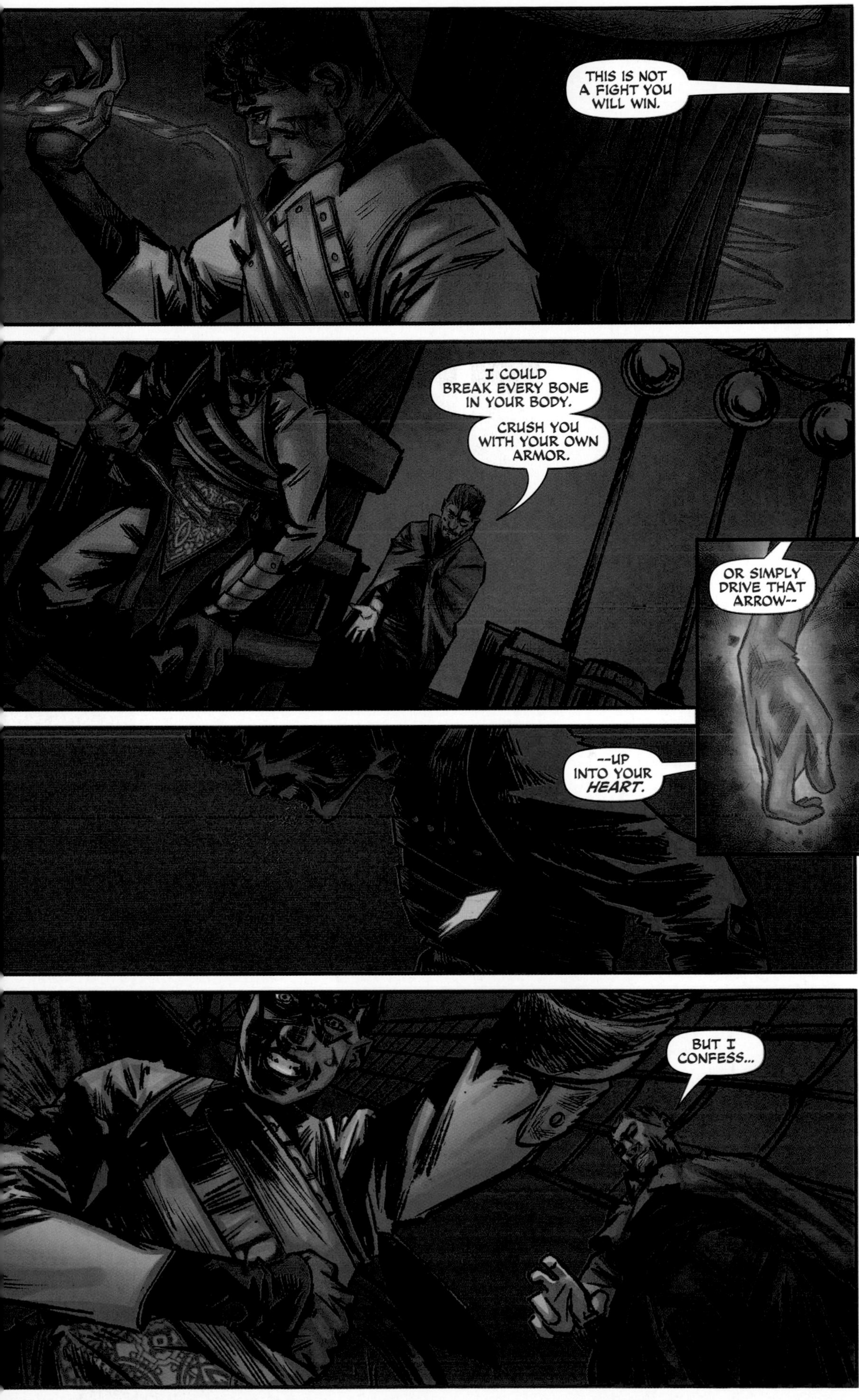
THIS IS NOT A FIGHT YOU WILL WIN.
I COULD BREAK EVERY BONE IN YOUR BODY.
CRUSH YOU WITH YOUR OWN ARMOR.
OR SIMPLY DRIVE THAT ARROW--
--UP INTO YOUR *HEART*.
BUT I CONFESS...

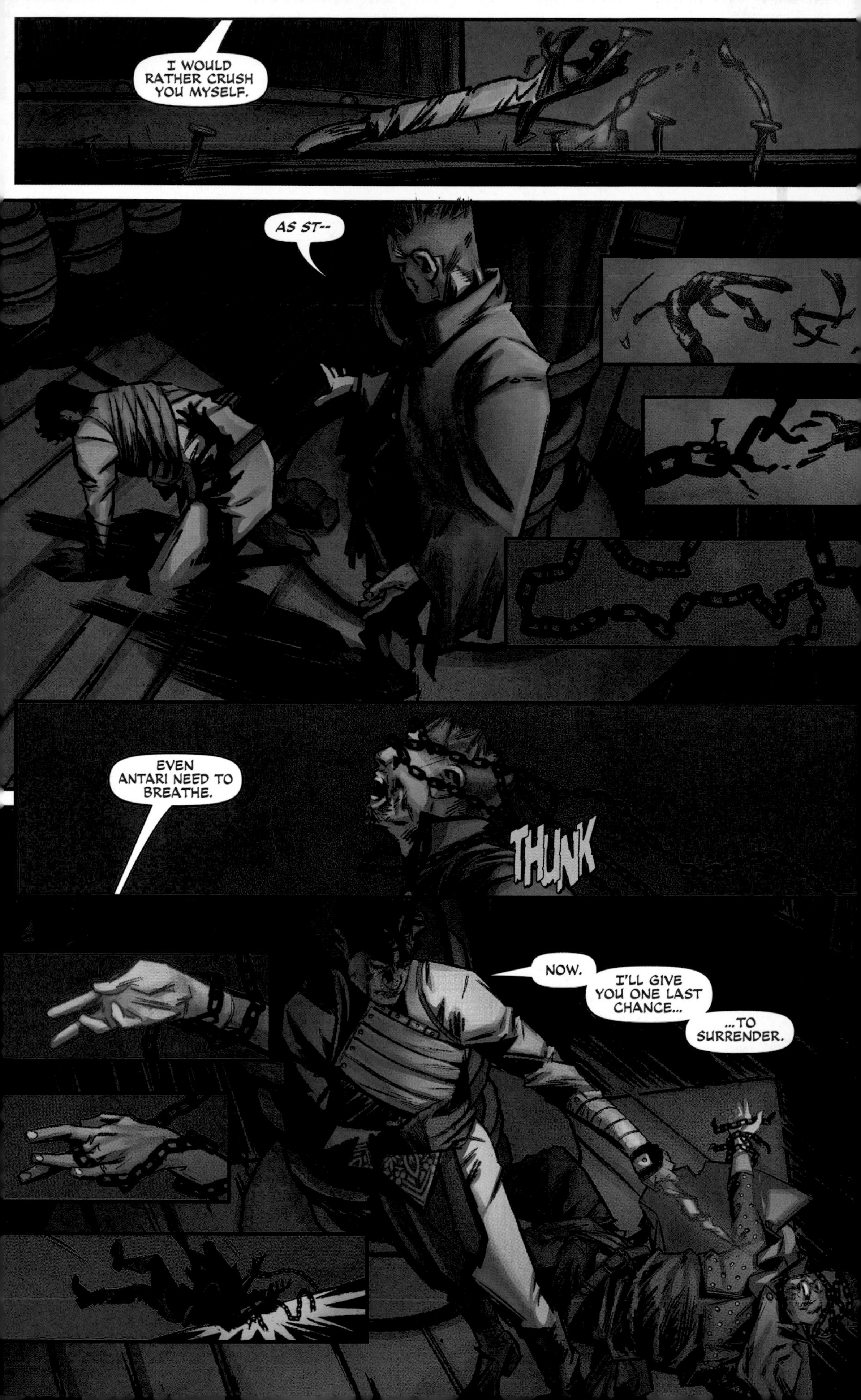
I WOULD RATHER CRUSH YOU MYSELF.
AS ST--
EVEN ANTARI NEED TO BREATHE.
THUNK
NOW.
I'LL GIVE YOU ONE LAST CHANCE...
...TO SURRENDER.

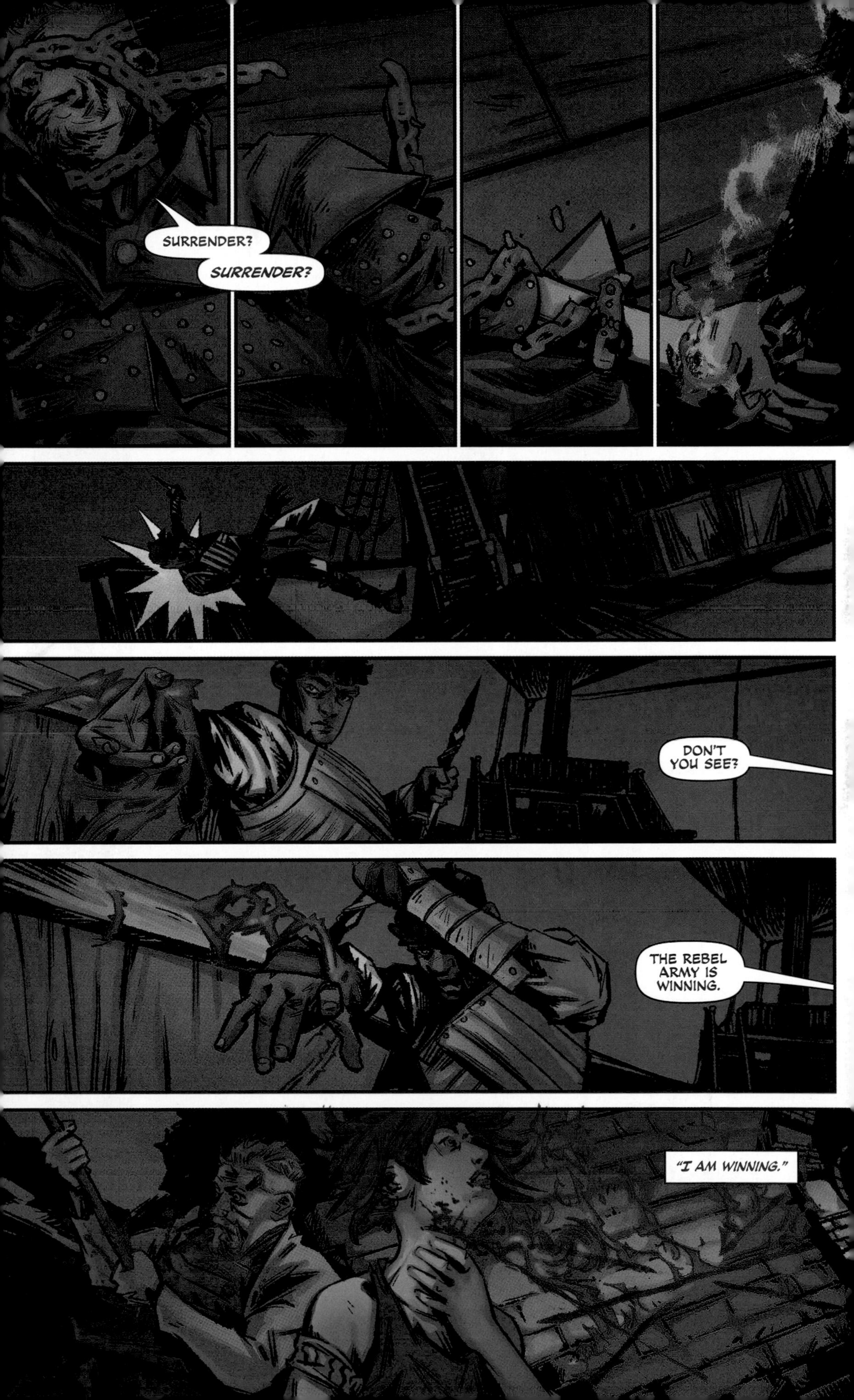
SURRENDER?
SURRENDER?
DON'T YOU SEE?
THE REBEL ARMY IS WINNING.
"I AM WINNING."

HAVING FUN YET?

"VEROSE WILL FALL, AS WILL EVERY PORT AND TOWN BETWEEN ME, AND THE CAPITAL.

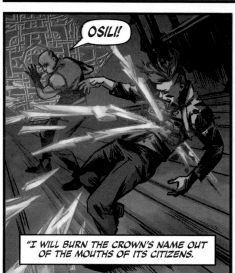

OSILI!

"I WILL BURN THE CROWN'S NAME OUT OF THE MOUTHS OF ITS CITIZENS.

"I WILL RAZE THIS EMPIRE IN MY WAKE.

"AND YOU WILL BE NOTHING BUT A MEMORY."

AN ARROGANT PRINCE, PARADING AS A SOLDIER.

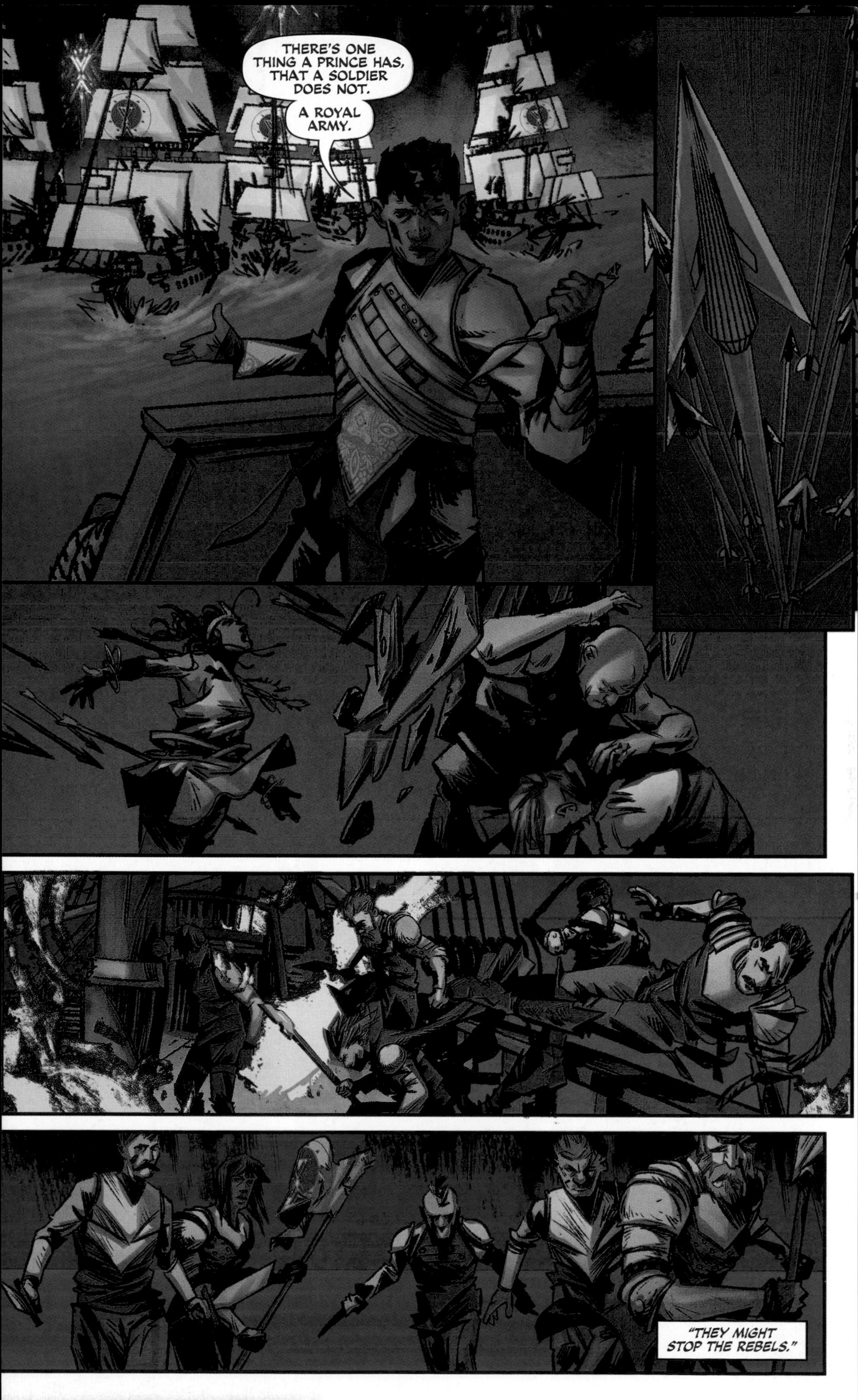
THERE'S ONE THING A PRINCE HAS, THAT A SOLDIER DOES NOT.
A ROYAL ARMY.
"THEY MIGHT STOP THE REBELS."

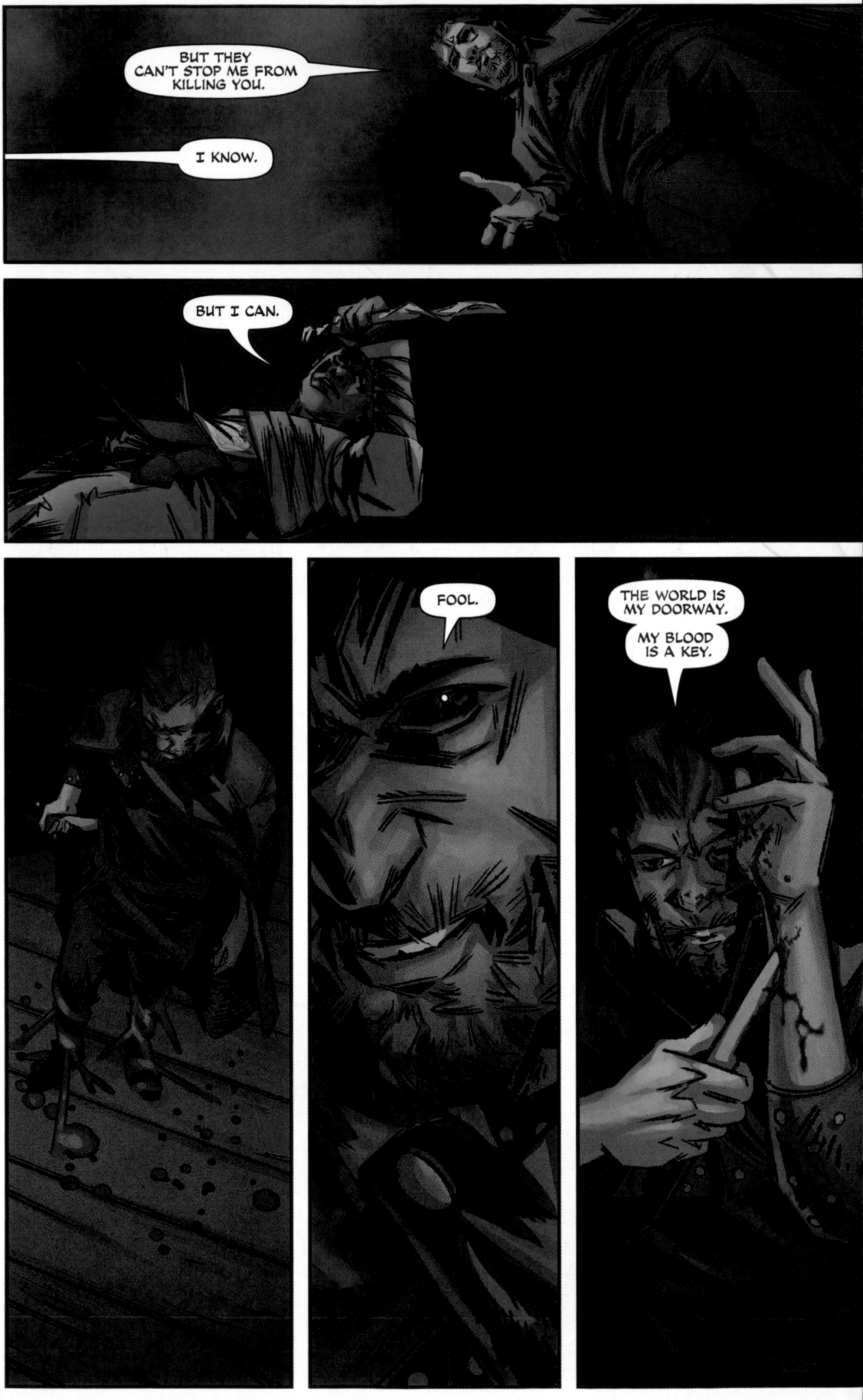
BUT THEY CAN'T STOP ME FROM KILLING YOU.
I KNOW.
BUT I CAN.
FOOL.
THE WORLD IS MY DOORWAY.
MY BLOOD IS A KEY.

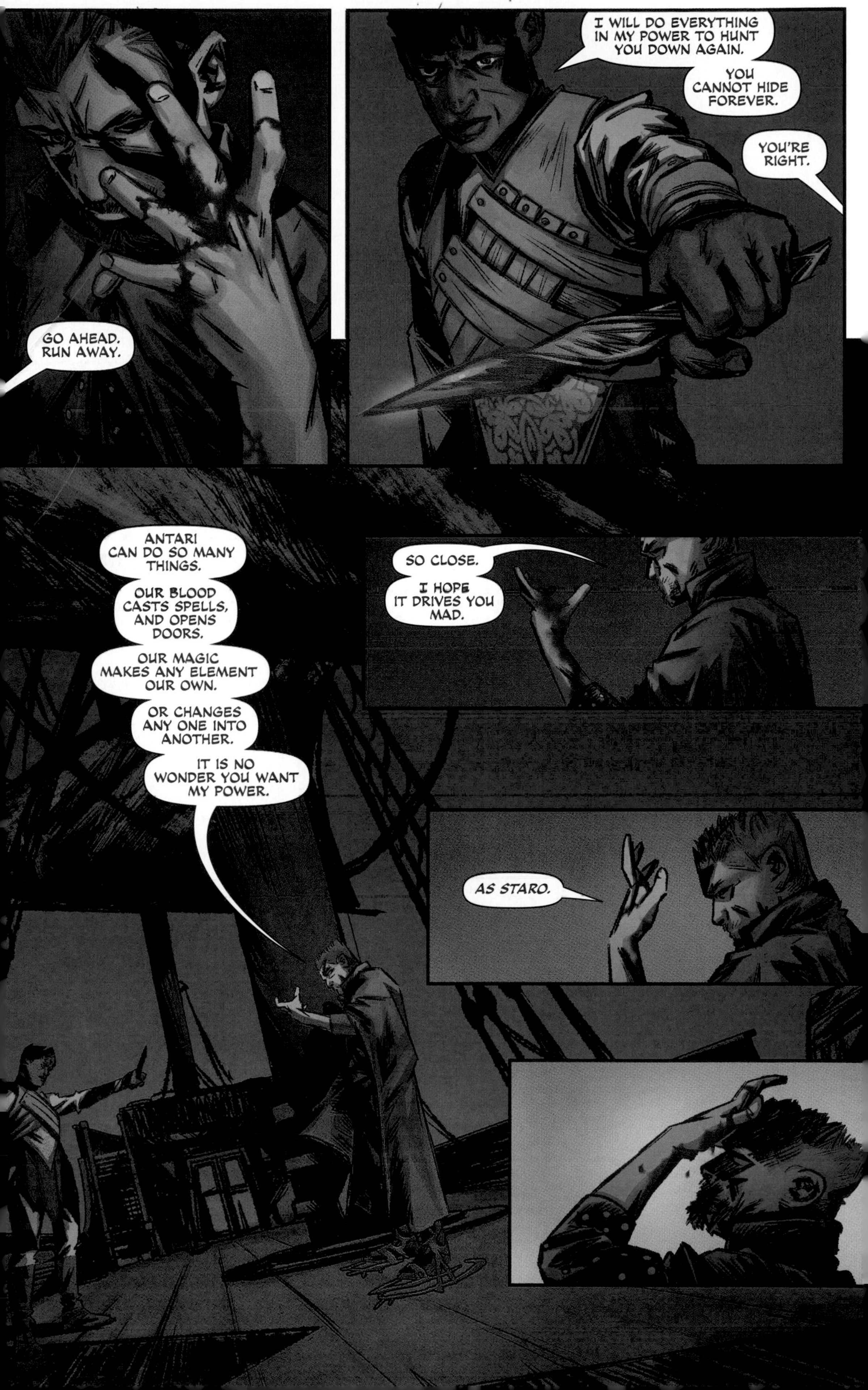
GO AHEAD. RUN AWAY.
I WILL DO EVERYTHING IN MY POWER TO HUNT YOU DOWN AGAIN.
YOU CANNOT HIDE FOREVER.
YOU'RE RIGHT.
ANTARI CAN DO SO MANY THINGS.
OUR BLOOD CASTS SPELLS, AND OPENS DOORS.
OUR MAGIC MAKES ANY ELEMENT OUR OWN.
OR CHANGES ANY ONE INTO ANOTHER.
IT IS NO WONDER YOU WANT MY POWER.
SO CLOSE.
I HOPE IT DRIVES YOU MAD.
AS STARO.

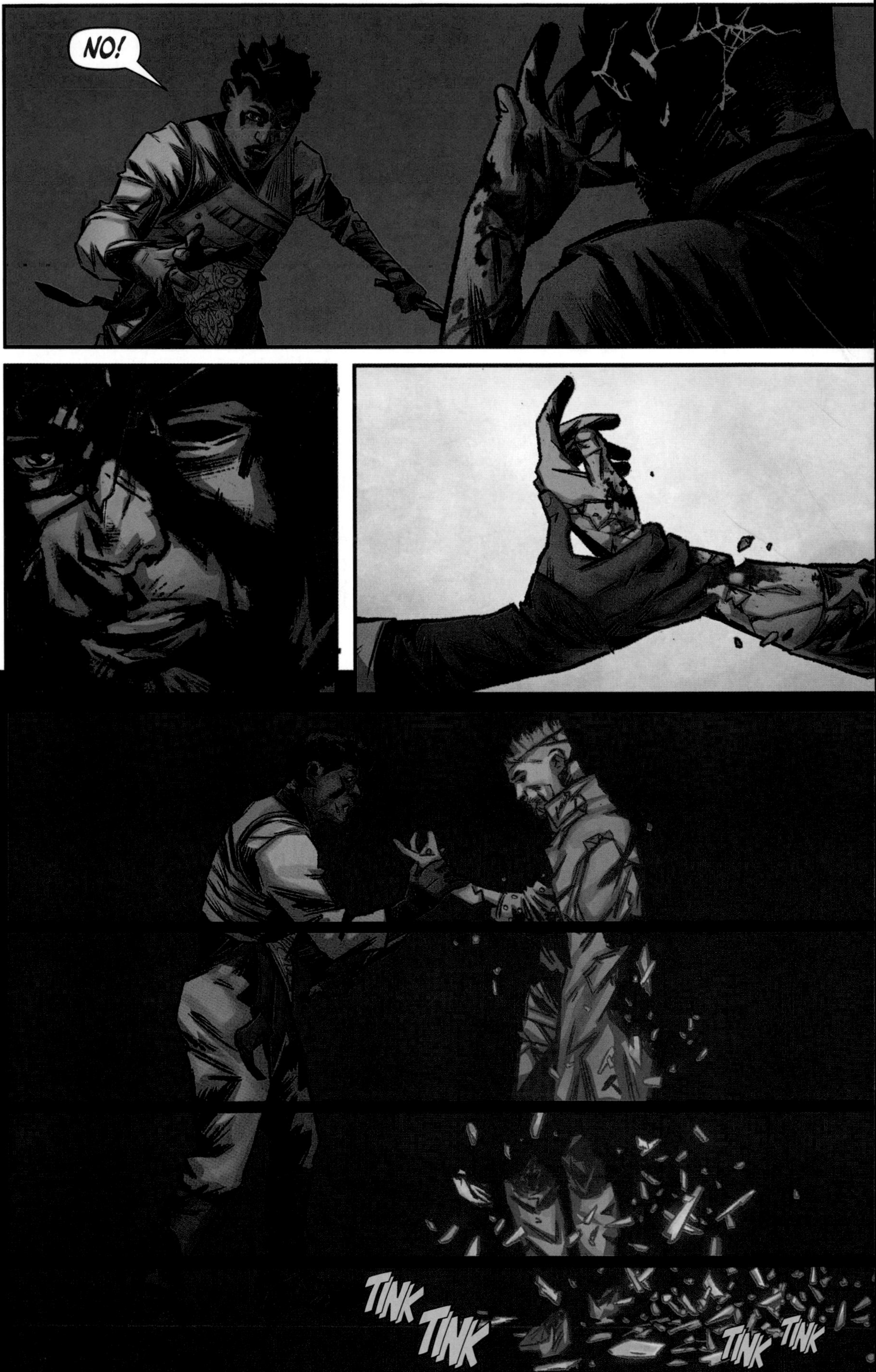
NO!
TINK
TINK
TINK
TINK

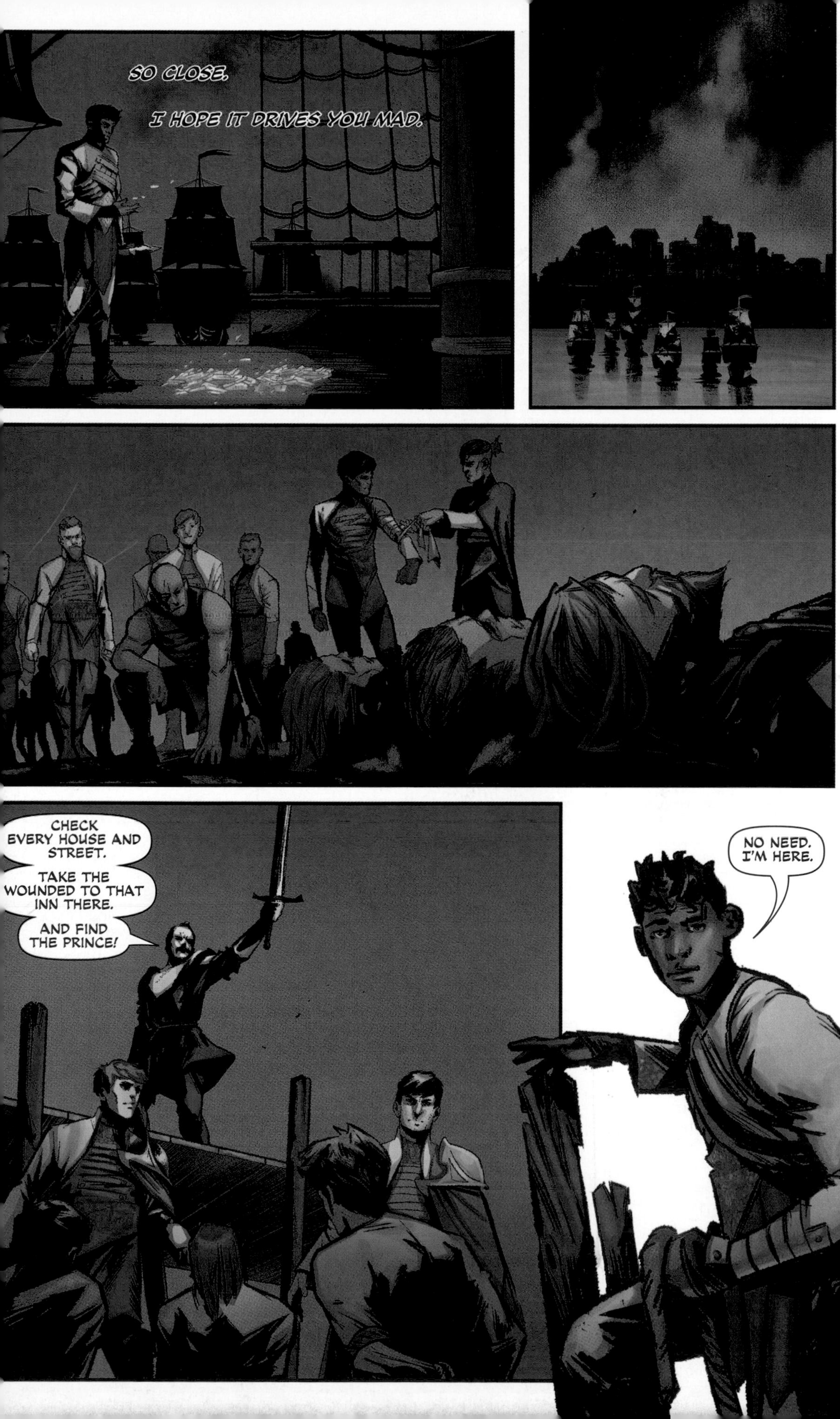
SO CLOSE.
I HOPE IT DRIVES YOU MAD.
CHECK EVERY HOUSE AND STREET.
TAKE THE WOUNDED TO THAT INN THERE.
AND FIND THE PRINCE!
NO NEED. I'M HERE.

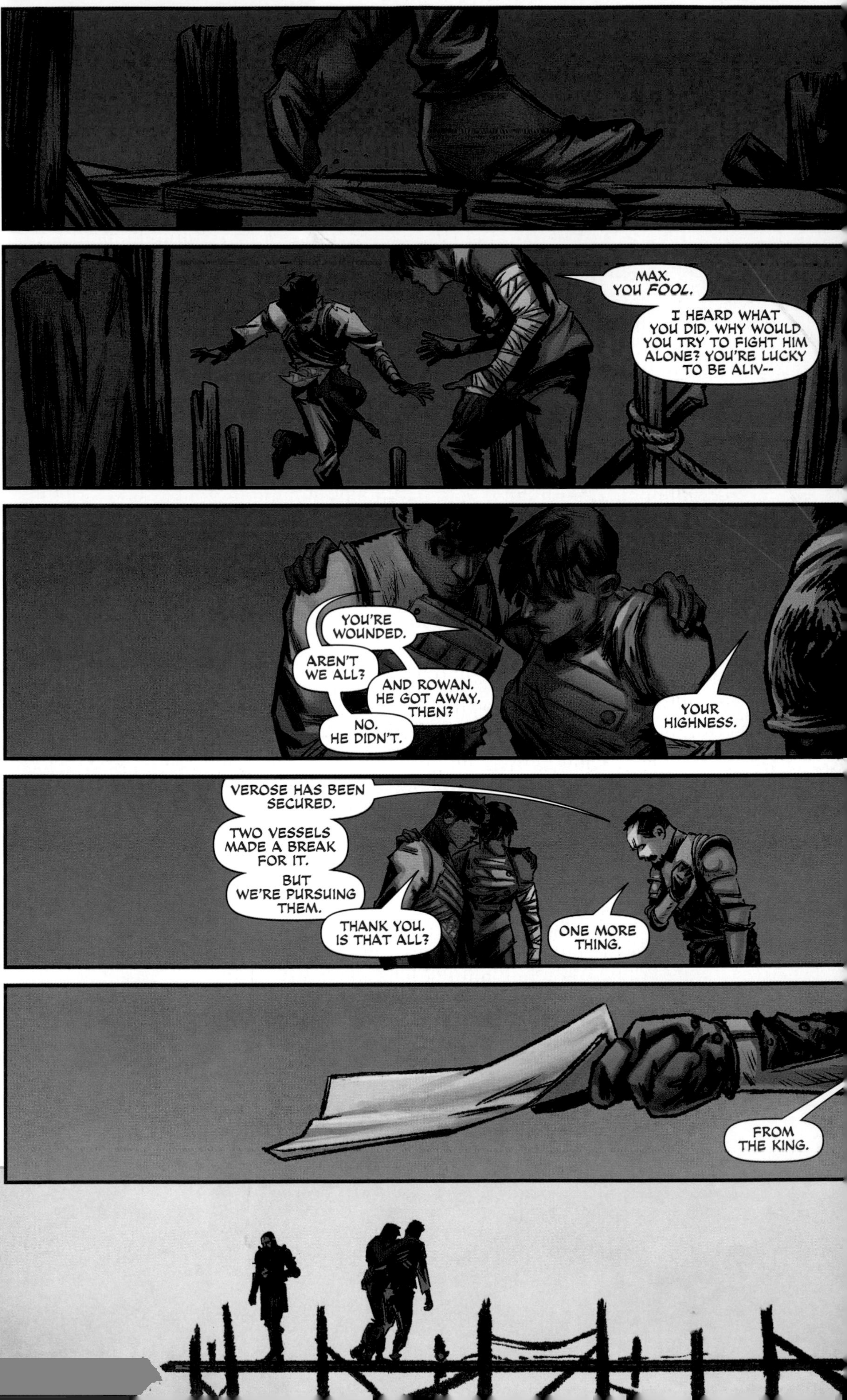
MAX. YOU FOOL.
I HEARD WHAT YOU DID, WHY WOULD YOU TRY TO FIGHT HIM ALONE? YOU'RE LUCKY TO BE ALIV--
YOU'RE WOUNDED.
AREN'T WE ALL?
AND ROWAN. HE GOT AWAY, THEN?
NO. HE DIDN'T.
YOUR HIGHNESS.
VEROSE HAS BEEN SECURED.
TWO VESSELS MADE A BREAK FOR IT.
BUT WE'RE PURSUING THEM.
THANK YOU. IS THAT ALL?
ONE MORE THING.
FROM THE KING.

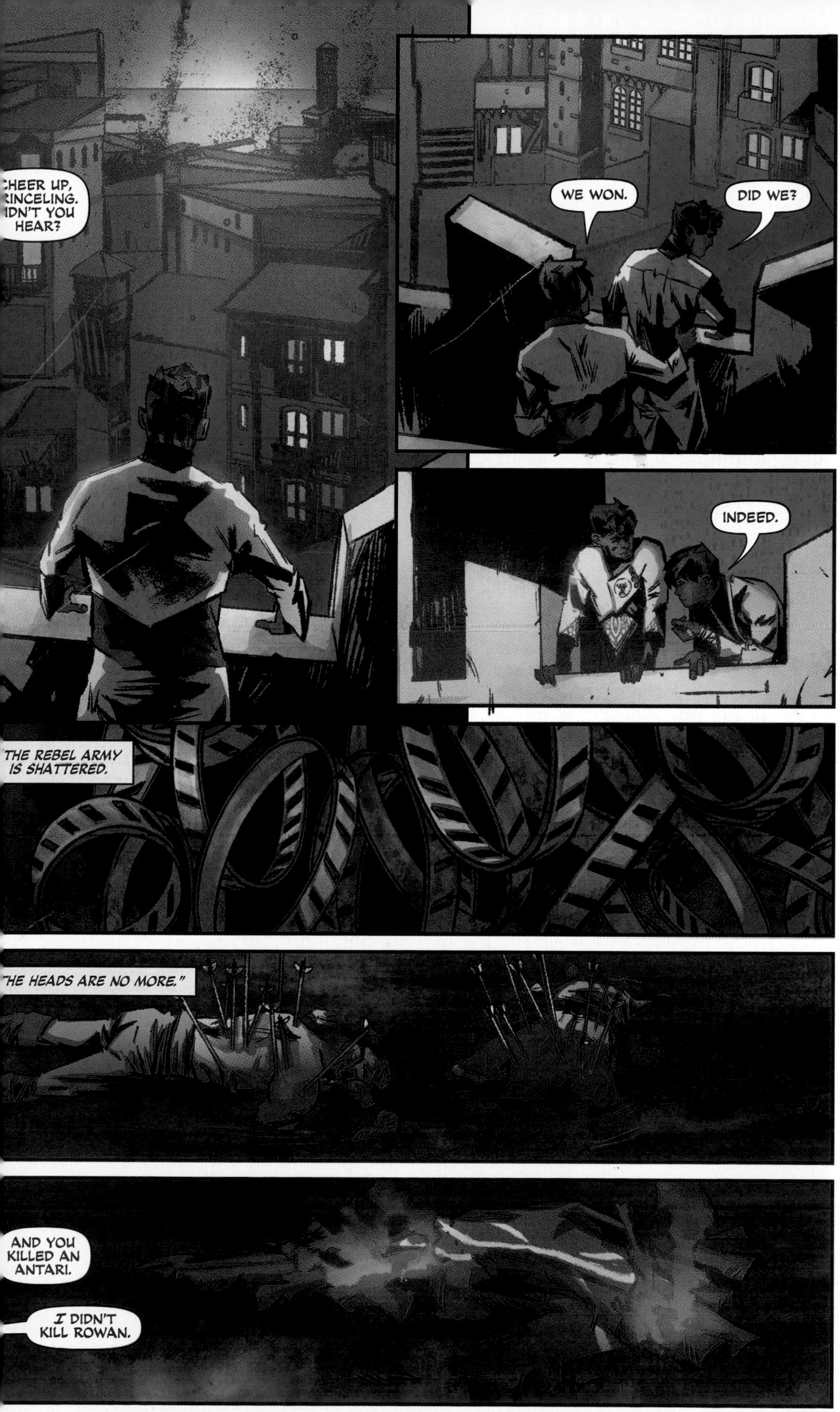
CHEER UP,
RINCELING.
IDN'T YOU
HEAR?
WE WON.
DID WE?
INDEED.
THE REBEL ARMY
IS SHATTERED.
"HE HEADS ARE NO MORE."
AND YOU
KILLED AN
ANTARI.
I DIDN'T
KILL ROWAN.

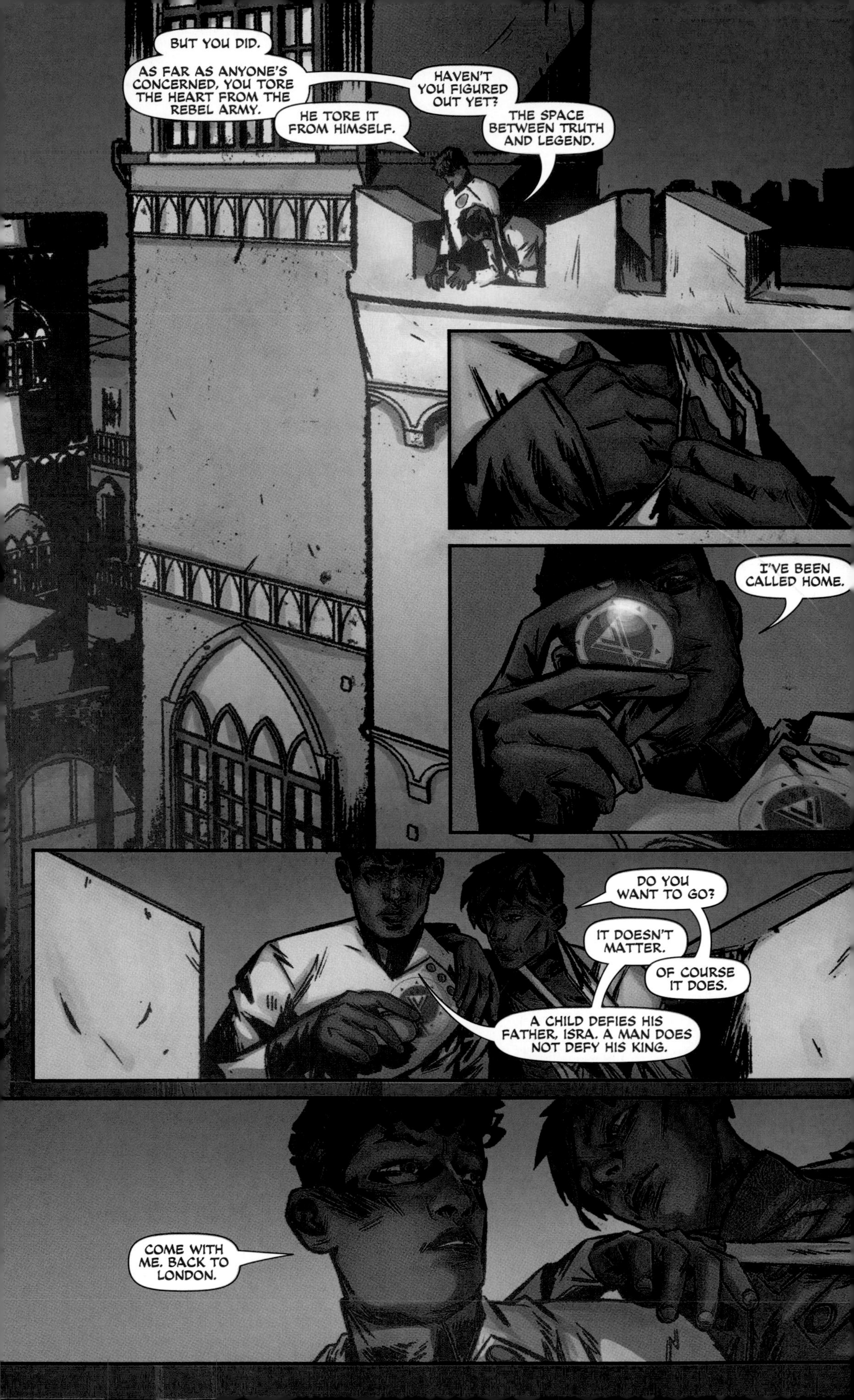
BUT YOU DID.
AS FAR AS ANYONE'S CONCERNED, YOU TORE THE HEART FROM THE REBEL ARMY.
HE TORE IT FROM HIMSELF.
HAVEN'T YOU FIGURED OUT YET?
THE SPACE BETWEEN TRUTH AND LEGEND.
I'VE BEEN CALLED HOME.
DO YOU WANT TO GO?
IT DOESN'T MATTER.
OF COURSE IT DOES.
A CHILD DEFIES HIS FATHER, ISRA. A MAN DOES NOT DEFY HIS KING.
COME WITH ME. BACK TO LONDON.

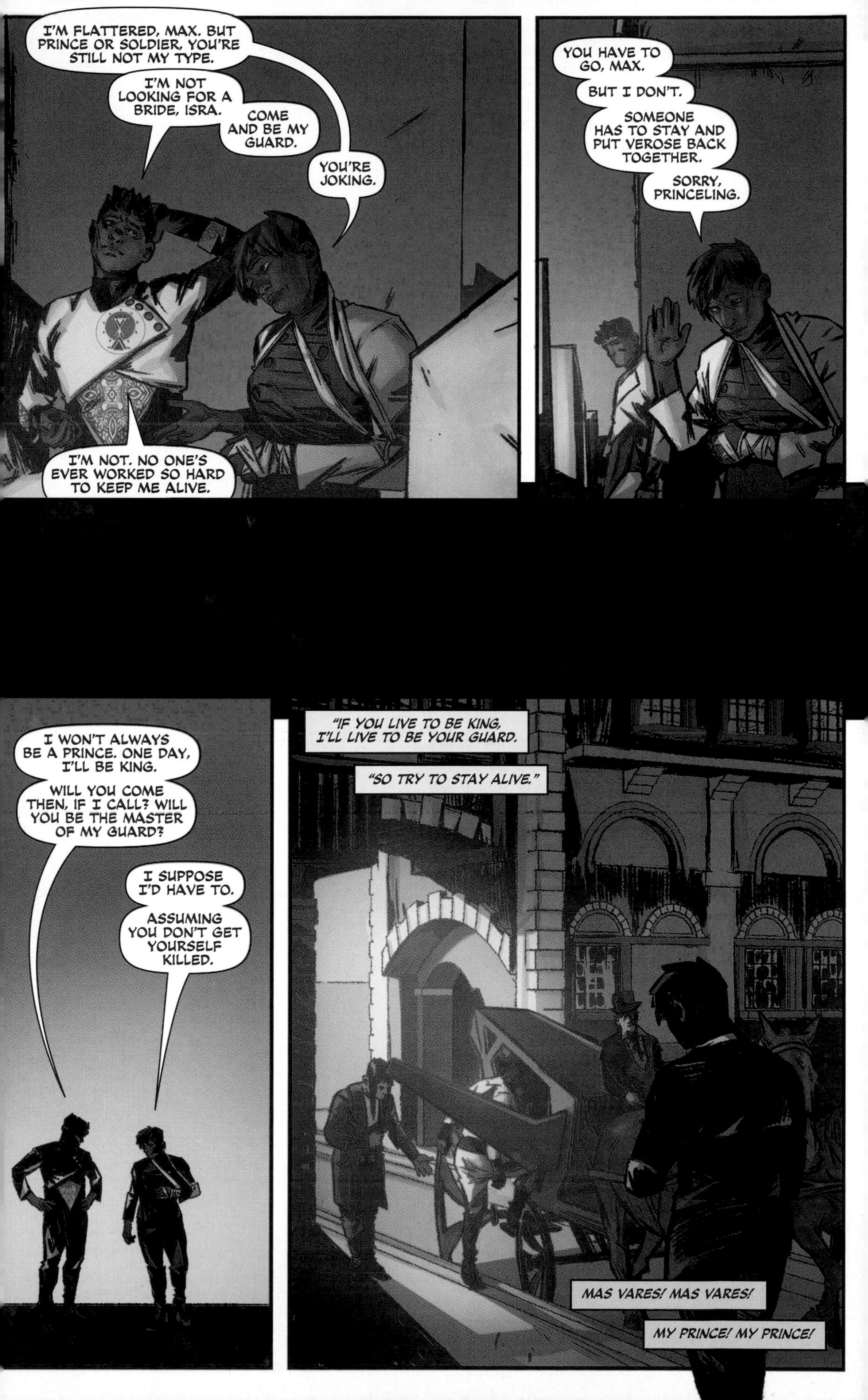
I'M FLATTERED, MAX. BUT PRINCE OR SOLDIER, YOU'RE STILL NOT MY TYPE.
I'M NOT LOOKING FOR A BRIDE, ISRA.
COME AND BE MY GUARD.
YOU'RE JOKING.
I'M NOT. NO ONE'S EVER WORKED SO HARD TO KEEP ME ALIVE.
YOU HAVE TO GO, MAX.
BUT I DON'T.
SOMEONE HAS TO STAY AND PUT VEROSE BACK TOGETHER.
SORRY, PRINCELING.
I WON'T ALWAYS BE A PRINCE. ONE DAY, I'LL BE KING.
WILL YOU COME THEN, IF I CALL? WILL YOU BE THE MASTER OF MY GUARD?
I SUPPOSE I'D HAVE TO.
ASSUMING YOU DON'T GET YOURSELF KILLED.
"IF YOU LIVE TO BE KING, I'LL LIVE TO BE YOUR GUARD.
"SO TRY TO STAY ALIVE."
MAS VARES! MAS VARES!
MY PRINCE! MY PRINCE!

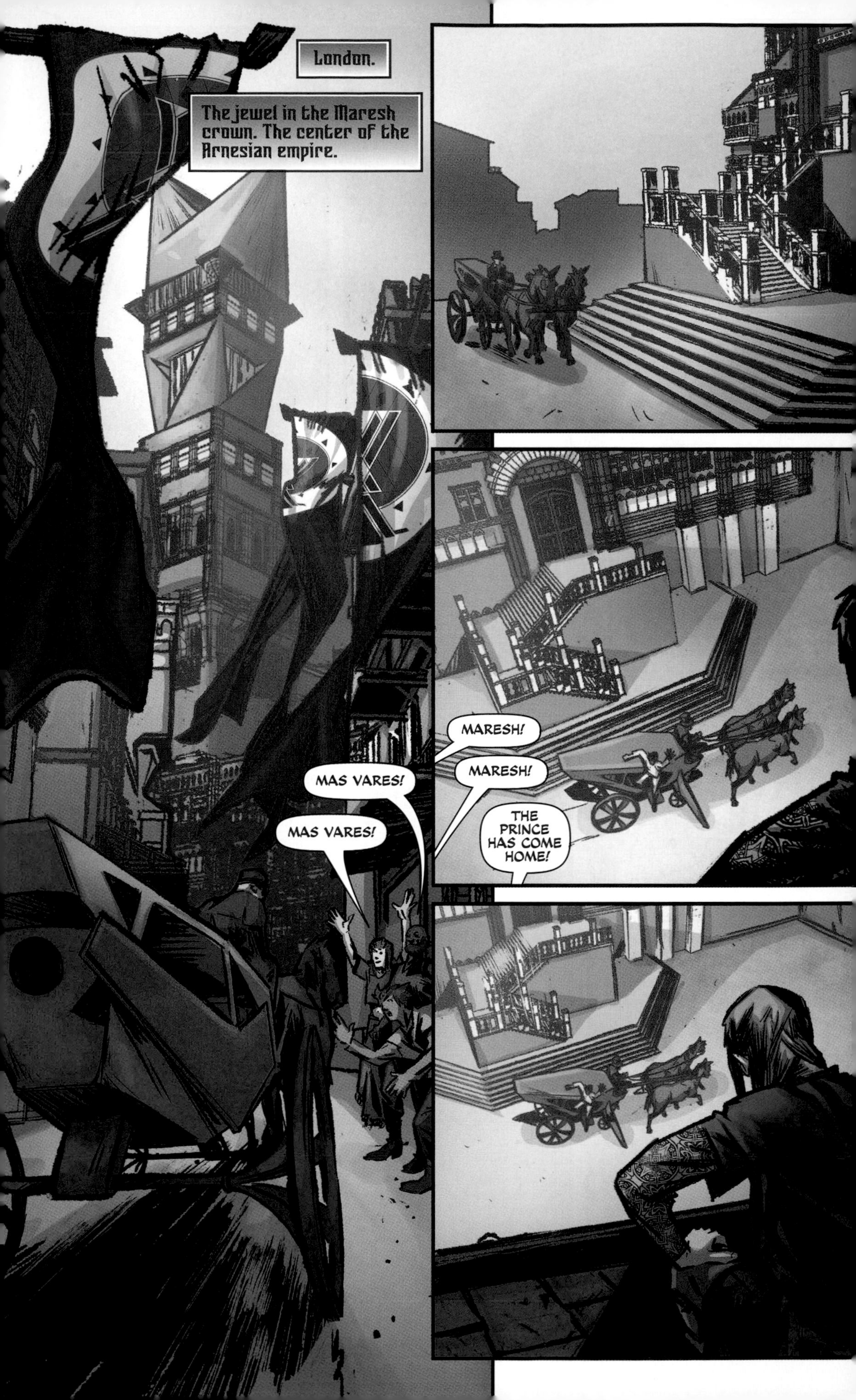
London.
The jewel in the Maresh crown. The center of the Arnesian empire.
MAS VARES!
MAS VARES!
MARESH!
MARESH!
THE PRINCE HAS COME HOME!

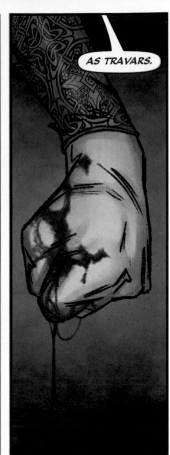

AS TRAVARS.

THE END

FROM SCRIPT TO ART

PENCILS & INKS: ANDREA OLIMPIERI COLORS: ENRICA EREN ANGIOLINI
FLATS: ALICE KINOKI LETTERS: ROB STEEN

THE STEEL PRINCE: The Rebel Army – Issue #1
V.E. Schwab

[Page 7]

Panel 1: Heads turning toward him, looking up from their food and drinks.

| Messenger: | I come with news. |
| Messenger: | The Rebel Army draws near. |

Panel 2: Insert shadowy image of a pirate fleet, sailing through the dark.

| Messenger: | They sail for no empire. They kneel to no crown. |
| Messenger: | They will free Milos from the bonds of the empire, and usher in a new age, where the might of magic reigns. |

Panel 3: The messenger presses his hand to the tavern wall, and fire licks out from his palm, scorching lines into the wood.

| Messenger: | Your liberators land at dusk. So you have until dark to decide. |

Panel 4: The sigil burning on the wall, the flag of the Rebel Army scorched into the wood.

| Messenger: | When you see the sign… |
| Messenger: | …will you kneel, or will you rise? |

Panel 5: The tavern door bursts inward. Soldiers coming in the doorway.

Panel 6: The messenger being dragged from the table, the sigil still burning on the wall behind him.

| Messenger: | You're too late! |
| Messenger: | The Rebel Army is on its way… |

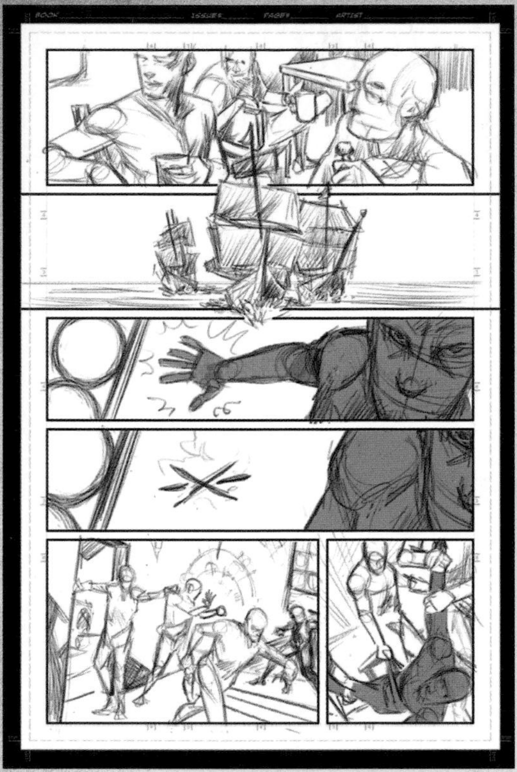

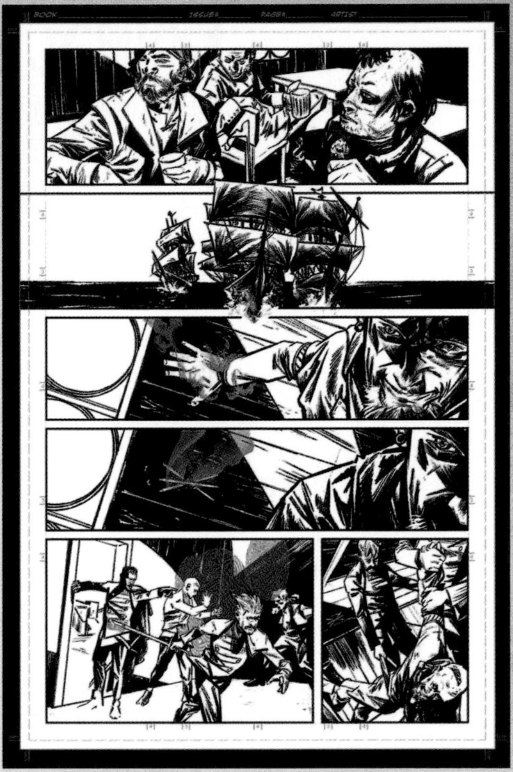

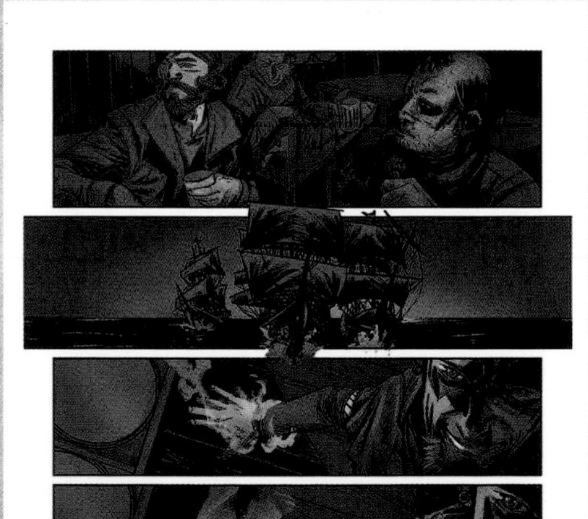

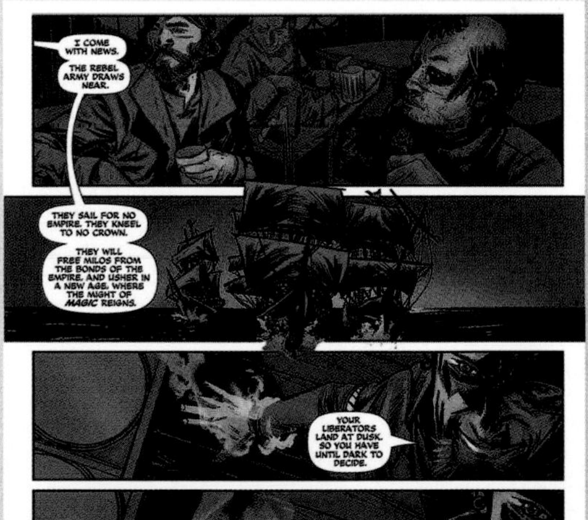

I COME WITH NEWS.
THE REBEL ARMY DRAWS NEAR.
THEY SAIL FOR NO EMPIRE. THEY KNEEL TO NO CROWN.
THEY WILL FREE MILOS FROM THE BONDS OF THE EMPIRE, AND USHER IN A NEW AGE, WHERE THE MIGHT OF *MAGIC* REIGNS.
YOUR LIBERATORS LAND AT DUSK. SO YOU HAVE UNTIL DARK TO DECIDE.
WHEN YOU SEE THE SIGN...
...WILL YOU KNEEL, OR WILL YOU RISE?
YOU'RE TOO LATE!
THE REBEL ARMY IS ON ITS WAY...

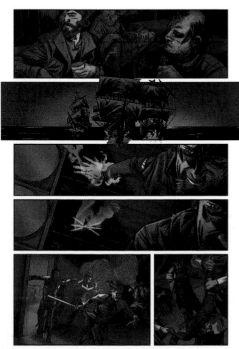

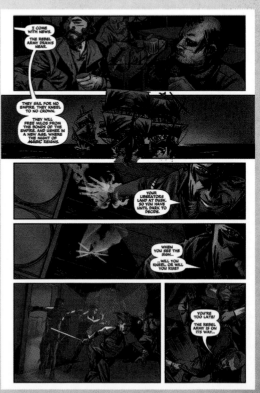

FROM SCRIPT TO ART

PENCILS & INKS: ANDREA OLIMPIERI   COLORS: ENRICA EREN ANGIOLINI
FLATS: ALICE KINOKI   LETTERS: ROB STEEN

THE STEEL PRINCE: The Rebel Army – Issue #1
V.E. Schwab

[Page 9]

Caption: "Milos."

Panel 1: The messenger from the tavern is bound, on his knees in a spelled circle, back arching as magic/electricity runs through him. The SFX of screaming continues from the last page.

Panel 2: The messenger sags forward, sweat dripping from his forehead onto the stone floor.

Caption: "Other ports have other soldiers, and those have bases of their own. And every base has a place like this, beneath the floor, or behind a wall. A place for prying truths from bodies."

Panel 3: The two soldiers looking down on the wounded prisoner.

Soldier 1:   Where is the Rebel Army now?
Messenger: Oh don't worry…
Messenger: …they're on their way.

Panel 4: The angle changes so we can see the messenger's expression. He bows his head against the floor. But he's smiling.

Messenger: The tide will roll over the empire, and sweep the crown from the king's head.
Soldier 2:   Send word to Verose.

Panel 5: Soldier 1 turns toward a black scrying stand (imagine a bird bath, or holy water receptacle, except the top is black stone instead of water). Behind him, Soldier 2 holds out his hand, and magic consumes the messenger again.

Soldier 2: Alert the prince.

FROM SCRIPT TO ART

PENCILS & INKS: ANDREA OLIMPIERI   COLORS: ENRICA EREN ANGIOLINI
FLATS: ALICE KINOKI   LETTERS: ROB STEEN

THE STEEL PRINCE: The Rebel Army – Issue #1
V.E. Schwab

[Page 21]

Panel 1: The RA—fighters and converts—stand in a crowd, all marked with the same Rebel Army arm band. The crowd looks up. Their details are obscured, but the arm bands stand out against their shadowy forms. (The size of the crowd will grow in each issue.)

        Rowan O/S: Welcome.

Panel 2: On a roof, the Faroan and Veskan stand upright, proud, but the voice comes from the shadow moving forward between them. Rowan.

        Rowan: You have chosen the path of power.

Panel 3: Rowan addresses the mass of RA fighters and converts.

        Rowan: And chosen well.
        Rowan: The Rebel Army will take the ports. And the cities.

Panel 4: Insert a tighter shot of Rowan's face, set, determined. This is personal.

        Rowan: And the thrones.

(Position the below dialogue back in main panel, not insert.)

        Rowan: For Magic knows no dynasty.

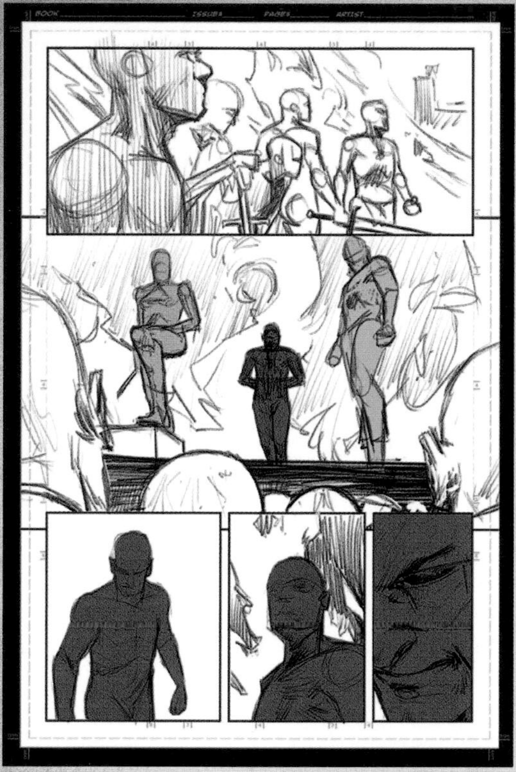

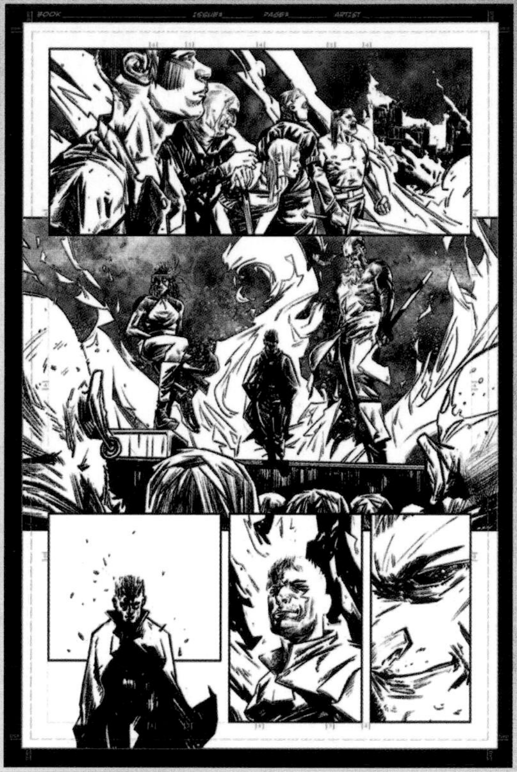

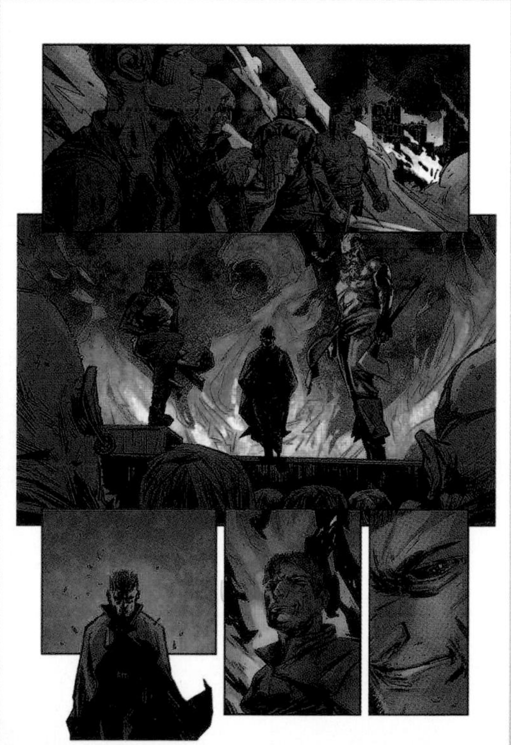

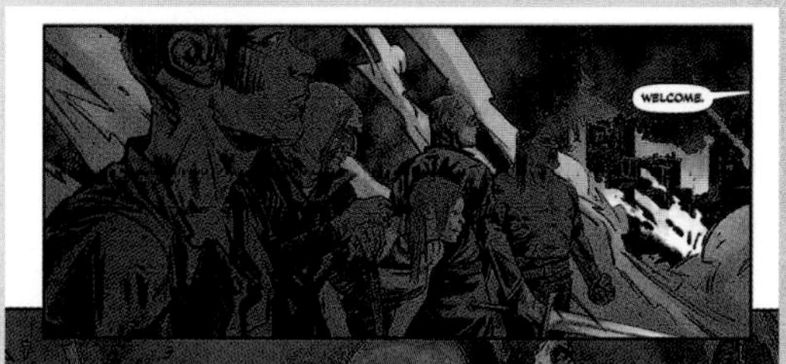
WELCOME.
YOU HAVE CHOSEN THE PATH OF POWER.
AND CHOSEN WELL.
THE REBEL ARMY WILL TAKE THE PORTS, AND THE CITIES.
AND THE THRONES.
FOR MAGIC KNOWS NO DYNASTY.

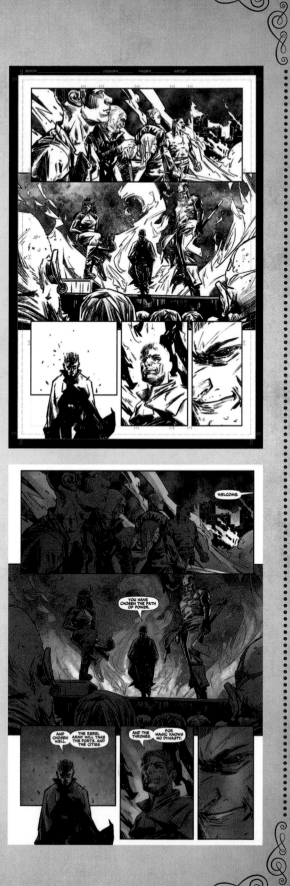

FROM SCRIPT TO ART

PENCILS & INKS: ANDREA OLIMPIERI COLORS: ENRICA EREN ANGIOLINI
FLATS: ALICE KINOKI LETTERS: ROB STEEN

THE STEEL PRINCE: The Rebel Army — Issue #2
V.E. Schwab

[Page 1]

Panel 1: A full-bleed image of the Rebel Army flag whipping in the background. Three white lines crossing against a black ground. The panels float over the top.

Caption:	The word spreads. The Army grows.
Caption:	And everywhere, the tide is rising.

Panel 2: A messenger stands, one foot up on a tavern table, addressing a crowd.

Caption:	Avena.
Messenger:	Rise up.

Panel 3: Another messenger in a public square.

Caption:	Corsalis.
Messenger:	Rise up.

Panel 4: A third messenger standing on the docks.

Caption:	Loran.
Messenger:	Rise up.

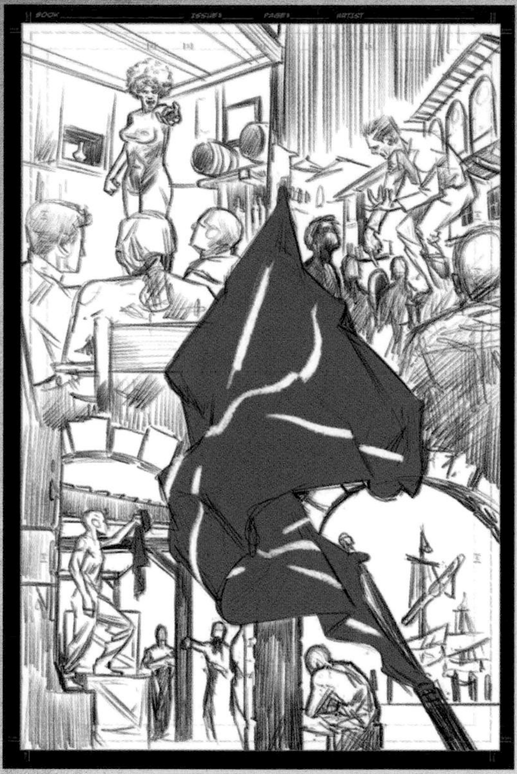

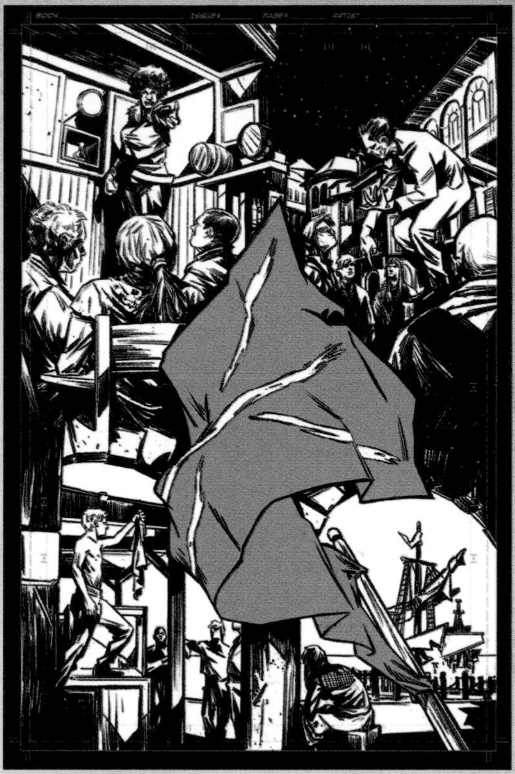

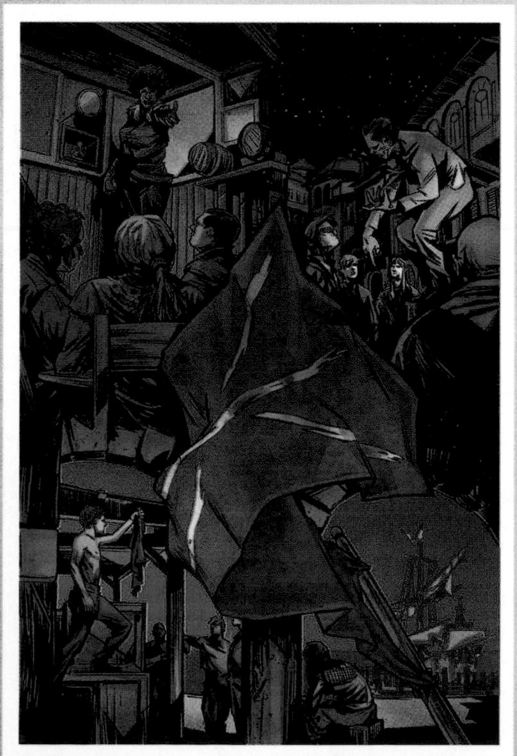

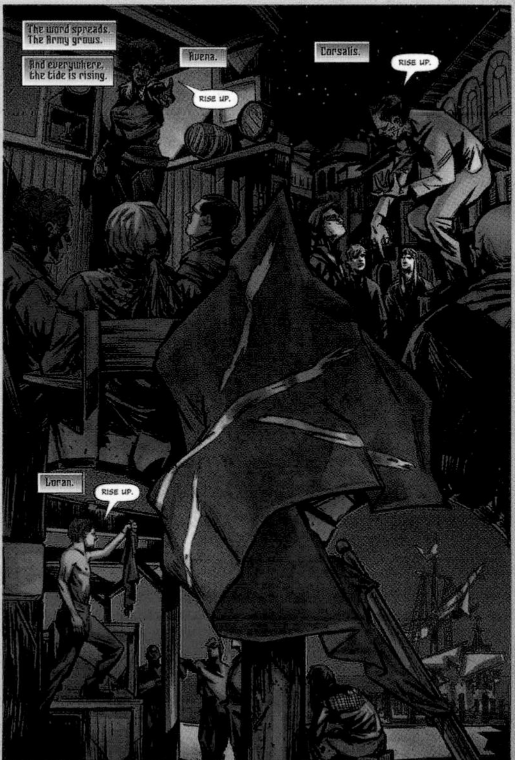
The word spreads. The Army grows.
And everywhere, the tide is rising.
Avena.
RISE UP.
Corsalis.
RISE UP.
Loran.
RISE UP.

FROM SCRIPT TO ART

PENCILS & INKS: ANDREA OLIMPIERI   COLORS: ENRICA EREN ANGIOLINI
FLATS: ALICE KINOKI   LETTERS: ROB STEEN

THE STEEL PRINCE: The Rebel Army — Issue #2
V.E. Schwab

[Page 13]

Panel 1: The metal of the knife begins to glow red and melt with the force of Maxim's power.

Maxim: Verose is like this blade.

Panel 2: Maxim guides the molten metal from the air to his own sword, driven into the crate.

Maxim: It is made stronger for every ounce of metal.
                   The Rebel Army will not forge anything with your strength.
Maxim: I may be a prince.

Panel 3: Maxim in profile, addressing the crowd. At his back, the image bleeds into one of the Pirate Queen on her knees, bound to the rail of her drowning ship.

Maxim: But I am also the one who slayed the Pirate Queen.

Panel 4: Maxim holds out his arm, displaying the four marks he earned in the Night of Knives.

Maxim: I am the one who bested the Night of Knives.
Maxim: And I will be the one who was not afraid to face the Rebel Army.

Panel 5: Maxim casts a glance over his shoulder at Isra.

Maxim: But I cannot fight alone.
Maxim: I have never fought alone.

Panel 6: Maxim high on the right, looking down. The crowd on the left, looking up.

Woman In Crowd: Why should we fight at all?
Maxim: The Rebel Army doesn't offer freedom. They conscript.
Maxim: And if you do not join their cause, they will slit your throats.
Man In Crowd: They will kill us faster if we're fighting for you.
Maxim: I'm not asking you to fight for me. Or the empire.
Maxim: I'm asking you to fight for Verose.

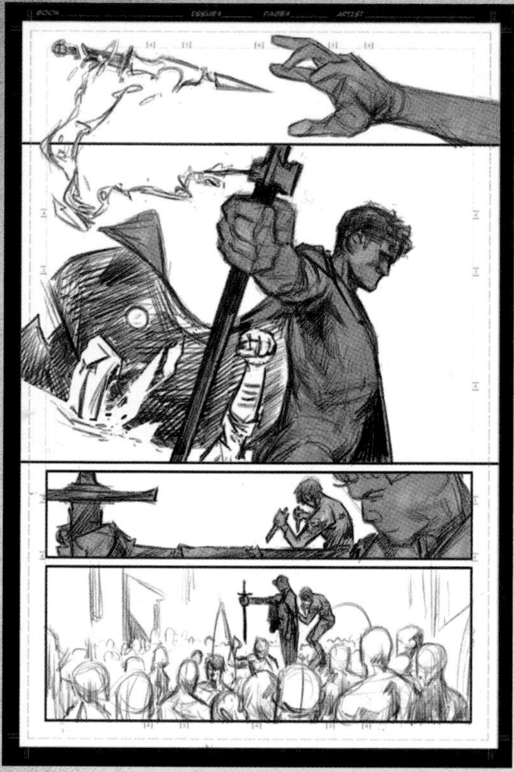

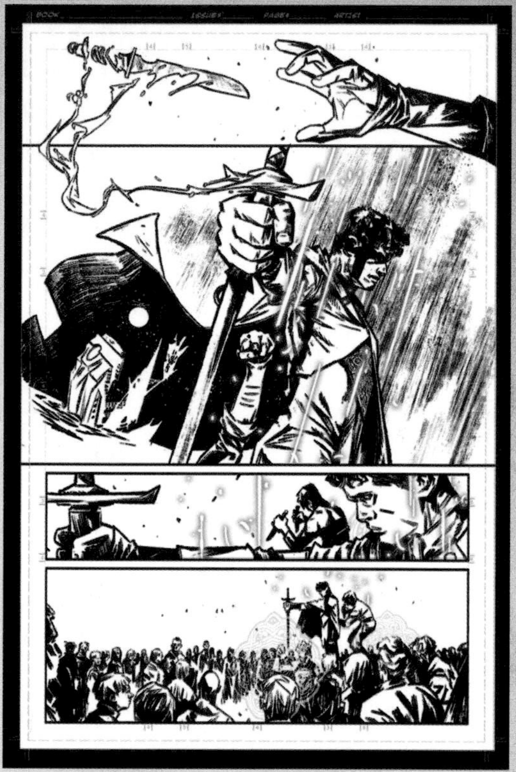

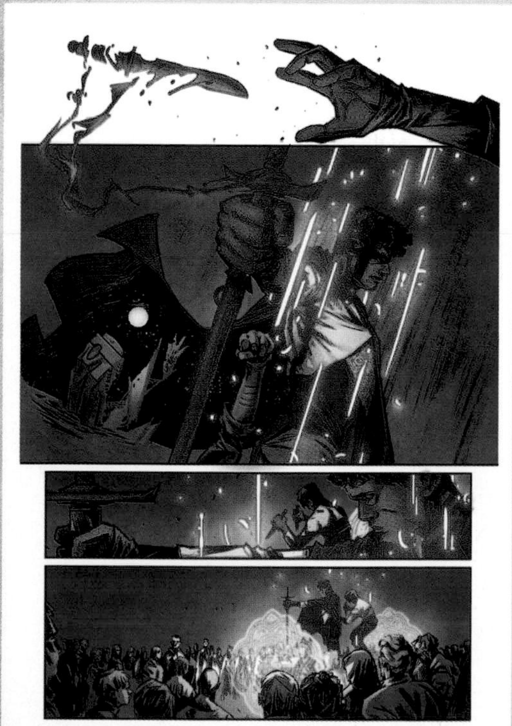

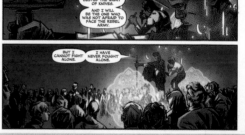

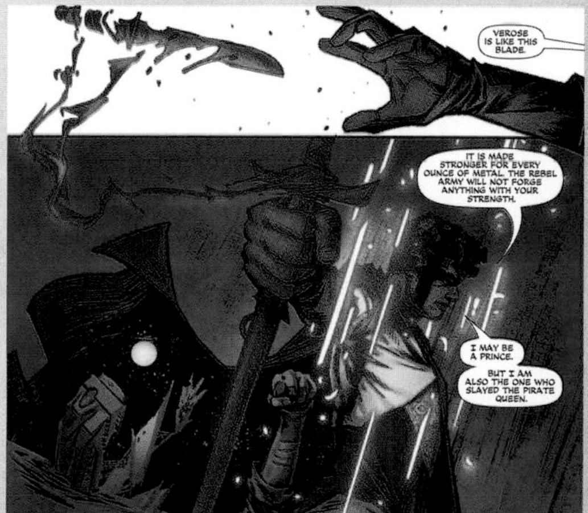
VEROSE IS LIKE THIS BLADE.
IT IS MADE STRONGER FOR EVERY OUNCE OF METAL. THE REBEL ARMY WILL NOT FORGE ANYTHING WITH YOUR STRENGTH.
I MAY BE A PRINCE.
BUT I AM ALSO THE ONE WHO SLAYED THE PIRATE QUEEN.
I AM THE ONE WHO BESTED THE NIGHT OF KNIVES.
AND I WILL BE THE ONE WHO WAS NOT AFRAID TO FACE THE REBEL ARMY.
BUT I CANNOT FIGHT ALONE.
I HAVE NEVER FOUGHT ALONE.

FROM SCRIPT TO ART

PENCILS & INKS: ANDREA OLIMPIERI COLORS: ENRICA EREN ANGIOLINI
FLATS: ALICE KINOKI LETTERS: ROB STEEN

THE STEEL PRINCE: The Rebel Army — Issue #3
V.E. Schwab

[Page 3]

Caption: "Meanwhile, in Loran."

Panel 1: A large, establishing shot of a ruined city, burned buildings, the outlines of bodies, and smoke billowing up against the sky.

Veskan O/S: See, Rowan?
Veskan O/S: We missed all the fun.

Panel 2: A lower body shot of three pairs of legs, and three pairs of boots, each belonging to one of the RA leaders. Three different styles. The Faroan's lean legs are sheathed in archer's lithe boots. The Veskan's are bulkier, adorned. Rowan's are the simplest, gold buckles with the Maresh seal scratched out.

Veskan: I'd rather get my hands dirty.
Faroan: Better than staying on the boats.
Rowan: A band of rebels brawls for fun. An army requires order.
                        A chain of command.
Veskan: Sounds like a coward's way to me.

Panel 3: Insert shot of Rowan's artificial hand curling into a fist, magic rising around it, then—

Panel 4: The same lower body shot as the Veskan pulls up short, Rowan's bone magic forcing his limbs to the ground. Rowan's legs and the Faroan's have both stopped at the right edge of the frame. SFX of the Veskan gasping in surprise and pain.

Panel 5: Rowan kneels in front of the Veskan's pinned and struggling form, inclines his head.

Rowan: I am not a coward, Veskan.
Rowan: I am a god.
Rowan: It would take nothing—nothing at all—for me to crush this town.
                        To grind it all to dust beneath my heel.
Veskan: —then—why—

Panel 6: Rowan rising back to his feet, looming over the Veskan's buckled form.

Rowan: Because I don't have to.

Panel 7: Rowan turns away, and the magic binding the Veskan dissolves. He collapses, gasping. Flames curl around his hands, a sign of his anger.

Rowan O/S: Get up.

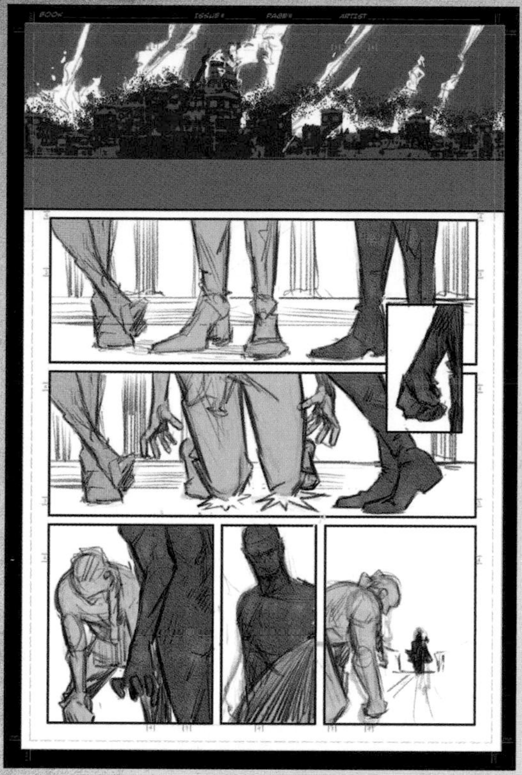

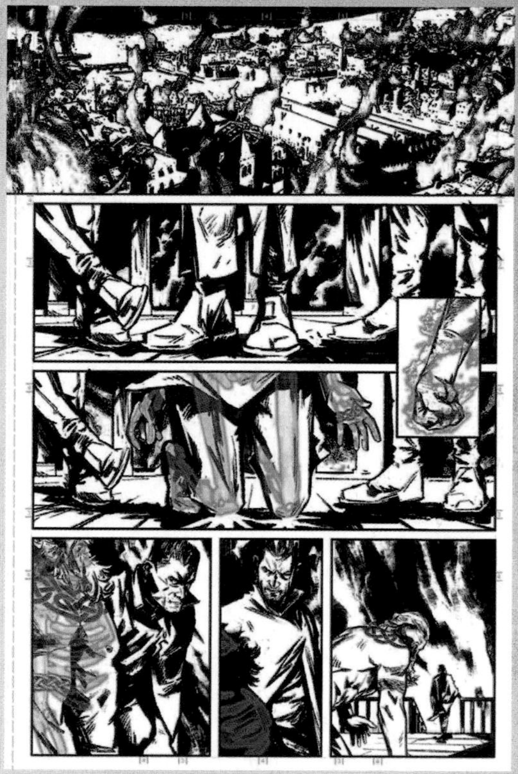

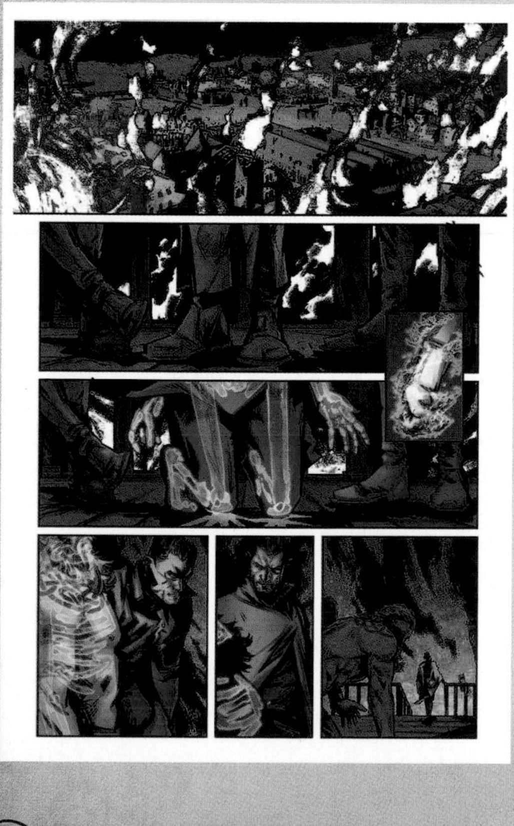

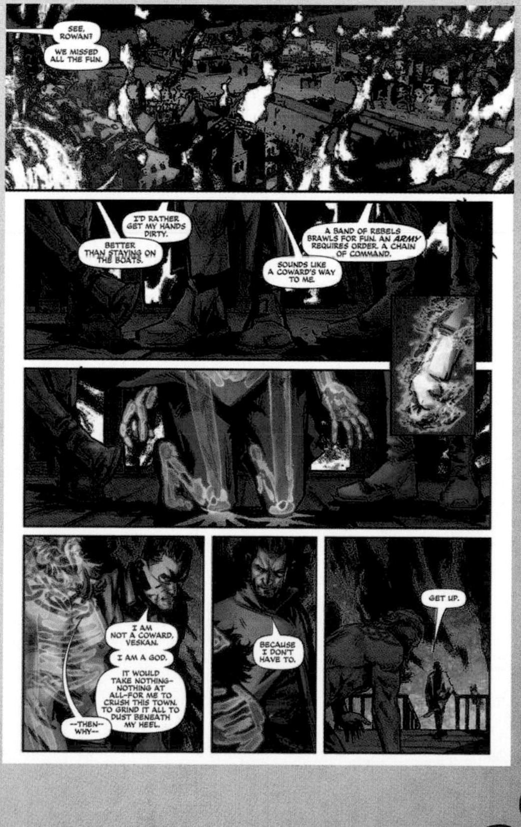

SEE, ROWAN?
WE MISSED ALL THE FUN.
I'D RATHER GET MY HANDS DIRTY.
BETTER THAN STAYING ON THE BOATS.
A BAND OF REBELS BRAWLS FOR FUN. AN *ARMY* REQUIRES ORDER. A CHAIN OF COMMAND.
SOUNDS LIKE A COWARD'S WAY TO ME.
I AM NOT A COWARD, VESKAN.
I AM A GOD.
IT WOULD TAKE NOTHING-NOTHING AT ALL-FOR ME TO CRUSH THIS TOWN. TO GRIND IT ALL TO DUST BENEATH MY HEEL.
--THEN--WHY--
BECAUSE I DON'T HAVE TO.
GET UP.

CREATOR BIOS

V. E. SCHWAB

Victoria "V.E." Schwab is the #1 NYT, USA, and Indie-bestselling author of more than a dozen books, including *Vicious*, the *Shades of Magic* series, and *This Savage Song*. Her work has received critical acclaim, been featured by *EW* and the *New York Times*, been translated into more than a dozen languages, and has been optioned for TV and Film. *The Independent* calls her the "natural successor to Diana Wynne Jones" and touts her "enviable, almost Gaiman-esque ability to switch between styles, genres, and tones."

ANDREA OLIMPIERI

Andrea is an up and coming comic book artist based out of Italy. He has been instrumental in creating the visual aesthetic for the *Shades of Magic* comic series. He has also contributed artwork to a number of high-profile titles, including *Monstri* and *True Blood*, and Titan Comics' *Dishonored*. He pencilled and inked *Shades of Magic: The Steel Prince* and inked issues 2 – 4 of *Night of Knives*.

ENRICA EREN ANGIOLINI

A skilled colorist and an accomplished fencer, Enrica has colored for books such as *Doctor Who: The Thirteenth Doctor*, *Warhammer 40,000*, *Terminator*, and *The Order of the Forge*. She lives and works in Rome, Italy.

ROB STEEN

Rob Steen is an experienced letterer whose skilled calligraphy has enlivened the comics of many publishers, from *Wolverine* and the *X-Men*, *Arrowsmith* and *Astro City*, *Harbinger* and *Bloodshot*, and Titan's own *Rivers of London* and *Warhammer 40,000* series.

BUDI SETIAWAN

Indonesian artist Budi Setiawan came to prominence in 2007 when he was nominated for the Russ Manning Most Promising Newcomer Award at the Harvey Awards. He has gone on to draw *Road Kill Zoo*, *Rex Royd* and the critically acclaimed four-issue mini-series *The Raid* for Titan Comics.